SAVING MIGRANT BIRDS

Number Fifty-five
THE CORRIE HERRING HOOKS SERIES

SAVING MIGRANT BIRDS
Developing Strategies for the Future

JOHN FAABORG

University of Texas Press, Austin

Requests for permission to reproduce material from this work should
be sent to Permissions, University of Texas Press, P.O. Box 7819,
Austin, TX 78713-7819.

⊗ The paper used in this book meets the minimum requirements of
ANSI/NISO Z39.48-1992 (R1997) (Permanence of Paper).

Library of Congress Cataloging-in-Publication Data

Faaborg, John Raynor, 1949–
Saving migrant birds : developing strategies for the future / John Raynor
Faaborg. — 1st ed.
    p.   cm. — (The Corrie Herring Hooks series ; no. 55)
Includes bibliographical references (p.).
ISBN 0-292-72544-2 (cloth : alk. paper) — ISBN 0-292-72548-5
(pbk. : alk. paper)
1. Bird populations.   2. Birds, Protection of.   3. Birds—Migration.
I. Title.   II. Series.
QL677.4 .F235   2003
333.95'816—dc21   2002005333

TO JANICE

You're the best!

Contents

ILLUSTRATIONS

PREFACE

I was one of those boys who became an adult during the 1960s. Looking back, we think of those as turbulent times because of Vietnam and all the demonstrations and disruptions associated with an unpopular war. As a college student during the end of that decade, I had to deal with whether or not I felt strongly enough about things to participate in anti-war demonstrations, and when I graduated from college in 1971, I had to live through several uncomfortable months as I waited to see if my draft lottery number would force me to become part of a war effort that by then was obviously winding down. (Fortunately, it didn't.)

As someone who started birdwatching while in elementary school and got a banding permit while still in high school, the 1960s were an exciting and turbulent time for other reasons. In 1962, Rachel Carson published her book *Silent Spring*, which suggested that the use of persistent pesticides such as DDT would lead to environmental devastation if continued at the levels common at that time. The importance of this single body of work in the development of the environmental movement is hard to estimate. I remember reading it first as a 12-year-old when parts of it appeared in the *Des Moines Register;* I certainly cannot remember anything else I read at that age that affected me as much.

Although numerous attacks on both the detail and the tone of *Silent Spring* occurred, and some of them were justified, too many pieces of evidence supporting Ms. Carson's thesis were appearing in the news to make *Silent Spring* go away. Bald Eagle (*Haliaeetus leucocephalus;* note that scientific names for Neotropical migrants are listed in the Appendix), Peregrine Falcon, and Osprey populations were declining rapidly, apparently because they were laying eggs with thin shells as a result of high DDT residues in their bodies. In the Midwest, where DDT was used to try to control the beetle that spread Dutch elm disease, many towns were losing not only their elms but their populations of American Robins as well. I will never forget the ritual of spring on the Iowa State University campus during the late 1960s. The robins would appear all over campus, set up territories, then start to die. By the end of the decade, only a few nests could be found, where literally hundreds had occurred before DDT.

So many observations suggested that something was wrong in the environment that many people did not believe those representatives of governmental agencies or big business who said that DDT was at best harmless or at worst a positive and cost-effective insecticide. I have often wondered how much the war-related turmoil of the 1960s aided the developing environmental movement; if government and big business would lie to us about how and why a war was being fought thousands of miles from home, why would they hesitate to lie about something as trivial to them as potential side effects of a pesticide?

The use of DDT in the United States was banned in 1972 (but it is still produced in the United States and exported in vast amounts). The recovery of those birds that were most obviously affected by DDT has been phenomenal. Despite warnings about the long-term effects of something with a half-life of around 10 years, robins are thriving throughout the Midwest, and the large raptors are coming back in impressive numbers. The Bald Eagle is off the endangered species list, and Ospreys are abundant. Peregrine Falcons are recovering more slowly (perhaps because they are still accumulating DDT on their tropical wintering grounds), but with the help of extensive restocking programs they are much more abundant than during their nadir.

Although all was not rosy on the environmental front during the rest of the 1970s and 1980s, for people whose focus was bird conservation in North America, this period seemed to be one of quiet progress. Those species that suffered the most from DDT seemed to be recovering rapidly, while most everything else seemed to be doing fine. There were species of concern, particularly those with limited populations and/or habitats; for these the Endangered Species Act was developed, which seemed as effective an approach to saving an endangered species as one could get.

This feeling that things were going well in the North American bird world was broken in the late 1980s. Several scientific discoveries that were counter to an "all's well" approach to avian populations appeared, and the patterns suggested by these studies were expanded in several articles, written for popular audiences, that painted a dire future for many North American bird populations.

The biggest scientific discovery that fueled a sense of doom was that of Chandler Robbins and his colleagues, who analyzed Breeding Bird Survey data for the period 1966–1988 and found that numerous species showed significant national declines during the period 1979–1988 (Robbins et al. 1989b). Most important, the species showing the most pronounced declines were those that winter in the Tropics of Central and South America and the West Indies. About this same time, numerous studies of so-called habitat fragmentation were appearing, nearly all of which showed that many species did not occur in remnant patches of habitats that at one time were more widespread, even when these patches were relatively large. Nearly all these studies agreed that the birds most affected by fragmentation were those that wintered in the Tropics. Concurrently, numerous studies detailed the loss of forest in the Tropics, with emphasis on loss of rain forest.

It didn't take a genius to start seeing a pattern in the above. Birds that wintered in the Tropics were declining at the same time that tropical habitats were disappearing. Soon, popular articles appeared, suggesting that the loss of the Tropics was causing declines in those birds that breed in North America and winter in the Tropics and featuring titles such as "Silent Spring Revisited," " 'Future Shock' for Birders," "Empty Skies," "Death of the Dawn," and "Birds over Troubled Forests." The most complete discussion suggesting a bleak future for migrant birds was John Terborgh's book-length treatise *Where Have All the Birds Gone?* (Terborgh 1989).

It did not take long for the conservation community to take note of such dire predictions and to respond. An international symposium of scientists in December 1989 was followed by an international gathering of both governmental and nongovernmental conservationists in December 1990. At the latter meeting, the Neotropical Migratory Bird Conservation Program (also known as Partners in Flight) was started to ensure survival of migrant birds while there was still time. By 1996, Partners in Flight was calling itself "the most comprehensive bird conservation program ever launched."

Were things really this bad? Did we face an imminent disaster? Even in 1997, popular articles appeared that showed how confusing the situation could be. Just one day apart, the *New York Times* published "Something to Sing About: Songbirds Aren't in Decline" (Stevens 1997), and the *Christian Science Monitor* published "Requiem for the Songbird: Perilous Decline Puzzles Scientists" (Schneider 1997).

The truth is that understanding migrant birds in enough detail to understand what regulates their populations well enough to save them is a complex task, one whose details do not fit easily within the confines of a newspaper article or an environmental organization's pitch for funds. In this book, I give an overview of how our concern about migrant birds came to be, what we need to know in order to save migrant birds, and what is currently being done. Although it is hard to fault an international conservation plan that is now focusing on virtually all birds, Partners in Flight is not without its controversies. The people who believe that breeding-season problems are at the root of declines argue with those who favor wintering-ground limitation, while those who think migration habitat may be critical feel they are being ignored. Managers want to manage now, while researchers (myself included) often argue that we don't know enough. At the extreme, we must ask if the evidence regarding declines of migrant birds is compelling enough to merit the most comprehensive conservation plan in history? Do we truly face a future of empty skies and silent springs? Are all migrant birds facing a similar future, or is our future one of different skies and different-sounding springs? Even if the evidence for declines is compelling, do we know enough about how migrant bird populations are regulated to design meaningful, effective conservation plans for them, recognizing that these may require multinational efforts?

I discuss these and other questions in this book, in many cases pointing out where the knowledge we need is missing and how it can be gathered. Along the way, I hope to provide insight into how science works (and sometimes doesn't work) and how the transition from science to management is not always a smooth one. The many ways that dedicated biologists work so hard trying to figure out how to save birds are also noted. Finally, and important, I hope to introduce the reader to many of the wonderful adaptations that characterize migrant birds; they truly are an amazing group of birds, without whom springtime in the New World Temperate Zone would not be the same.

Acknowledgments

This book would not have been possible without the help of a lot of people, although none of them should shoulder any blame, if blame needs to be dished out. My colleagues Scott Robinson, Frank Thompson, Jeff Brawn, and Mark Ryan have had a tremendous impact on my thinking, although they do not always agree with my final conclusions. Scott and Robert Askins read the entire manuscript and made a number of comments that have improved its quality. Thanks also go to my buddy Will Carter, who commented on the first half of the book and who continues to be one of my best contacts with serious naturalists.

I have been blessed with a large group of wonderful graduate students who have forced me to think a lot harder than I had planned. Many are now off establishing their own careers and bridging that gap between former student and colleague. Many appear in this book in one fashion or another; rather than risk leaving someone out and hurting feelings, I will thank them as a group for all the good times, good ideas, and hard work. I was blessed with some exceptional guidance myself, and special thanks go to Milton Weller, Henry Horn, Robert May, John Terborgh, and the late Robert MacArthur for the examples they set for me while I was in school. In particular, John Terborgh showed how one could combine science and conservation; I hope that he sees those occasions when I disagree with him in this book as a step toward determining the final truth. Although not my students, Katie and Bruce Dugger have become great colleagues and friends.

Shannon Davies, formerly of the University of Texas Press, encouraged me to put my ideas about Neotropical migrants on paper, something I probably would never have done without her encouragement. William Bishel and Leslie Tingle of UT Press and copyeditor Rosemary Wetherold helped tremendously with getting this book into its final form.

Finally, I thank my wife, Janice, for her love and support during the long process of getting this project done. My children, Jason, Jodi, Claire, and Miles, and all the livestock also helped me stay sane as I tried to put this science into a form that anyone who cares about birds can understand.

SAVING MIGRANT BIRDS

1 | WHAT ARE NEOTROPICAL MIGRANTS AND WHY ARE WE CONCERNED?

Before we begin examining the development of the concerted effort to save migrant birds, we must define what Neotropical migrant birds are (which you will see is not such an easy task) and go over the evidence that resulted in the Partners in Flight response. This will take us to the state of knowledge about migrant birds around 1990. We can then try to examine both the validity of data up until 1990 and the developments since then with regard to understanding and conserving migrant birds.

WHAT IS A NEOTROPICAL MIGRANT?

The Neotropical Migratory Bird Conservation Program (Partners in Flight, PIF) considers a Neotropical migrant bird to be a species that breeds completely or primarily in the New World Temperate Zone (the United States and Canada) and winters completely or primarily in the Tropics (Mexico, the West Indies, or anyplace south). Ideally, this distinguishes Neotropical migrants from so-called short-distance migrants, which spend both the breeding season and the winter primarily in the United States and/or Canada, although they may migrate great distances. To try to deal with the variation in migration strategies among these birds, the official PIF list of migrants has subdivisions A through D: "A" migrants are those species that winter south of the United States, "B" migrants are those that winter only partly south of the United States, and "C" and "D" migrants are subtropical birds whose ranges barely penetrate California, Arizona, Texas, or Florida. (The Appendix lists the common names of the species involved, along with their scientific names.)

Of course, with hundreds of species of migrants found in North and Central America and the occurrence of the northern boundary of the true Neotropics somewhere in the middle of Mexico, definitions for these migrants can get both geographically and biologically confusing. Rappole et al. (1983) used the term *Nearctic migrant* to describe those species that breed north of the tropic of Cancer and winter south of that line, which reinforces the temperate-tropic transition and makes it easier to separate tropical migrants from shorter-distance temperate migrants. This label presents two problems, because it ignores the tropical nature of many of these migrants (which may spend up to 8 months residing in the Neotropics) and it leaves us with the problem of what to call the within–Temperate Zone migrants whose whole lives are spent in the Nearctic (effectively the United States and Canada).

Part of the problem with nomenclature for these tropical wintering migrants has to do with concepts of how such long-distance migration evolved. Prior to the first international meeting on such migrants, sponsored by the Smithsonian Institution in 1977 (Keast and Morton 1980), workers from the tropics considered these migrants to be North American birds that "invaded" the Tropics during the winter but "belonged" to the North American avifauna. For most tropical ornithologists, such migrants were something that one ran into while studying the really exciting tropical species such as motmots, trogons, jacamars, and the like. I know that when I first visited Puerto Rico, I got much less thrill catching a Black-and-white Warbler or an American Redstart than when I caught any of the Puerto Rican endemics. (I must admit, though, that when I returned to the same site the next winter and caught many of the same individual black-and-whites and redstarts in exactly the same location as the year before, I was hooked on migrant studies.)

At the first meeting on migrants, several of the tropical ornithologists who resided in the Tropics argued that because of the length of the annual cycle spent in the Tropics and the fact that most species seemed to have well-established niches within tropical communities, we should think of these as tropical birds, which would justify calling them Neotropical birds. The logic used by some was that these migrants were not temperate birds that invaded the Tropics to avoid winter, but they were tropical species whose reproductive strategies in the highly competitive Tropics involved a trip north to raise young. Thus, if they were part of the Neotropical bird community and they migrated, they must be Neotropical migrants.

To this messy mix of North American breeding birds that spend half or more of the year in the Tropics but migrate to the Temperate Zone must be added species that live their lives totally within the Tropics but also migrate. Originally, this seemed to include just a relatively small group of so-called austral migrants, which breed in temperate parts of South America and winter to the north, and a handful of other tropical species known to move through the year (so-called intratropical migrants). Recent work has shown, however, that elevational migrations are widespread in tropical species that were once considered very sedentary. Some of this evidence came from banding studies, where it was shown that different individuals of a species occurred in a site through the year, which documented migration in a way that pure observational studies could not. Other support came from more detailed studies through the year, which showed that species occupied different habitats or elevations at different seasons. In some cases, a species leaves a site where it bred but is replaced by a migrant that seems ecologically identical, which led Steve Fretwell (1980, 518) to state, "For most communities we must be genuinely puzzled by all the comings and goings."

A more recent attempt to clear up the nomenclature was made by Floyd E. Hayes (1995). Hayes noted the discrepancies above, plus the fact that the term *austral migrant* actually applied to any bird that bred in the Southern Hemisphere and moved northward, so it was not limited to New World systems. Yet, even with six categories of New World migrants (altitudinal, austral, boreal, intratropical, Nearctic, and Neotropical), confusion reigns in separating birds that breed in North America but migrate different distances. Only with the use of such terms as *Nearctic-Nearctic migrants* or *Nearctic-Neotropical migrants* is this confusion avoided.

Even if one defines these categories of migrants precisely, the reality is that there are still species whose movements and distribution patterns do not fit into any category cleanly. In addition, using the hyphenated names ignores the arguments about origins of migration and the amount of time spent in different areas; one could easily argue that a migrant that spends 7 months in the Tropics and only 5 months in the Temperate Zone should be a Neotropical-Nearctic migrant, rather than the reverse.

As we go through this book, the difference in migration strategies will occasionally be important. Most of the time, though, we will be dealing here only with those migrants that breed in the Temperate Zone of the United States and Canada and migrate to somewhere in the Tropics, and we are going to call them Neotropical migrants. Although this is a bit simplistic, it matches the definition of the Partners in Flight program, and *Neotropical* migrants is the term used most commonly for this group of species in recent literature.

WHAT IS THE EVIDENCE SUPPORTING NEOTROPICAL MIGRANT DECLINES?

In general, Neotropical migrant birds are still exceedingly abundant, and because they are small, don't congregate in specific sites, and are quiet during much of the year, they are also difficult to count. Most have relatively large breeding ranges, and although the wintering range is often much smaller, we rarely have good information about which habitats are actually needed in the wintertime and if the amount of such habitats might be a problem for a specific species. Few studies have looked at populations over a long period of time in the same site, and even those studies must be interpreted with care because population changes may be due to local habitat change rather than population-wide phenomena. Given that individual migrants may travel thousands of miles between breeding and wintering sites, one must be careful in generalizing about population levels from a study done in a single location.

Despite these difficulties, scientists have presented enough information suggesting widespread population declines in these migrants to cause concern and to justify the development of the massive Partners in Flight program. One of the best things about PIF is the simple fact that the conservation community is responding to declines at a time when most migrants are still abundant, but one also must be careful about overreacting to what may be in truth short-term trends, local population changes, or questionable data.

Thus, to understand arguments about the notion of possible migrant declines, we must examine the evidence used to justify the development of PIF. As was noted in the Preface, three major patterns were used to convince the world that PIF was needed: (1) declines in migrants shown on Breeding Bird Surveys, (2) widespread discoveries that migrants suffered most as habitats were fragmented, and (3) general patterns of deforestation in the Tropics. We will look at each of these briefly here and then examine them in more detail in later chapters.

Breeding Bird Survey Declines   The Breeding Bird Survey (BBS) was developed following the DDT scare and was designed as a way to monitor bird populations. Although there was evidence that local bird populations were declining due to the effects of DDT, scientists found that it was hard to make a case that populations in general were declining, because no baseline data on bird populations were available. The BBS was designed to fulfill this need and to provide scientifically sound data on population patterns of North American birds. Each Breeding Bird Survey route is a roadside census done during June, with 3-minute stops every half mile for 24.5 miles (50 stops). Ideally, surveyors are hand-picked by regional supervisors so that they are experienced birders who know the local birds and will follow the census rules, a process that minimizes observer variability. Locations were picked randomly, with routes starting in the eastern United States and Canada in 1966 and the whole of both countries in 1967. More than 3,100 routes exist, most of which are run annually, which makes for a censusing effort that is unmatched anywhere else.

Early results from the BBS provided baseline data on populations on a national scale. A publication highlighting the first 15 years of the BBS provided lots of data and range maps but did not argue that negative trends were dominant. Only by the late 1980s did such trends appear. Robbins et al. (1989b) analyzed patterns of abundance for birds in the eastern BBS region (the United States and Canada east of the Mississippi River) for two periods, 1966–1978 and 1978–1987. They found striking differences in patterns between these two periods for the 62 species with the most data: 15 species showed negative trends but 47 species showed positive trends during 1966–1978, whereas 44 species showed negative trends and only 18 had positive trends during the period 1979–1987. In looking at characteristics of the species involved, it was found that permanent-resident and Temperate Zone migrants generally had positive trends or showed no change, whereas species that wintered in the Tropics showed general declines. Among these Neotropical migrants, the data suggested that species that wintered in forest rather than scrub declined more dramatically, as did those migrants that breed in forest in the Temperate Zone.

In many cases, the declines shown by migrant birds were pronounced, with rates of decline exceeding 5% per year for the period 1978–1987 shown by such species as Yellow-billed Cuckoo, Black-billed Cuckoo, Olive-sided Flycatcher, Tennessee Warbler, Bay-breasted Warbler, Blackpoll Warbler, and Wilson's Warbler. Numerous other species showed statistically significant declines of more than 1% per year, which, when extrapolated over this 10-year period, suggested major population declines, particularly for Neotropical migrant birds (Fig. 1.1). The appearance of population declines in such a massive censusing effort is certainly something that is not easily ignored, and BBS patterns were (and continue to be) the main justification behind the PIF response.

Population Loss through Habitat Fragmentation Several studies appeared during the mid- to late 1980s that looked at the negative effects of habitat fragmentation on bird populations and distributions. Habitat fragmentation occurs when naturally contiguous habitats are broken up into scattered remnants and separated by altered habitat types. Fragmentation was a common part of the advance of civilization across North America, as forests and native grasslands were converted into farms and cities, with native habitats left (if such occurred) in bits and pieces for any number of reasons.

Two major forces occur as habitats are fragmented. First, the total amount of original habitat is reduced, sometimes by a great amount. One cannot ignore that massive loss of habitat often results in massive reductions in the total populations of birds occurring in these native habitats. Second, the remaining habitat occurs in pieces of varying sizes and shapes, in most cases separated from one another by the new habitat of farms or subdivisions. In central Missouri, for example, the 302,000 acres of Howard County were originally nearly all forested but are now only about 18% forest, with this forest occurring in 617 separate parcels, of which only 6 parcels are 1,000 acres or larger. This 18% looks good, though, compared with Greene County, Iowa, where I was raised and where all the native habitat (prairie) has been converted to agriculture in some form. For North America, most of such habitat loss and fragmentation occurred at least 100 and as long as 300 years ago, with the advance of European civilization. Native birds have been contending with such fragmented habitats for a long time, and in the eastern United States, fragmentation may be less of a problem now than it was in the past.

Well-publicized evidence of the potentially devastating effects of habitat loss and isolation came from long-term studies of Rock Creek Park in the Washington, D.C., area (Robbins 1979). When bird surveys were started in the 1940s, this park was part of a green corridor that was connected to large tracts of natural habitat; we assume that, at that time, birds could move along this corridor searching for breeding habitat. With the development of the area, the connections disappeared and the park became an isolated fragment. After becoming isolated, breeding birds in the park had to maintain populations by reproduction, or new colonists had to find the park in the spring by crossing expanses of suburban

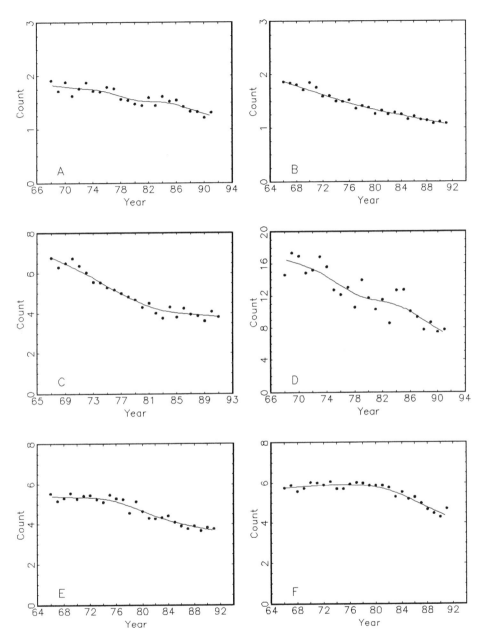

FIGURE 1.1. *National declines of species from Breeding Bird Survey data. Species shown are Rock Wren (A), Prairie Warbler (B), Painted Bunting (C), Black-throated Sparrow (D), Wood Thrush (E), and Bobolink (F). From Robbins et al. (1992a).*

sprawl. Apparently, neither of these options was working well, for the park showed a strong pattern of population decline for many species, with local extinction occurring for six once-abundant species. Although some of the declines might be because forests had matured over time, in most cases the habitat in the park was getting better for birds. However, because the park was now small and isolated, bird populations were declining and going extinct in the park.

Because most fragmentation studies did not have the time line that the Rock Creek Park study had, one could not say how recent the population declines might be in fragmented regions. But virtually all fragmentation studies showed that many species do not occur on habitat fragments, even when these fragments were dozens or even hundreds of times the size of an individual territory. Because growing human populations and high rates of timber harvest seemed to be breaking up the remaining patches of many habitat types, it was easy to think that many species might be declining because of fragmentation of the breeding grounds.

It also was shown in numerous studies that birds that migrated to the Tropics were generally most sensitive to habitat fragmentation. It was suggested that this was related to several factors, which we will discuss in detail later. For example, most tropical migrants are single-brooded, in contrast to multibrooded, short-distance migrants or permanent residents. These migrants also usually use open nests, often on the ground, whereas short-distance migrants and residents are more often found nesting in cavities. Both these factors might make Neotropical migrants more susceptible to the effects of nest predation in fragments. There was also evidence that long-distance migrants might be more susceptible to parasitism by the Brown-headed Cowbird. Whatever the reason, the patterns suggested strongly that Neotropical migrant populations did not do well in a fragmented world.

The Loss of Tropical Rain Forest   Because Neotropical migrants may spend up to 8 months of the year living in a little piece of tropical forest, it is not unreasonable to think that loss of wintering habitat could lead to population decline. John Terborgh noted at the first symposium on migrants that the potential for winter limitation in Neotropical migrants is extreme because most North American breeding migrants winter in Mexico, Central America, or the West Indies. The potential wintering area is only about one-seventh to one-eighth as large as the potential breeding range, which led Terborgh to suggest that the loss of an acre of wintering habitat could result in the loss of breeding birds on 7 to 8 acres in the Temperate Zone (Terborgh 1980).

Because most migrants winter in the "near" Tropics (Mexico, Central America, and the West Indies), most of the focus on habitat loss has been on this region. This is not to say that habitat loss in South America is not important, for numerous species winter exclusively on that continent and a few have wintering ranges restricted to fast-disappearing habitat types. Yet most migrants do not travel to South America, and the occurrence of the still-vast Amazon basin makes summaries of habitat loss less dramatic, so the focus has been on Central America and the West Indies.

Gary Hartshorn, then of the World Wildlife Fund and currently director of the Organization for Tropical Studies, reviewed forest loss in Central America in the symposium volume that followed the second migrant symposium (Hartshorn 1992). He noted that most forest loss had occurred since 1950, with the pairing of modern technology and increasing population pressures. Since then, rates of forest loss had been high, with Costa Rica, for example, having lost over 50% of its tropical forest since 1950. Although much of the forest loss was in arid environments before 1977, a sharp increase in forest loss during 1977–1983 involved tropical wet and montane forests that were converted to cattle ranches for raising beef for export. Little of the timber harvest was done with any thought toward sustainable harvest, and most timber extraction was followed by human colonization, where agriculture exacerbated and extended the damage done by timber harvest.

Although Costa Rica is often used as an example of enlightened protection of natural areas, it also serves as an exceptional example of habitat loss in recent decades. It is clear that there is much less primary forest available to wintering migrants than even 20 years ago, and all types of forest cover have declined. That similar forest loss has occurred throughout Mexico, Central America, and the Caribbean makes it easy for one to argue that winter habitat limitation is a cause of declines of Neotropical migrants. As we shall see later, the relationship between forest loss and declining migrant populations is not as simple as this, but the current levels of forest loss are frightening and the future does not bode well even if winter limitation is currently not in effect.

Other Evidence for Declines   Other evidence suggesting declines appeared in the late 1980s and early 1990s but was generally not as broad in scope and compelling. My colleague Wayne Arendt and I presented 15 years' worth of monitoring data from a site in Puerto Rico, which showed a steep decline in the number of winter-resident warblers caught in a standard-effort mist net sample there (Faaborg and Arendt 1989). A line of nets that caught as many as 30 winter residents in the early

1970s yielded only 11, 8, and 5 captures during the period 1986–1988. These were the first long-term data that suggested population declines from the wintering grounds and were compelling enough that John Terborgh added a figure to his 1989 book *Where Have All the Birds Gone?* By itself, though, I am not sure what such a study shows, and some of the alternative explanations for our observed declines will be discussed later.

Sidney Gauthreaux of Clemson University made a convincing case at the 1989 migrant symposium for declines of trans-Gulf migrants (those individuals that fly a nonstop route across the Gulf of Mexico in both spring and fall) from his analysis of radar records (Gauthreaux 1992). Because these migrants show up on radar screens and there is a filmed record of these screens, he was able rather quickly to compare general levels of movement across the Gulf between the 1960s and the 1980s. His first analysis suggested that the fraction of days with weather conditions appropriate for migration in which a migration occurred had declined from 95% in the 1960s to only 44% in the 1980s. After two days of presentation of papers at this symposium arguing about what was or wasn't going on with migrants, Gauthreaux's data convinced a lot of people that a real decline was evident. As we shall see later, though, even these data are not without their difficulties.

Additional evidence suggesting declines arose from other sites. In many cases, natural factors such as succession or human factors such as fragmentation might have explained the declines, but an almost overwhelming data set showing population declines arose. Those studies with data showing stable or rising populations seemed to get lost in the furor over potential population declines. New potential limiting factors also were presented, including such things as acid rain and its ability to reduce productivity of northern or high-elevation habitats, pesticide residues (including the possibility that DDT picked up on the wintering grounds was at work), cats, dogs, reflective windows, radio towers, and almost anything else that kills a migrant bird. Although each of these can result in impressive losses of birds in some situations, the extent to which they affect bird populations on a regional or national scale is less clear.

JUSTIFYING THE PIF RESPONSE

By the end of 1990, the impressive array of evidence summarized above had appeared in both the scientific and the popular press. The evidence was alarming at best, and downright frightening if true to the extent that some believed. Any person or agency concerned about the conservation of birds would have been totally remiss not to express concern about the situation and put major effort into trying to understand what was going on so that the declining trends, if they proved to be real and long-term, could be stopped while most of these species were still quite abundant. There was too much evidence suggesting long-term declines for the situation to be ignored.

On the other hand, were we truly facing a situation as severe as suggested by some, with their references to silent springs and empty skies and curtain calls for songbirds? Was the evidence for declines so compelling that one would dare talk about Neotropical migrant declines as though they definitely existed and were occurring everywhere? Did conversion of tropical forests to other, often second-growth, forested habitats mean the end of wintering habitat for all Neotropical migrants? Numerous questions needed to be answered about migrant ecology to be able to answer these and the myriad other questions that suddenly arose as our concern for Neotropical migrants mounted. Alternative questions arose. Could the declines be real reflections of an adjustment to recent habitat change somewhere along the line, but adjustments that did not require extrapolations to zero?

At the end of 1990, there was a real asymmetry in knowledge about what was going on, because a number of sources had documented the declines in quite convincing fashion. To test whether or not the declines reflected long-term patterns and to understand the causes of these declines, whether they were of a long-term or short-term nature, required detailed work on reproduction, wintering ecology, migration ecology, demography, and a host of other aspects of bird ecology where, it turns out, we didn't know much about what was going on. Additionally, these topics often required years of data to achieve conclusive results, years that some suggested we couldn't afford, given the nature of the declines.

A lot has happened since 1990, both on the research front and with regard to Neotropical migrant conservation. In subsequent chapters, I hope to show you some of this, with a focus on both the strengths and the weaknesses of the data that resulted in the establishment of Partners in Flight. As you shall see, it is a complex, challenging puzzle, but one whose solution is critical to the conservation of Neotropical migrants in the future, if not in the present.

2 | THE BREEDING BIRD SURVEY
So Simple Yet So Complex

I think it is safe to say that without the evidence of declines from the Breeding Bird Survey (BBS), there would not have been enough evidence to justify a massive response such as Partners in Flight. There is no evidence much more simple or meaningful than a nice graph showing declining migrant populations, particularly when we know that the annual averages are based on the thousands of counts that constitute the BBS across the country.

Certainly, scientists studying habitat fragmentation had some detailed examples of how loss and isolation of habitat could result in reduced densities or loss of species at a local level, but it was hard to extrapolate such local results to a regional, let alone national, level. This was particularly true because it appeared from the first that individual species responded to fragmentation differently across their ranges, so simple patterns about which species might be lost did not appear. In addition, the loss of tropical habitats has been going on for much longer than the apparently recent declines of Neotropical migrants, so a simple explanation of cause and effect does not work. Finally, we have known so little about what migrants do on the wintering grounds and how this time of the year could cause population limitation that to make a cry for conservation based on wintering data alone is difficult. Even the startling evidence from radar about trans-Gulf migrants would seem empty if the BBS was not showing accompanying declines. Given the importance of these data to the Neotropical migrant conservation program, we must ask ourselves just how good the BBS is at measuring bird populations and showing us that populations are in decline.

THE SIMPLICITY OF BBS

The BBS was designed by scientists to balance simplicity of operation with the potential for powerful results. The simplicity was expressed in the experimental design:

1   Points were picked randomly by computer (two per degree block in the eastern part of the country, and only one per degree block in the western part because there aren't enough birders there) to ensure that representative habitats were covered by the census (Fig. 2.1).
2   Direction of the count from the randomly selected point was based on the coordinates selected, so that direction was random and not determined by the desire to cover particular sites or habitats.
3   The nearest road to this point was designated to be followed in the direction selected, which made accessibility for counters fairly easy. (Heavily traveled roads were not used, but the alternative routes were selected, with a distinct set of rules that avoided any bias by the counters.)
4   Observers were selected by a state coordinator to ensure that the censuses were done by experienced birders familiar with the birds of the area and able to follow the censusing guidelines.
5   The census route started at the randomly picked site on a road and proceeded for 24.5 miles in the appropriate direction, with stops every one-half mile (50 total stops).
6   Each stop was to be 3 minutes long, with the observer counting each bird seen or heard within one-fourth mile of the point (which ensured that an individual bird would not be counted twice unless it moved along with the census taker).
7   Counts were done in June to control for seasonal variation in the ease that species are counted, particularly because birdsong is still prevalent in June. (Ideally, routes were done at the same general time in June to minimize variation.)
8   All counts started one-half hour before sunrise at the initial point, so that the observer visited each point at approximately the same time each year.
9   Counts could be done only when weather conditions were favorable, such that the birds were active and the observer could see and hear them.
10 Detailed maps and easy-to-read forms were provided to make the job of doing the counts as easy as possible for the volunteer workers.

Ideally, these simple guidelines were accompanied by the participation of the same observers year after year, little habitat change along the census

FIGURE 2.1. *Breeding Bird Survey routes (dots) and physiographic provinces (lines) used for regional analyses. From Peterjohn et al. (1995).*

routes, minimal seasonal variation in breeding phenology, and little variation in any other factors that might mess things up. With more than 3,000 BBS routes scattered across the United States and Canada, the folks who compile the BBS data would have the potential to get annual information from about 150,000 individual point counts from across North America (because each BBS route is a 50-point transect).

The point count in one form or another has become the favorite tool of avian census takers for a variety of reasons. It is a discrete sampling unit, and the technique is easily learned in the field (although for those doing point counts that are supposed to be some fixed distance, say 50 m, it is often difficult to guess where the 50 m boundary is). When statistical analysis is performed, a point is a sampling unit, so the sample size on a BBS route is 50; this contrasts with such bird-counting techniques as spot mapping or territory mapping in which a person covers a fairly large area and may count many birds, but the sample size is limited to the number of plots on which these labor-intensive activities are performed.

If all the above guidelines are followed, it seems like an easy chore to just add up the counts for each species for each route and compare them for patterns over time. Of course, with a nationwide census, a lot of different habitats and species are involved, so one might want to break the country down into some sort of ecologically meaningful subunits. This was done with the use of 64 physiographic provinces (see Fig. 2.1), which are areas with similar ecological, geological, and ornithological conditions. These provinces were small enough to combine areas with similar conditions, but large enough that a fairly large number of census points occurred in each, so that adequate samples for analysis of patterns over time were obtained. BBS results have also been summarized by state, which is an ecologically more questionable division but is of obvious value to those employed by state agencies whose job is to protect songbird populations.

THE COMPLEXITY OF BBS

The design of BBS as a monitoring tool is about as good as it could get, but it is not perfect. Although it might be easy to visualize taking the long-term data from all these routes and combining them for simple comparisons of trends in totals or averages either nationwide or within the physiographic provinces, in truth it is not nearly that easy. Largely because there is a lot of variation both in how the censuses are run (for reasons beyond the control of the people in charge of BBS) and in how bird populations vary, the types of analyses that are needed are often complex and regularly confusing to those who don't converse comfortably in the language of statistics. Although one might come up with a list of dozens of problems with the data set and the analysis of BBS routes, here we will focus on four major problems that make the analysis of BBS routes problematic.

Variability in Data Gathering Despite all the efforts of the people who designed BBS to control conditions, variation is inevitable, particularly when the goal is to run the same procedures with the same people in the same place for several decades. It simply cannot be done.

One can summarize the guidelines of the BBS and point out how every procedure has its own source of variation on some time scale. Although the census locations chosen for the start of a route have not changed position over time, the roads that were selected sometimes did, so the routes might not be exactly the same. I remember a stop in Iowa near an old wooden bridge surrounded by giant cottonwoods that always contained a Warbling Vireo; when the bridge was "improved," the cottonwoods were cut and the vireo was gone.

Observers for particular routes have changed with time; many of the people I remember running routes in central Iowa when the BBS was initiated are now long dead. Although their replacements were presumably selected for their ability to identify the birds of the region, individual observers are different, so the shift from one observer to the next involved changes in species recorded or bird numbers that were related to observer differences.

Running counts at about the same time in June can be a problem, sometimes because of personal schedules of the counters, but other times because of weather. Since the counts don't end until around 9:00 in the morning, people with typical working hours are confined to weekends for their counts (daylight saving time accentuates this problem). A couple of rainy weekends in early June can easily shift the best-planned counting schedule to something very different from what was originally conceived. Even if the counts are run at the same time, the phenology of reproduction in birds can vary greatly from year to year, so that singing rates may vary from one June 5 to the next, even if everything else is done uniformly. Of course, the worst result of delaying the counts happens when weather cancels all the available mornings for a season, resulting in a route with gaps in the counts over the years.

The time constraints of running counts are accentuated by the vagaries of weather. The rules state that counts can be done only when weather conditions do not exceed certain standards of wind and other weather features. With 50 stops of 3 minutes each, and a minute or so between stops, it is hard to predict at 4:00 or so in the morning (the time you leave your house for the drive to the route starting point) what the weather will be like at 8:00 or 8:30. I know I have gone back to bed when a bank of clouds full of lightning seemed the dominant force in the weather, only to awaken to a beautiful, calm morning that would have been perfect for counting. On the other hand, I have started counts in perfect conditions and then had to quit when gale-force winds arose halfway through the route.

All sorts of other variations may occur. Some observers seem to focus on rare species, so they are good at attaining large species lists but provide less reliable census data. Others are meticulous at counting the most abundant birds but may miss uncommon species. There has been a fair amount of research in recent years on how an individual's ability to hear changes with age, with the suggestion that some sort of standardized testing might be appropriate when picking people to do point counts such as BBS routes. I know that a couple of my elderly friends were exceptional birders but could not hear a Grasshopper Sparrow if their life depended upon it. Such omissions could be critical, but in most cases these sorts of variations are not that important, because the summaries of BBS routes often look at species densities by fairly broad abundance categories. It is interesting to note that Sauer et al. (1994) found that the number of birds counted by observers has increased, independent of population trend, for the majority of species in BBS; what this means is more difficult to say.

Other information is recorded in addition to the abundance data for any route, to provide information on weather conditions that may be of help in doing analyses over time. But the truth of the matter is that BBS routes are going to vary because that is how nature works and how people work. All the guidelines in the world won't get around the occurrence of variation in these counts; even the use of paid professionals would not fix this problem, because they vary in their abilities too. (And think about what it would cost to get 3,000 routes run each spring at the going wage for a federal employee!)

Ups and Downs Occur Here and There   Although one might expect that a species would show declines throughout its range if winter limitation was at work or if the factors that limited breeding were uniform throughout the breeding range, the truth is that one should realistically expect a species to decline more in some regions than in others. Certainly, this is an easy argument to make if breeding-season limitation occurs, because some physiographic regions have undergone much more change in recent history than others and bird populations should reflect this. Even if winter limitation is at work, one might expect to be able to document declines more readily in some regions than others, because densities of breeding birds vary regionally.

Given such regional variation, a population can do three things over time in a region: stay stable, increase, or decline. With 64 physiographic regions, a widespread species might be stable in one-third, increasing in one-third, and decreasing in the other third. Depending upon how densities were distributed, this species could show stable populations overall, or it could be showing an increase or decrease. Which is the important story? If we see no change in population overall, do we put the species into a "no problem" category, despite having one-third of the regions showing declines? Obviously, each species may have a complex pattern with regard to how, where, and when population change may be occurring, so before we start sounding the alarm for a species, we must try to understand what is really going on with the species overall.

The potential confusion that can occur when one tries to summarize the overall population change of a single species from BBS routes is compounded if one tries to look at groups of species all at once. BBS data have been summarized in this fashion repeatedly, often with maps showing the proportions of populations that are increasing or decreasing in a physiographic region (Fig. 2.2). Such maps may have important conservation implications because they have the potential to draw attention to physiographic regions that seem to have high proportions of declining populations. On the other hand, there is so much going on that determines these patterns that the maps are of little value to the conservation of any particular species, even though it may be contributing to the patterns of the maps in any number of ways.

To determine true population change throughout a physiographic province or for a species throughout its range, one would like to have some measure of how density (number of birds per area) varies throughout the range and how it has varied over time. Despite their favor among avian ecologists in recent years, point counts are notoriously bad measures of actual bird density, and this may be particularly true of short-duration counts such as the 3-minute counts of the BBS. The weakness with measuring density occurs because each point is a circle of some radius (often 50 m, but up to one-fourth mile in the BBS) that is superimposed upon the various territorial boundaries of the species being censused. This area may include just part of a territory or perhaps several territories. The number of detections of a species on a point count will reflect this variation in density and territory size, but unless one takes detailed measurements of the distance that each bird is away from the point, there is little way to convert these detections into a true density measure. As a result, although the BBS may provide an index to changes in populations within

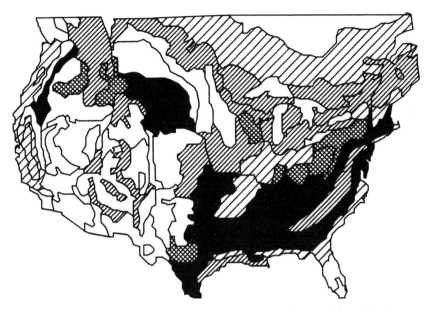

FIGURE 2.2. *Summary of regional population changes from BBS data. Dark areas have a higher proportion of declining species, but an individual species could appear as both increasing and decreasing on these maps. From Sauer and Droege (1992).*

regions or overall by recording a change in the average number of birds recorded per route, one cannot easily extrapolate such a change into some kind of meaningful regional total population change.

How Long Does It Take to Make a Trend? As was stated earlier, summaries done after the first 15 years of the BBS failed to note any general pattern of decline among species of Neotropical migrants or other birds (Robbins et al. 1986). It was analyses covering the period 1979–1988 that suggested that declines were widespread, particularly for birds that wintered in the tropics (Robbins et al. 1989b). The situation was made more complex because a number of species actually showed increasing populations during the period 1966–1978, followed by declines (Fig. 2.3); these species often had similar levels of abundance in 1966 and 1988.

Thus, some populations declined only during a small portion of the BBS sampling period, and others showed declines that brought them back to their initial levels of abundance. Yet, all these were being noted as declining species in 1989. As a result, some scientists have raised valid

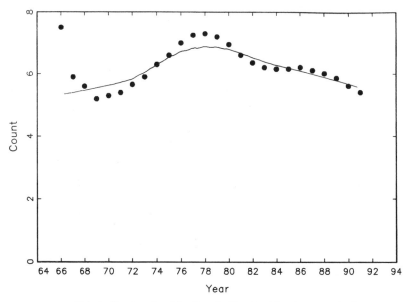

FIGURE 2.3. *Population trends of the Purple Martin. Note that populations are stable over the total length of surveys but have declined in recent years. From Peterjohn et al. (1995).*

questions about the period of time one should examine trends in order to make valid statements about their direction. Although a decline for a period such as 1979–1988 might be real, it is somewhat less shocking when put in the context of an increase in the prior decade, such that the long-term (1966–1988) population trend is one of no change.

Because large-scale censuses such as BBS are so new, we really have no idea what sorts of general patterns are shown by bird populations over long temporal scales. Many populations in nature show cycles as an inherent part of their basic biology. Other populations might fluctuate in response to climatic cycles, particularly those related to drought conditions. It is interesting to note that the final years of the period of purported declines (1985–1988) were years characterized by widespread drought conditions throughout the United States and Canada, particularly in the eastern United States, where the bird declines seemed most pronounced. A number of biologists found greatly reduced reproductive success during these years; with nearly half of all migrant birds dying each year under good conditions, it takes only a couple of years of reduced reproductive success to bring about a general population decline. (And, of course, a couple of good years can result in rapid population increases.)

Of course, one never wants to ignore statistically significant trends in populations that have a downward direction, but a good scientist should also take into account the context in which this occurs. Not all downward trends extrapolate to zero and result in the extinction of the species. Some may reflect natural ups and downs related to a variety of ecological factors, among them rainfall, wind conditions during migration, and temperatures during the breeding season.

Lies, Damn Lies, and Statistics   Although the sheer volume of numbers involved in averaging the results of as many as 150,000 point counts seems intimidating, the logic behind the process of counting birds at the same place and same time each year and seeing how numbers change seems simple enough. Unfortunately, it is not as simple as it may appear. To analyze trends in such an enormous data set, with its inherent sources of variation, requires some sophisticated statistics. The office that handles BBS data has several full-time employees whose primary job is to develop the appropriate statistical models to determine what the BBS data really mean with regard to population trends. These are folks with strong statistical training from the best universities in the United States, and they have developed what they believe are the best models available for dealing with the BBS data set. These "official" BBS trends are what were presented by Robbins et al. (1989b) and others when pointing out their generalization that Neotropical migrant birds were declining during the period 1979–1988. These have also become the official trends used by most PIF committees and numerous state agencies.

Unfortunately, other statisticians, also highly trained and experienced, have other opinions about which statistical models are most appropriate for a data set such as BBS. As Thomas (1996) pointed out, nearly everyone agrees that some sort of regression-based approach is required, but there are at least four major types of regression models that might apply (these are called linear multiplicative models, polynomial multiplicative models, additive models, and rank models, for those with a bit of training or interest in statistics). These all vary in their assumptions about how trends occur and in their abilities to denote changes in trends over time. Depending upon which model one uses, the same data set can provide quite different patterns with regard to population trends over time.

Those of us who do not have degrees in statistics or are not wise enough to understand the differences between methods are left with the question, Who do we believe? Although it has been stated that trends that indicate clearly declining populations will be shown by all the models, many of the BBS trends are not yet that clear. Thus, using different analysis techniques can give us different patterns of trends for species and regions. James et al. (1996) used BBS data and two different models (in this case nonlinear models, which adds a linear-versus-nonlinear-model argument to the whole discussion of which models are best) to show that the widespread declines suggested by Robbins and others were really confined to only two ecological regions and that they occurred mostly in the 1970s, not the 1980s. James et al. conclude their article by noting that "the issue of generally declining populations of Neotropical migrant land birds has been subject to such a degree of overgeneralization that, unless the situation is clarified, we risk undermining the credibility of avian conservation programs." On the other hand, they point out that their analyses show declines in a number of species in highland regions of the eastern United States, and they believe that conservation efforts should focus on these populations rather than on populations that are not really declining.

The thing we must remember is that all of these people are bright, well trained, and concerned about the future of Neotropical migrant birds. The whole situation points out how we must be careful, though, about falling into the Chicken Little syndrome of declaring that the sky is falling when it is not. All of the models seem to have their inherent strengths and weaknesses; if one were far and away the best, I think that the strength of the discussions concerning which model to use would have led to a consensus on which model is best.

THE TAKE-HOME POINT

What is one to believe? First of all, I think we must agree that the BBS is a useful thing, because it provides a data set that has the potential to detect declining trends while birds are still relatively abundant. At its best, bright people using sophisticated techniques of analysis of BBS data have suggested that a number of species were showing declines over a period of time; this alerted us to a potential problem while the problem was still potentially fixable, with populations still large and habitats still widespread. At its worst (excluding the possibility that this is some sort of nefarious plan concocted by biologists working with BBS data), the BBS data have shown us that a few species are declining dramatically throughout their range and that a number of species have shown strong enough regional patterns of decline that conservationists should be concerned.

This is not to say that the BBS data have not been misused by folks with their own political agendas or those who do not understand all the variation within the methodology. On many occasions, the generalization that BBS data have shown declines for some species has been overused and extended into the statement that the BBS shows that all Neotropical migrants are declining and, in a case or two, that the end is near. BBS never said that, and we must remember that any trends unveiled by BBS must be evaluated within the context of the strengths and weaknesses of this technique.

3 | IS THERE OTHER EVIDENCE FOR LARGE-SCALE POPULATION DECLINES?

If the Breeding Bird Survey is functioning as it is intended, and therefore it is true that populations of Neotropical migrants, or at least some species, are in a general decline, one would expect these declines to show up in other studies that do sweeping surveys of populations and that involve large geographic areas. Unfortunately, there are very few situations in which both of the above criteria are met (many species covered and a large geographic area included).

In an attempt to come up with data either to substantiate or to refute the patterns of the BBS, a variety of approaches have been used. These all cover a variety of species (although some focus on a subgroup of birds such as raptors) and a fairly large geographical area.

THE BREEDING BIRD CENSUS

The Breeding Bird Census (BBC) was started in 1914 with the support of the U.S. Biological Survey. These censuses involve intense measures at single sites, ideally for a long period of time. BBC data are now published by the Association of Field Ornithologists, although they once were published by the National Audubon Society.

Although often of great interest (see Chapter 4), most BBC sites do not fit the criteria we are considering in this chapter because they involve a single site. A variety of local factors (forest succession, isolation of the study site, change in the surroundings of the study site, etc.) can affect the patterns shown by a single study site, no matter how meticulously the birds are counted.

Johnston and Hagan (1992) attempted to analyze the available BBC data for long-term patterns. They were able to find only 13 surveys that fit their criteria of being situated in mature forest (so that habitat change is not a factor) and having lasted at least 10 years; only 6 of these surveys lasted 20 years or more. The authors found many more significant negative trends among Neotropical migrants than among residents or short-distance migrants. Interestingly, their data suggested that the major declines in Neotropical migrants had occurred in these sites earlier than the time suggested by BBS data.

Although these long-term data sets are valuable by themselves to tell us what is going on within individual sites, and the attempt by Johnston and Hagan to look for broad-scale patterns within them was admirable, we must examine each of these sites individually to see if local factors are determining population trends before we start generalizing across regional or national scales. As we shall see in Chapter 4, a piece of forest or prairie that is surrounded by some other habitat does not support birds the way it does when it is surrounded by similar habitat.

THE CHRISTMAS BIRD COUNT

The Christmas Bird Count (CBC) is a tremendous method for monitoring changes of bird populations in the winter. Counts are done at the same time of year in the same general area, often with similar effort. Although the focus may be on species lists, a strong attempt is made to do actual counts of individuals within the count circle. Because counts have been done in some locations since 1900, they have the potential to uncover long-term trends in populations. A number of excellent studies have been done incorporating CBC data (discussed below).

The CBC has an immediate disadvantage for the study of Neotropical migrants because virtually all of these counts are done in the United States or Canada at Christmastime, which means that these counts are not in a location to count Neotropical migrants. Those few done on the Neotropical migrant wintering grounds often tend to focus on counting the many resident tropical species; although some effort is made to count winter residents, most of these species are secretive at this time of year, so observations through this form of censusing do not give an accurate measure of winter-resident populations.

Since the development of PIF, there have been more CBCs conducted in tropical habitats, and these have made a stronger effort to count wintering birds. In most cases, however, the Christmas Bird Count methodology will not provide strong quantitative data from a study site, but poor data are better than no data at all.

Although not of much use for finding trends in Neotropical migrants, the CBC is of great value to the story about possible Neotropical migrant declines because of the information it has provided about short-distance migrant populations and populations of nest predators and brood parasites. For example, CBC trends can be compared to BBS trends for those species that winter within the area of CBC coverage. Permanent residents and short-distance migrants in general seem to be doing fine.

CBC data have also shown that populations of some species have increased dramatically over time. Most interestingly, CBC data have shown that populations of the Brown-headed Cowbird have risen pretty much continuously through this century (Fig. 3.1). Brittingham and Temple (1983) have suggested that this is the result of additional food throughout the wintering grounds of the cowbird due to both shifting agricultural practices (more grain crops) and the use of mechanical harvesters that leave lots of waste grain. As we shall see in Chapter 5, more cowbirds mean lots of problems for breeding birds, especially Neotropical migrants.

CBC data also have shown changes in populations of such potentially important predatory species as the Blue Jay (*Cyanocitta cristata*) and the American Crow (*Corvus brachyrhynchos*). In the case of the Blue Jay, it has been suggested that our propensity to provide winter food for birds may in fact be leading to reduced reproductive success for many migrants because of the high populations of predators it subsidizes. So CBC data have been of great interest to students of Neotropical migrant birds, but they do not provide direct substantiation of population change in these species.

An exciting new way to monitor winter bird populations in North America has been developed in recent years as part of the citizen science program at the Cornell Laboratory of Ornithology. Called Project FeederWatch, this program recruits people to do systematic counts of birds that use their feeders. In recent years, many of these have even become hooked up to computer systems, so that the data on population trends at feeders can be spread on a website within days of their being

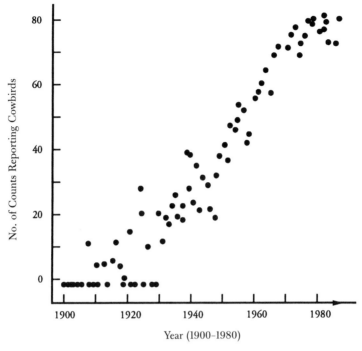

FIGURE 3.1. *Increase in cowbird populations on Christmas Bird Counts, 1900–1990. Reproduced from M. C. Brittingham and S. A. Temple, 1983, "Have Cowbirds Caused Forest Songbirds to Decline?"* BioScience *33:31–35, by permission of the American Institute of Biological Sciences.*

taken. Project FeederWatch has done a marvelous job of documenting the annual variation in finches across North America, and it has provided invaluable data on House Finch population change as this species expanded its range, then declined in numbers due to disease. Unfortunately, despite its glamour, Project FeederWatch does not tell us what is happening to Neotropical migrants on their wintering grounds, so it shares many of the limitations of the Christmas Bird Count.

BANDING STATIONS

A number of bird banding stations exist in North America, mostly along ocean shores, but sometimes also at strategic locations near the Great Lakes, in mountain passes, or at other sites where migrant birds may congregate. These stations are put in locations where often spectacular numbers of birds can be caught and studied during migration. These banding stations have been of utmost importance in providing information about migration. For example, they have shown that different species have different migratory schedules, that the different ages or sexes of some species migrate at different times, and how weather conditions affect movements.

Many of these banding stations have been in operation for years and have consistent netting efforts each year, such that one can compare captures of different species across time. When concern was rising about population trends within Neotropical migrants, a number of these banding stations analyzed their data to see if banding trends matched those of the BBS. As presented at the 1989 meetings on migrants, the results were a mixed bag.

Data from Long Point Bird Observatory in Ontario over a 28-year period were standardized for the effects of weather, lunar cycle, date, and study sites to produce counts of migrants that could be compared with BBS results for Ontario for the same period (Hussell et al. 1992). Trends from the two techniques were positively correlated for 45 species, which suggests that both sources of data reflect real population change. Of 33 species of Neotropical migrants, 29 decreased during the study and only 4 increased, whereas short-distance migrants showed an equal number of increases and decreases. Some of the declining species showed lots of variation with time, and some of that variation could be correlated with causal factors such as regional spruce budworm outbreaks or extremely severe winters. Nine Neotropical migrant species and 3 short-distance migrant species had consistent downward trends throughout the 28-year period, a finding that differed from BBS trends for the region.

Banding data from Manomet Bird Observatory (located in coastal Massachusetts) and Powdermill Nature Reserve (in the mountains of western Pennsylvania) showed rather different patterns (Hagan et al. 1992). Although both sets of data showed that capture rates of recently invading species tracked their population increases well and that declines in some wintering species could be correlated with particularly hard winters, neither had many correlations with local or regional BBS patterns, and there were few correlations between the two stations. The Manomet data actually suggested that short-distance migrants that winter in the southeastern United States were showing the most distinct declines, while Neotropical migrants were holding their own.

A recent paper attempted to combine banding data with a number of other measures of bird abundance taken at the same time to look for long-term trends in populations (Francis and Hussell 1997–1998). Working at the Long Point Bird Observatory in Ontario, these authors used "migration counts" that involved numbers of birds mist-netted at their banding station, birds seen along standardized census routes that were operated daily, and incidental observations. There were enough data for 64 species to use a multiple regression model to compare population trends with a variety of other factors (weather, date, lunar cycle, etc.) and search for patterns. It is interesting that these data tended to show a number of declining trends until 1988 but have shown increases since that time. The majority of these species now show a net increase since 1961. These trends tend to be similar to those found in Ontario BBS data, although the increases in the Long Point populations seem stronger than those shown in the BBS data. Despite the generally more positive results of this study, the authors point out 9 Neotropical migrant species with strongly negative trends that are worthy of further investigation.

Over the past decade, there have been attempts to combine data from a wide variety of banding stations to see if national patterns might appear from such a large analysis. These attempts have produced few clear patterns, in part because of the great variability inherent in trying to track populations on such a large scale with high variability at each of the monitoring sites. Francis and Hussell (1997–1998) concluded their Manomet/Powdermill paper by suggesting that migration capture data can track changes in populations but will probably be more corroborative in nature and may be restricted to the general region of sampling. Certainly the many things we have learned from these banding stations about Neotropical migrant birds justify their continued operation, but their role as population monitoring sites probably does not.

COUNTING HAWKS

Hawk Mountain in eastern Pennsylvania has been famous as a concentration point for migrating raptors for years. Originally, the ridges of this site were where hunters stood and shot at the thousands of raptors that flew by, sometimes resulting in massive kills. In the 1930s this area was purchased by people who wanted to protect hawks from this barbaric activity. Systematic counts of the migrating raptors began in 1934.

Obviously, a data set extending from 1934 to the present is potentially extremely valuable for looking at population trends. Not surprisingly, though, this data set is full of possible biases. The amount of time spent counting was variable from year to year, including many years when either "full-day" or "half-day" counts were done, with no exact times. Only since 1966 have exact hours of coverage been recorded. Yet, hours of daily coverage were quite consistent over a 50-year period; if one assumed that weather patterns varied randomly from year to year, a massive data set is available for examination.

Jim Bednarz and a number of colleagues did this (Bednarz et al. 1990) with some interesting results. They massaged the data in an attempt to smooth out the problems with sampling effort, and then they analyzed trends in three time periods, the pre-DDT period of 1934–1942, the DDT period of 1946–1972 (no counts were done during 3 years of World War II), and the post-DDT period of 1973–1986. The results were generally clear, showing that many species responded negatively to DDT use and, in some cases, showing that the effects of DDT appeared in populations of immature birds before those of adults. For smaller raptors that apparently were not as strongly affected by DDT, long-term trends suggested either increasing or stable populations. The only exceptions to this generalization involved the American Kestrel and Red-tailed Hawk, both of which showed significant declines at Hawk Mountain in later years. It is interesting to note that Breeding Bird Survey data for these species in that region do not match these declining trends.

That the Hawk Mountain data did such a good job of noting the declines of those species that were most affected by DDT provides support for the strength of this monitoring tool. The fact that most species showed apparently stable populations, including such Neotropical migrants as the Broad-winged Hawk, did not indicate declining raptor populations for the eastern United States.

RADAR ORNITHOLOGY

At the 1989 Neotropical migrant symposium in Woods Hole, Massachusetts, there was a lot of rather contentious discussion about the "real" situation with regard to Neotropical migrant bird populations. Although the Breeding Bird Survey data seemed pretty clear in suggesting that many Neotropical migrants were declining, the story for each species was often a mix of pluses and minuses. Additionally, some symposium participants believed that the BBS analyses were done improperly and suggested that the BBS data, reanalyzed their way, showed completely different patterns. Local studies in fragments showed extremely poor nesting success, but other studies, often in bigger forests, showed good reproduction and populations that were just fine. After a couple of days of this back-and-forth evidence, symposium participants had a right to be a bit confused. But near the end of the symposium, Sidney Gauthreaux of Clemson University gave a talk that stopped us in our tracks and made nearly all of us believe that we might have a problem.

Gauthreaux is one of the champions of radar ornithology, a field that uses radar to track bird movements and populations. He did his doctoral work at Louisiana State University, looking at the factors that seemed to affect the migration patterns of those Neotropical migrants that use a trans-Gulf of Mexico route. A large variety of Neotropical migrant birds favor the trans-Gulf route, including thrushes, tanagers, and even hummingbirds. These birds fatten up on land, then head either north or south (depending upon the season) and fly nonstop across the Gulf of Mexico, provided that flying conditions are right. Ideally, they continue past the coastline and settle a few miles in the interior, but if conditions become unfavorable during their flights, they may stop at the coastline itself. If conditions get awful, massive losses of birds may occur as they simply drop into the ocean from exhaustion. Recent work has shown that oil drilling platforms in the Gulf may be important sites to help save birds from this fate until conditions get better for flight.

These migrating birds appeared on the old weather radar screens as little blips, but this blip was enough to provide information about movements and direction, and a whole bunch of blips could tell you something about general abundance patterns (Fig. 3.2). Much of Gauthreaux's original work looked at the conditions that seemed to affect trans-Gulf migration over coastal Louisiana in spring and fall. After finishing his degree at LSU, Gauthreaux got a job at Clemson University in South Carolina, where he proceeded to study other aspects of bird migration.

When the discussion about Neotropical migrant population declines was starting, Gauthreaux was not involved, for his recent work had little to do with population levels. At some point, though, it dawned on him that he might be able to provide quantitative evidence of Neotropical migrant population changes from his studies of radar ornithology. All of the weather radar screens were photographed periodically throughout their operation. Therefore, there was a record of how many blips appeared each year from 1958 until these radar units were replaced in the 1990s. All one had to do was look at all the blips, quantify them in some fashion, and compare numbers over time.

At the 1989 symposium, Gauthreaux reported on his initial work of

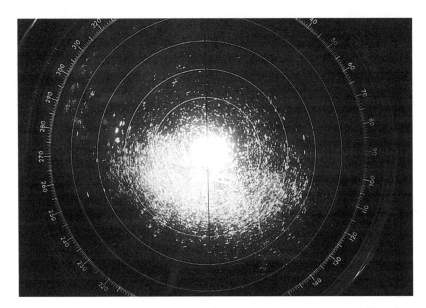

(A)

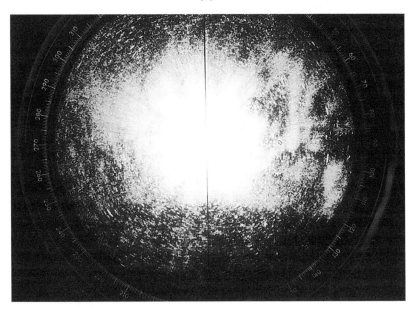

(B)

FIGURE 3.2. *Bird migration as shown by radar. Both images are from WSR-57 radar at Lake Charles, Louisiana. (A) Birds about to end their trans-Gulf migration (12:23 CST, 8 May 1965). The range marks are 20 nautical miles apart, with echoes from migrating flocks visible as far as 80 nautical miles to the east-southeast. (B) Evening exodus of migrants at distances up to 50 nautical miles (19:34 CST, 7 May 1965). The patterns on the eastern edge of the image show the locations of riparian bottomland hardwood stands where many migrants spent the day. Photographs courtesy of Sidney Gauthreaux.*

trying to analyze these patterns in spring (Gauthreaux 1992). He looked at trans-Gulf flights for two radar stations (Lake Charles, Louisiana, and Galveston, Texas) for the years 1987–1989 and compared them with his earlier work done in 1963–1967. Although he did not have good data on actual numbers of birds, he showed clearly that there were only about half as many flights in 1987–1989 as in the 1960s. He also showed that flights during the 1960s occurred almost always when weather conditions were suitable, whereas in the 1980s they occurred only on 36% to 53% of the acceptable flying nights. Finally, he showed that the movements that used to occur in early spring (until mid-April) had declined dramatically.

As Gauthreaux ended his talk at the Woods Hole meeting, a hush fell over the crowd. This was scary. Unless more birds were flying with each flight, he may have presented data showing a 50% loss in population over a 25-year period. Although one could reassure oneself that the data were preliminary and only from a couple of stations for a short period of time, it also was a data set for 3 recent years compared with a similar data set from the past. It was hard not to believe that trans-Gulf migrants had declined dramatically.

Since 1989, Gauthreaux and his students have been working diligently to analyze this data set properly. It is not an easy job. Their goal was to include data from all of the weather stations that circle the Gulf for the whole period that films are available (1957–1990). This would allow them to be sure to catch the entire migration, and it also would allow them to see if flights from different parts of the wintering range (such as the West Indies) had changed. In addition to counting flights, Gauthreaux and his students hoped to develop a way to quantify flights, so that some index to populations could be compared (in essence they are making a quantitative measure of the "cloud" of birds on the radar screen). Because they know the timing of migration of different species, they would be able to estimate the extent that different species had changed numbers over time. It was a major undertaking, to be sure, but one with incredible importance to our understanding of Neotropical bird migration and population change.

As this book was being finished, Gauthreaux and his assistants had not completed the whole task. Some of the data from farther west in the Gulf suggested that the low years for the Louisiana and east Texas radar stations may have been higher years for the Corpus Christi station. But trying to put all the pieces together has taken a lot longer than they had hoped, so the story is still somewhat up in the air.

As part of doing this work, the Gauthreaux laboratory has also been looking at flying conditions across the Gulf of Mexico over the period of study (around 1960 to the present). It is interesting to note that they have discovered what seems to be a long-term deterioration of flying conditions during the 20 to 30 years prior to 1989, then an improvement in conditions in the 1990s. They don't know if this reflects some sort of long-term weather cycle or just random events, but it suggests that trans-Gulf migrants in the 1980s faced increasingly harsh conditions during their spring migration. The extent to which these weather conditions might have caused high mortality of migrating birds, reduced body condition upon arrival on the breeding grounds, or delayed arrival times on the breeding grounds, all of which might reduce overall population levels, is not yet known, but it certainly suggests some tough conditions for this subset of migrants during this period of time.

WHAT DOES IT ALL MEAN?

As you can see, some of the non-BBS evidence that deals with long-term population trends supports the BBS patterns, but some of it does not, and all of these data sets have problems with biases, variability, and the like. I think it is safe to say that, without something as powerful as the BBS analysis, it would have been difficult to make sweeping generalizations about widespread Neotropical migrant population declines. Rather, we would have had local evidence about alarming population trends in some species and bleak trends in only a few species. On the other hand, the other forms of evidence have been highly valuable in noting the details of declines (e.g., where are the birds declining the most) and in indicating possible causes (e.g., the great increase in cowbird and jay numbers).

4 | FRAGMENTATION STUDIES
Real Evidence of Local Declines

Long before the possible widespread declines of populations from Breeding Bird Survey data and other sources were brought to the public's attention, a number of well-documented cases of local population decline and extinction had appeared in the scientific literature. Nearly all of these fit into the category of what are known as "fragmentation" studies, although a few of them were not initially presented as such.

Fragmentation is the term used to describe the process of habitat loss that usually accompanies human development. Portions of a habitat type that is originally large and fairly continuous are converted to some other habitat type by human activities, reducing the amount of remaining original habitat and often leaving it in pieces (fragments) that are separate from the other remaining pieces. Ideally, some portion of the original habitat is left as nature preserves or for other reasons, such that the original habitat does not disappear. The classic example of fragmentation that has appeared in numerous books, articles, and lectures and shows how this process has proceeded over time in a county in Wisconsin was that of Curtis (1956); I also offer my own example (Fig. 4.1), which involves five counties in central Missouri both before and after European settlement. The forested area in this region was reduced to about 25% of the original area and fragmented into more than 1,000 separate units.

Some people have argued that our concern with studying fragmentation has resulted in our ignoring the main problem with fragmentation, which is the overall loss of habitat in a region. They have a point, because loss of a majority of the habitat is probably more important than what we do with the remaining pieces, but the reality is that we did not under-

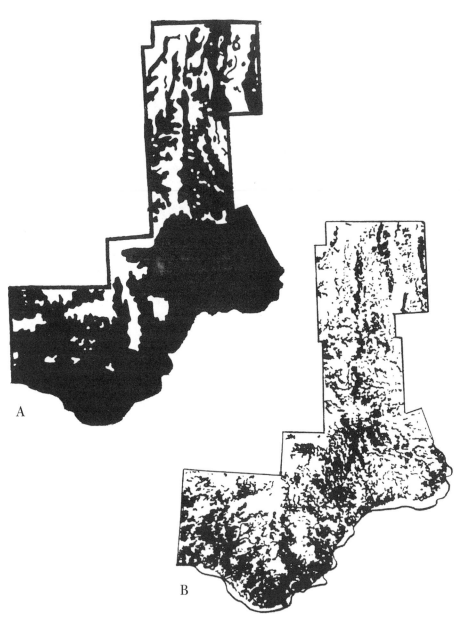

FIGURE 4.1. *Forest fragmentation in central Missouri. This five-county area was fairly heterogeneous before European settlement* (A) *with forest shown as dark, prairie as light, but most prairie and forest areas were connected. Today* (B), *the light area is farmland, and forest area has been reduced 75% and is found in more than 1,000 separate tracts.*

stand much about fragmentation and how it works until long after most habitats had been fragmented. Now that we have seen that patterns in the size, shape, and location of fragments can be of ecological and conservation importance, we have no choice but to find out how best to conserve what we have left.

The seriousness of fragmentation depends upon a variety of factors. First of all, the type of habitat that results following conversion of the original habitat type is critical. Converting prairies to pastures or hay meadows certainly is hard on plant species diversity but has less effect on grassland bird species that can use both the original prairie and the converted habitats to some degree. In addition, the new habitat type is not much of a barrier for movement of birds between remaining prairie fragments. Converting prairies or woodlands to intensive agriculture, especially row crops, means that few or none of the original species can live in the new habitat type, and the remaining habitat fragments can exchange birds only if the birds are willing to fly across the fields that isolate these remaining fragments.

The amount of fragmentation is also important to how birds respond to it. If virtually all the original habitat is destroyed, as occurred in the prairie regions of Iowa and northern Illinois, only tiny, isolated fragments are left, and, as we shall see, usually few birds remain. If some larger proportion of the original habitat (say, 20%) is left, then more widespread opportunities exist for populations to survive in the remnants and to support each other by exchanging individuals. Obviously, how this remaining habitat is distributed can be important, because having one big piece that is 20% of the original area has the advantage of supporting a large local population, but the disadvantage of being either the only such piece remaining or being isolated from other large pieces by the new habitat type.

APPLIED BIOGEOGRAPHY

Given that the process of fragmentation usually results in a group of habitat patches of varying size and shape surrounded by alien habitat, it was easy for scientists to approach these fragments as "habitat islands." This connection was natural because during the late 1960s and most of the 1970s island biogeography had been an active field of ecology. Activity in this area was stimulated by a model of dynamic zoogeography developed by Robert MacArthur of Princeton and E. O. Wilson of Harvard in the 1960s (MacArthur and Wilson 1967). In an attempt to explain the

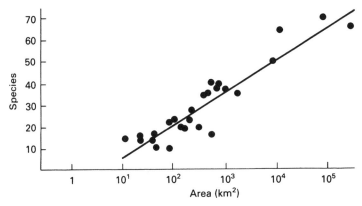

FIGURE 4.2. *A species-area curve for West Indies landbirds. From Faaborg (1988).*

generally linear relationship between the area of an island within an archipelago and the species occurring on that island (Fig. 4.2), MacArthur and Wilson suggested that each island supported an equilibrium between two rates, the rate at which new species visited and established themselves on the island and the rate at which species already established on the island went extinct (Fig. 4.3). It was suggested that the colonization curve should decline as the number of species on an island increased, which makes sense for several reasons. Certainly, as species are added to an island, fewer new species were left to colonize it. More important, as species become established on an island, their large populations and ability to use the resources available on that island may make it harder for the next colonizing species to find enough food or other resources to establish itself. For example, the first species colonizing an "empty" island may have no competition and unlimited food, but by the time 30 species have established themselves, the 31st species will have to deal with those established species to be able to survive.

MacArthur and Wilson suggested that the extinction curve would be the inverse of colonization. When few species existed on an island, one would expect them to do well and rarely go extinct, but as more and more species tried to coexist and subdivide the resources available, the probability of some species going extinct should increase.

The authors suggested that each island had reached a point over time where the rates of colonization and extinction were in balance, which gave that island its characteristic species number. Small islands might have low colonization rates both because they are smaller targets for species roaming across the ocean and because they have fewer resources and less space in which species can live. These latter factors also suggest that small islands should have higher extinction rates, because small populations specializing on specific resources probably go extinct quickly on small islands. In contrast, large islands are big targets and have lots of space and resources (including many habitat types), which means they have higher colonization curves and lower extinction rate curves. The size (area) of the island is the dominant factor in these equations, but the effects of the distance of the island from other islands or sources of colonists are also important. As a result, one might expect islands that are small but close to a larger island to have more species than a like-sized island off by itself. This phenomenon helps explain much of the variation one sees in species-area curves for an archipelago (Fig. 4.2). Finally, history has a role in species densities on islands. One must distinguish between oceanic islands, which have always been surrounded by water, and land bridge islands, which were once connected to the mainland but have lost that connection, most often because of sea level fluctuations. Land bridge islands often have more species than oceanic islands of the same size,

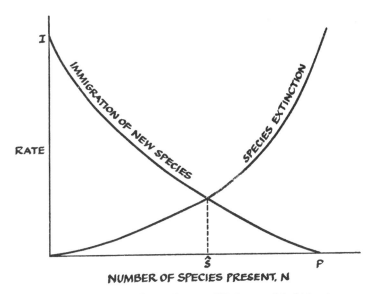

FIGURE 4.3. *The MacArthur-Wilson equilibrium model of island biogeography. Reproduced from R. H. MacArthur and E. O. Wilson, 1963, "An Equilibrium Theory of Insular Biogeography," Evolution 17:373–387, by permission of the Society for the Study of Evolution.*

particularly if the separation occurred recently such that the island has not had time to lose all the species it will eventually lose. Jared Diamond (1972) found that many small land bridge islands of the southwestern Pacific had species densities similar to those of like-sized oceanic islands, whereas large land bridge islands still contained "too many" species.

The MacArthur-Wilson model provided a chance for scientists to predict how bird species might respond to the fragmentation of their habitat. Did birds in habitat fragments show species-area patterns similar to those of real islands? If so, could one use similar logic to explain why these patterns occurred?

ROCK CREEK PARK

We won't spend a lot of time on this example, because it has been described in detail in many other publications (Robbins 1979; Terborgh 1989). Rock Creek Park is a large park that cuts through much of Washington, D.C. As such, it is easily accessible and has been studied for many years by ornithologists. As time went on, these studies showed that many species experienced population declines, then local extinction. In a few cases, it appeared that the habitat the species used had disappeared through natural succession, but in many other cases the habitat had not changed or had seemingly improved.

By looking at how the habitat around Rock Creek Park had changed, the scientists studying birds there were able to come up with an explanation for the many local extinctions they had witnessed. Not that many years ago, Rock Creek Park was just a segment of a long, wooded stretch of riparian habitats, with eventual connection to the vast forests of the Appalachian Mountains to the west. With the development of the area around Washington, these connections were reduced and eventually severed. By the 1980s, Rock Creek Park, although its habitat was perhaps in better condition than ever, sat all by itself, surrounded by the city of Washington and then miles and miles of suburbs. The local populations of each species within the park were relatively small, and if they did not have good reproductive success (see "Generalizing about Area Sensitivity," below) or if individuals did not survive for whatever reason, the chances that replacement individuals of that species would recolonize the park were less than when birds could move easily along the riparian corridor. Over time, many species disappeared from the park; this isolated habitat island could no longer support as many species as before.

ARCHIPELAGO STUDIES

Rock Creek Park is a good example of what can happen to an isolated park, particularly because of the time line involved. It cannot tell us much, though, about how different species vary in their response to fragmentation, since it is just a single unit. Fortunately, because of the interest in island biogeography and its models, several studies on habitat fragmentation were done in the 1970s and 1980s that gave us great insights into how birds respond to fragmentation of their habitats (see Whitcomb et al. 1976, 1981; Hayden et al. 1985; Robbins et al. 1989a; and Wilcove and Robinson 1990).

Many of these studies were done in the Midwest or settled parts of the East Coast, in part because fragmentation characterizes these regions more than others and in part because these regions do not have a lot of topographic variation, so one could control for nearly all ecological variation except fragment size. In contrast, trying to study fragmentation in a mountainous area is confounded by all the habitat change associated with changes in elevation.

To understand the role that area plays in local species extinction, most of these studies began by selecting fragments with the same habitat but covering a wide range of sizes. Ideally, each was isolated from other fragments by a similar distance and had a generally similar shape, such that the experimental units were as similar as possible except for their size. Each "habitat island" was then surveyed for birds, with methods ranging from simple presence and absence through measures of density and, in more detailed studies, measures of nesting success (see Chapter 5). In most of these studies, no time component was involved, because prior studies had not been done on any of these sites. The Trelease Woods site in central Illinois is an interesting exception to this pattern; this remnant had been censused annually for many years, so one could see the extent to which time might affect these patterns (Brawn and Robinson 1996).

Virtually all of these studies showed distinct species-area relationships, such that the number of bird species recorded increased as the area of the fragment increased (Fig. 4.4A). In most cases, this was a logarithmic increase, such that it took a 10-fold increase in area to double the species list, but that also often occurs among real oceanic islands. Of equal importance was that qualitative patterns of species occurrence appeared; that is to say, some species occurred only in fragments of a certain size range (Fig. 4.4B). Some species were present, or were most abundant, only on small fragments but disappeared on larger fragments. In

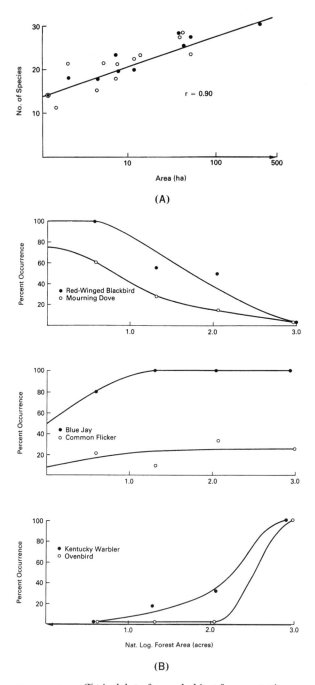

FIGURE 4.4. *Typical data from a habitat fragmentation study. Censuses of forest fragments of different sizes produced a typical species-area curve (A), but the occurrence of species varied with fragment size, with some species occurring only on large fragments (B). From Faaborg (1988).*

many cases, these were species associated with the edge of the forest or other disturbed habitats.

Most important, a number of species occurred only on large or relatively large fragments. Despite the presence of seemingly adequate habitat that might be large enough to support dozens of territories, these species only occurred when fragment size had exceeded some required minimum area. Not surprisingly, scientists rather rapidly tried to determine what these minimum critical areas were and quickly labeled these species as "area-sensitive" (although one could also argue that those species found only on small fragments were also area-sensitive, but in a less worrisome way).

Using the above logic, scientists (including my students and me) quickly rushed to provide refuge managers what were called "minimum area requirements" for area-sensitive species. These preliminary estimates were usually naively based simply on the regular presence of a particular species on a fragment of a particular size. Some even used the size of a forest fragment that had a 50% chance of containing the species. As a result of these rather loose definitions, we computed a minimum area requirement of 300 ha for the Worm-eating Warbler in mid-Missouri, but this was based on the fact that one of our study sites had a single male Wormie in our censuses each summer, although we never saw it with a mate.

Even with these crude estimators, though, it was clear that habitat fragmentation had severe consequences. If many species would not occur on fragments of less than 300 ha (750 acres), controlling fragmentation was necessary to maintain these species in the regional avifauna.

Generalizing about Area-sensitivity: Good News and Bad

As more information about area sensitivity came to light, a general pattern became apparent: the most area-sensitive species were Neotropical migrants. In other words, species that migrated to the Tropics tended to be much more area-sensitive than permanent residents or species that migrated shorter distances. Obviously, when evidence such as the BBS data showed that Neotropical migrants were declining the most, it was easy for people to suggest cause and effect to explain declines.

As with many other things associated with Neotropical migrant birds, the story is more complex, with both good news and bad. Let's begin with the bad news. It is clear that habitat fragmentation can have highly detrimental effects upon birds, with Neotropical migrants perhaps suffering the most. In truth, the situation with regard to habitat fragmentation may be much worse than the earlier estimates of minimum area requirements suggested. Studies have shown (and these will be discussed in more detail in Chapter 5) that populations existing in fragments near the minimum size for that region often are basically "unhealthy." For example, although birds may exist from year to year, pairing success rates for males may be reduced in habitat fragments (Gibbs and Faaborg 1990). In central Missouri, we have found some forest fragments with up to five singing male Ovenbirds but no evidence that any of them attracted a mate (Van Horn et al. 1995). Because these males continue singing in hopes of finally attracting a mate, these sites are often full of song in mid-June, which might suggest that they are preferred habitat over a larger forest where little Ovenbird song occurs at that time of the year. Of course, the reduction in song in large forests is because male Ovenbirds are busy being good fathers at that time of year, rather than trying to attract mates.

Other studies have shown that even if pairing success rates are normal, in many fragments, including some that are very large, nests face unusually high rates of both brood parasitism (from the Brown-headed Cowbird in most of the United States) and nest predation. As a result, a fragment that is thousands of acres in size may show reduced reproductive rates when compared with what we see in the largest forests in existence today and what we think occurred before fragmentation. In small fragments in the Midwest, and these may include forests of up to several hundred acres, most birds have only a small chance of producing young. Although most of these species are incredibly persistent and will attempt many clutches through the breeding season, in some locations the predation rates are so high that success is almost impossible. Brawn and Robinson (1996) suggested that many Neotropical migrants living in small forest fragments in Illinois had nest predation rates high enough that it would take 20 nesting attempts for a pair to be successful. Obviously, the temperate breeding season doesn't allow time for this many attempts, so the birds living in these fragments are usually doomed to failure.

As my colleagues and I started gathering and sharing our data showing such incredibly low reproductive success on fragments, we got pretty depressed. If it took forests that were many thousands of acres in size in order for these birds to reproduce (and most states did not have forests of this size), it seemed inevitable that Neotropical migrant populations would have to decline. When the BBS data appeared, it was hard to argue with people who said that habitat fragmentation was driving population declines.

But one puzzling observation appeared in most of our studies—this is the good news. Although we were finding horrible reproductive success in forest fragments year after year, populations of breeding Neotropical migrants seemed to be doing just fine in these very same fragments. If populations were regulated by local reproduction, then we must not have been finding lots of nests that were successful; perhaps we found only nests that did not succeed, or the act of monitoring nests led to higher predation. Although we knew we weren't finding all the nests, we were not convinced that this was the answer, and several studies showed that nest monitoring did not increase predation rates.

Another possibility was that migrants were very mobile, such that young birds produced in good habitats could wander off to colonize fragments and keep populations there at a stable level. We will discuss the details of this phenomenon in Chapter 6; for now, all we need to point out is that those sites that were providing the most convincing data about reproductive failure, data that might be used to explain regional or national declines in populations, were also sites where populations tended to be doing just fine.

It is this inconsistency that makes it difficult to provide sweeping blame to habitat fragmentation for the recent declines shown by Neotropical migrants. For habitat fragmentation to account for population declines such as those evidenced by BBS, it seems that the failure of reproduction in fragments should express itself both along BBS routes and in the fragments under study themselves. It is much more of a stretch to suggest that reproductive failure would reduce populations where the census routes are but not where the birds are failing to reproduce.

Additional evidence regarding the time frame of fragmentation also works against fragmentation as an explanation for population declines. Population declines were associated with the late 1970s and 1980s, but fragmentation of breeding habitats tended to occur long before that. What could have changed about the distribution of fragmented habitats on a regional scale during the 1970s to drive the decline? If anything (as we shall see in Chapter 6), parts of the United States, particularly in the east, were becoming less fragmented during this period.

Thus, while habitat fragmentation can cause numerous problems for local populations of birds, and particularly Neotropical migrants, it is harder to see how some general change in fragmentation patterns on the breeding grounds could have caused the BBS declines at the time they occurred.

EVIDENCE FROM NONFRAGMENTED SITES

An interesting sociological phenomenon may help explain the ease with which many reputable scientists (myself included) jumped on the fragmentation bandwagon as at least a partial cause of population declines of migrants. Because fragmentation was inherently interesting as science and conservation, even without Neotropical migrant declines, a number of us were working on it at the same time, before the days of Partners in Flight. To do these studies we, of course, chose fragmented habitats, usually with study sites no larger than a few hundred or maybe 1,000 acres. We limited ourselves to areas of this size partly because we had no idea what the appropriate spatial scale was with regard to avian responses to fragmentation and often, pragmatically, because forest fragments larger than this were not available.

The result was that we all were studying sites with lousy reproductive success. When we would get together over beers at ornithological meetings, we would exchange horror stories about failed nesting. (Scott Robinson usually "won" these rather twisted bragging contests, citing the incredibly high parasitism and predation rates he found at his seemingly large Shawnee National Forest study sites in Illinois.) After a few beers and lots of negative examples, extinction of everything seemed certain and soon. Even when we talked about the fact that populations weren't declining the way reproductive success might suggest, it was hard to visualize where the birds were coming from, at least until we started studies within some nonfragmented sites.

What we needed were long-term data from mature habitats (so habitat change was not much of a factor) situated in locations where fragmentation was also not a factor (or was becoming less of one). Fortunately, there were a few of these sites that both gave us hope and provided some interesting insights about population change in migrants and its possible causes.

Hubbard Brook   Richard Holmes of Dartmouth College started studying the bird community of Hubbard Brook, New Hampshire, in the late 1960s. The Hubbard Brook location was already famous for work on ecosystem traits such as energy flow and nutrient cycling, and

Holmes's initial goal was to look at the interactions among ecological energetics, food supply, forest composition and structure, and the bird community. To do this, he needed detailed measures of the density of each species within his study sites for comparison with the other ecological measures. This information was compiled for many years, with some of the most detailed community ecology of birds ever recorded resulting from the work of Holmes and his students (who include such important figures in Neotropical migrant biology as Scott Robinson, Tom Sherry, and Peter Marra).

When the discussion about population declines and its possible causes became heated, Dick Holmes and Tom Sherry realized that their long-term data set from a nonfragmented site was valuable, so they published a paper comparing population trends from their intensive study site with those found in all the BBS routes of New Hampshire (Holmes and Sherry 1988). Although they found that more of the 19 mostly migratory species for which they had data were declining in both habitats (8 declining and 1 increasing in the unfragmented forest; 5 declining and 1 increasing statewide), they were quick to point out that the declines were not necessarily the result of winter limitation. Because the authors had such detailed knowledge of the specific characteristics of breeding habitat used by the declining species, they were able to come up with compelling causes for declines that did not involve winter habitat. Rather, such factors as food limitation, habitat change (both through the natural process of succession and from human land-use changes), and climatic events on the breeding areas were shown to be possible explanations for many of the declines. The only strong evidence suggesting some sort of winter limitation concerned a set of species (Hermit Thrush, Dark-eyed Junco, and Winter Wren) that may have had populations affected by severe winter conditions. In addition, these species were not hard-core Neotropical migrants but species that wintered primarily in the United States. The authors presented no strong evidence that any of the declines in populations they studied were caused by loss of wintering habitat in the Tropics, although they noted the variety of problems associated with determining cause and effect on such a large scale. They ended their paper with a strong warning that we must be sure to consider alternative explanations for population declines before we conclude that a factor such as tropical wintering limitation is at work.

Great Smoky Mountains   David Wilcove, currently with the Environmental Defense Fund, was the first ecologist to examine some of the factors causing population declines in forest fragments. Largely because he had worked in small forest fragments with only a small portion of the possible species living there, Wilcove wanted to see if the bird community within large tracts of forest had changed over time (Wilcove 1988). To do this, he returned in 1982–1983 to the site of 10 Breeding Bird Censuses made in the Great Smoky Mountains by B. Fawver in 1947–1948. Great Smoky Mountains National Park is certainly one of the largest and least disturbed tracts of forest in the eastern United States; no fragmentation effects would be expected.

Wilcove's surveys found no change in the populations of Neotropical migrants over the 36-year period of study, but he did find great increases in the populations of three species—Common Crow (*Corvus brachyrhynchos*), Blue Jay (*Cyanocitta cristata*), and Dark-eyed Junco. For all of these, he suggested that human activities in the general vicinity of the park might be at work. Wilcove pointed out that these observations showed that one need not use winter limitation to explain population declines in fragmented habitats and that large, unfragmented sites may be critical to the future conservation of migrant birds.

GENERAL CONCLUSIONS AND MISCONCLUSIONS ABOUT FRAGMENTATION

Studies from within large forests served as reference points for studies of fragmentation, because one could see how trends related to fragment size often extrapolated directly to characteristics of these large sites, which perhaps serve as "mainland" sites for habitat islands. The general pattern seemed to be that species dropped out of these forests as the forests became fragmented, with more species disappearing as the fragment got smaller and smaller. Neotropical migrant species seemed to drop out first with declining fragment size, while some short-distance migrants or permanent residents actually increased in abundance or frequency as fragments got smaller.

If a species would occur only in a forest of at least some particular size, it was clear that fragmentation had to be controlled to maintain populations within a particular region. Many studies in the 1980s showed that a 1,000-acre fragment of woodland was not enough forest to support the full potential complement of breeding bird species found in that region, even though this same area might support hundreds of territories of many species if it were part of a large, contiguous forest. The development of conservation guidelines that used the minimum area of occurrence of these area-sensitive species was certainly a step in the right direction, but several problems immediately arose with these suggestions. First, studies on the same species showed that the minimum area of occurrence in one region could be different from that in another. If we didn't have the time or resources to study the species in our state, did we use the suggested minimum area requirement for Maryland or for Missouri? For the Ovenbird, the minimums for these states differed by a factor of 3.

More important, the suggested minimum areas were nearly always based on minimum areas of occurrence. Thus, if a bird species occurred on a 1,000-acre forest most of the time, that area was listed as its minimum area requirement, no matter how many individuals occurred there. As noted earlier, in Missouri we were disturbed because the presence of a lone Worm-eating Warbler on a 300 ha tract year after year suggested that that area was suitable for conservation purposes. After all, the species showed 100% occurrence over a several-year period, which fit the criteria designed by some for determining minimum area standards. Yet, the species was always represented by just a single male on that tract, and observations suggested that he never attracted a mate. On a more general note, even if lots of individual Neotropical migrants occurred on a large fragment, did we have any evidence that the birds on that fragment were producing enough young to maintain populations? In many cases, when migrant abundances approached what we thought was normal, we just assumed that reproductive success would be normal too. This assumption was a big mistake, as we shall see in Chapter 5.

Nearly all studies of fragmentation have shown that small fragments do not support the complete bird community one would expect if that habitat were part of a larger habitat complex. Not only has fragmentation become a standard part of the lexicon of avian ecologists and professional conservationists, but it is used regularly by any layman who is well versed in modern conservation. Although most studies showed nothing but bad news with regard to birds, there were a few bright spots among fragmentation studies of the 1980s. Robert Askins and Margaret Philbrick (1987) of Connecticut College showed that the birds found in a fragment they studied were increasing, primarily because this fragment was becoming less fragmented and isolated as the surrounding countryside reverted back to forest. Thus, there was hope both that fragments could be restored and that large areas could support bird populations, but by the 1990s the need was to figure out how big an area was necessary for a population to be able to maintain itself and what sort of distribution of these areas might be necessary for some sort of regional conservation plan. To reach the former goal, we needed more detailed information on avian demography, which is discussed in Chapter 5. To reach the latter goal, we needed to change the whole way we thought about populations and population regulation, which is covered in Chapter 6.

5 | WHAT HAPPENS ON HABITAT FRAGMENTS?

There is now overwhelming evidence that larger pieces of habitat are necessary to support many species of birds. In many cases, a species may occur with regularity only in habitat blocks that could contain dozens if not hundreds of territories, even though smaller fragments may seem to contain ideal habitat conditions.

Thus, to understand why species do not occur on smaller fragments, we need to examine the possible limiting factors that may be at work on smaller fragments. We have already alluded to higher parasitism and nest predation rates. Recent work has suggested that changes in the habitat or food supply may be associated with fragmentation. Not surprisingly, an additional factor may be behavioral responses of the species involved to fragmentation, such that the birds attempt to maximize nesting success when possible by avoiding the above factors. Of course, all of these factors may be at work, leading to the messy patterns and convoluted answers typical of ecological studies. Before we look at these factors in more detail, though, we must examine another part of the story about fragments, a part that may play an important role in explaining patterns in all of the above factors. This is the role of habitat edge and so-called edge effects.

WHAT IS EDGE AND WHAT ARE EDGE EFFECTS?

Edge is the general term used to describe any discontinuity between habitat types. Where a forest ends and a field begins, or where a pasture ends and a cultivated field begins, there is an edge. A large contiguous forest or prairie has little edge, unless the forest is full of small clear-cuts or other openings, all of which create edge.

As fragmentation occurs, the amount of edge found in a region inevitably increases, because small pieces of habitat have relatively more edge than do large blocks. If we look back at Figure 4.1, we can see that the original situation had a reasonable amount of edge due to the heterogeneous nature of the forest-prairie transition, but most of the forested area was some distance from this edge. Today the remaining fragments are small enough that the forest edge is always relatively near. The total amount of edge around prairie and forest fragments undoubtedly reached a maximum at some point, then started to decline as the total number of remaining fragments became fewer. Much of the modern agricultural land may contain edges, but these involve differences between crop types or the existence of wooded fencerows and the like, so they are of less concern to the birds that lived in the original habitat. If these wooded fencerows attract predators or cowbirds, they may affect nearby grassland birds.

Because an edge of an original habitat type lies adjacent to a different habitat, the properties of the original habitat along the edge may be different from those of the habitat farther from the edge. If one visualizes a mature forest with a closed canopy, one might think of a relatively dark, damp habitat, but if that habitat is right next to a soybean field, it will undoubtedly be drier and brighter than the forest well within the fragment's interior. Desiccation of the habitat near the edge is termed an edge effect. If cowbirds or predators prefer to search for nests along the forest edge (and they often do), their behavior would be an edge effect.

Although *edge* is defined as the point where two habitats come together, it is unlikely that negative edge effects occur only at this point. Rather, we would expect that if the occurrence of edge increases predator numbers or densities of cowbirds or affects the habitat near the edge, this effect should extend some distance into the original habitat. Much of the recent work on fragmentation and edges has involved trying to figure out how far these edge effects actually extend into the affected native habitat.

Edge effects and fragmentation effects may go hand in hand in explaining why many bird species disappear from fragments. Certainly, there is a statistical relationship between the ratio of edge to area as fragment size changes, provided one keeps the fragment shape constant. But in the real world, this shape is not always constant, so some fragments that are long and thin may have the whole habitat exposed to edge effects, while another fragment of the same size but in a circular shape might have some core area that is not exposed to these edge conditions. As we shall see below, edge effects and area effects may not always be the same.

Nearly all the recent evidence on edge effects has shown edges to have negative values for forest birds. Obviously, edge effects favor edge species. Many studies with Neotropical migrant forest birds have shown that edges are bad and should be avoided whenever possible. These findings conflict strongly with several decades of wildlife management theory, much of which promoted the creation of edge in order to increase wildlife populations. Certainly, it creates a conflict between what is good for many Neotropical migrants and what is good for turkey, deer, and quail, as well as migrants that like edge.

Much of this conflict has to do with history; in the old days, *wildlife management* meant management of game species, most of which prospered in situations with lots of edge. To increase the deer or turkey populations, you increased the amount of edge. In many cases, this involved wildlife openings in the forest or rows of trees next to a prairie. These openings or trees would bring a whole new set of species to these habitat types, among them the turkey, deer, quail, and pheasant targeted by the managers. If the forests with the openings or the prairies with the tree rows were large enough, this would still preserve all the species needing large habitats and would add those favoring edge. Problems occurred when the management practices opened up enough of the forest to chase away the species that had large area requirements or when enough trees were put into the prairies to chase away the true prairie birds. Of course, if the managers were evaluated with regard to how many deer or quail they produced and not how many Ovenbirds or Dickcissels they had chased away, their decision-making process could not be questioned. But as the definition of *wildlife* expanded in the 1980s and the concern with migrant birds grew in the 1990s, the conflicts between classical wildlife management and Neotropical migrant bird management became apparent.

As we look at some of the more specific reasons why many birds cannot exist on habitat fragments, we will regularly examine the role of edge and edge effects in explaining these patterns. These effects are often a clear cause for the declines that we see associated with the area of remaining habitat fragments, but we will see that edge effects also may depend upon other, larger-scale factors such that edge effects may be muted in some situations.

THE BROWN-HEADED COWBIRD:
A SUCCESSFUL GENERALIST PARASITE

The Cowbird Strategy   The Brown-headed Cowbird has received
much of the blame for declines of Neotropical migrant bird species, and
in a few cases this blame may be legitimate. Of course, we shouldn't blame
a species for doing what it was meant to do, and in many ways the problems associated with the Brown-headed Cowbird are problems that are
the result of human activities that have increased cowbird numbers.

Before we go out casting blame, we should recognize the Brown-
headed Cowbird as a prime example of evolution in action. It is a species
whose reproductive strategy takes advantage of the work ethic of other
species. By laying its egg in another bird's nest, a single cowbird not only
avoids "putting all its eggs in one basket" with regard to possible predation but also takes advantage of the parental care provided by the host
birds. With 30 or more eggs laid annually (which, interestingly enough,
develop in the bird in "clutches" of 4 or 5, which may reflect the original
clutch size of this species when it actually raised its own young), a single
female cowbird has an incredible potential productivity, all with minimal
work. By being a generalist brood parasite, the cowbird can take advantage of a large range of potential hosts; cowbird eggs have been recorded
from nests of more than 200 other species of birds.

Although the scenario presented above may suggest a situation in
which female cowbirds are running across the environment and dumping eggs in any nest they see, the reality is that female cowbirds have
constraints on where they put their eggs to increase their probability of
success. The cowbird egg must be deposited in the host nest before incubation starts, so that the cowbird egg can hatch either with or before the
host young. A cowbird egg deposited in a nest well into incubation will
never get the chance to hatch, even though cowbirds often have shorter
incubation periods than other species of similar size. Additionally, the
cowbird should try to choose a host that feeds an appropriate diet to its
young; otherwise that egg is wasted too. Finally, the cowbird should be
careful not to parasitize birds that are much bigger than it is, because
the cowbird baby will likely not get enough food when in competition
with the larger host young. On the other hand, cowbirds can parasitize
smaller species, because the host parents will compensate for the baby
cowbird's needs by increasing delivery rates and food sizes (Dearborn
et al. 1998).

Host Responses Of course, the host birds would rather not raise cowbirds, because, in nearly all cases, doing so reduces the number of young of their own that they can raise. As a result, another set of constraints arises for cowbirds as hosts evolve responses to parasitism.

Some species will desert a nest if a cowbird lays an egg in it, particularly if the cowbird egg is the first egg laid. Obviously, the cowbird should wait until at least one egg has been laid before laying its own egg. Desertion of the nest following parasitism may be related to the egg-laying behavior of the host. A former student of mine, Dirk Burhans, discovered that Field Sparrows (*Spizella pusilla*) lay their eggs early in the morning, before the time cowbirds do, such that Field Sparrows were on the nest when the cowbird arrived to lay (Burhans 2000). When a cowbird tried to lay in a Field Sparrow nest, a fight would ensue, which usually was followed by desertion of the nest. In contrast, Indigo Buntings in the same field didn't come to lay their eggs until well after the cowbirds had visited the nests. Unless the cowbirds laid first, Indigo Buntings accepted cowbird eggs willingly. We suspect that the few cases in which Field Sparrows accepted cowbird eggs may have involved situations in which the timing precluded the interaction between host and cowbird.

Because cowbirds lay only a single type of egg, white with brownish splotches, in many species it is obvious if the nest has been parasitized. For example, the blue eggs of a Wood Thrush look quite different from those of a cowbird. One would think that host birds that could distinguish cowbird eggs from their own would try to get rid of the parasitic eggs, and in some cases they do. In many cases, birds will remove the cowbird eggs and leave only their own, but the requirement here is that the host bird is large enough to be able to grab the egg and carry it away. Poking the cowbird egg and breaking it before removal causes several possible problems. First, breaking the egg may mess up the nest, causing problems with raising the host young. Secondly, cowbird egg shells are unusually thick, which may result in the host bird's blows deflecting off the cowbird egg and into one of the host eggs.

Depending upon how a host species responds to cowbird eggs, hosts can be categorized as either accepters or rejecters. Accepters seem to accept cowbird eggs without any response, whereas rejecters will remove these eggs. Within a species, though, there is often individual and sometimes regional variation in behavioral responses to cowbird eggs, sometimes related to the frequency with which birds historically are exposed to parasitism.

Costs to the Host With hundreds of potential hosts, it is hard to make concrete statements about the effects of cowbird parasitism. For most species, raising a cowbird means raising fewer host young. One reason for this is that the female cowbird often removes a host egg as she lays her egg, so the clutch size of the host starts out smaller in a parasitized nest than in an unparasitized one. (The cowbird often eats this egg for the nutrition it offers.) After hatching, the cowbird young is often much larger and more active than the host young, which means it can monopolize the food brought by the parents, sometimes to the point that host offspring starve. The hosts often show remarkable efforts in their attempts to raise all the young in their nest. One of my students, Donald Dearborn, used video cameras to record food deliveries to numerous nests (Dearborn et al. 1998). After hundreds of hours of analyzing these films, he found that Indigo Bunting parents would increase feeding rates nearly threefold when raising a cowbird, and they would begin bringing in larger food items more quickly when raising the larger bird. As a result, the parents were sometimes able to raise both the cowbird young, which weighed more than 30 g, and one or two of their 11 g young.

Some of the world's brood parasites are notorious for the things they do to their nest mates. Cuckoos in the Old World (family Cuculidae) usually hatch before their nest mates and proceed to push the remaining eggs or other young out of the nest, using their backs to push the eggs or young over the nest rim. African honeyguides (family Indicatoridae) parasitize cavity-nesting species, and they are equipped with a sharp egg tooth that is used to slash the nest mates to death following hatch. Obviously, the above species are careful not to lay two parasitic eggs in a single nest, for an ugly battle would eventually ensue.

Cowbirds have generally not been thought to engage in such brutal within-nest rivalries, but while studying feeding rates of Indigo Buntings, Don Dearborn did record a case in which a young cowbird obviously pushed a baby Indigo Bunting out of the nest. How often this occurs remains to be seen, but another aspect of cowbird nestling behavior may be equally deadly. Baby birds help stimulate their parents to feed by the chirping they do at the nest while being fed. Cowbird nestlings, which are trying to coerce host parents to greatly increase their feeding rates, are unusually noisy, both with regard to the strength of the begging call and the frequency with which it is given. By combining their data, Dirk Burhans and Don Dearborn found evidence that nests with cowbird nestlings exhibited higher predation rates than those with just host young. To test this, Dearborn set up an artificial nest experiment in which he put out artificial nests in sets of three; one nest was next to a speaker that played Indigo Bunting nestling calls in typical fashion, one nest was next to a speaker that played cowbird nestling calls with their louder sound and higher frequency, and a control nest was next to a speaker that played a tape that made only the slight hiss that tape recorders make. Don found that predators ate more of the eggs from the "cowbird" nests than from either the bunting nests or the controls (Dearborn 1999).

A final potential cost that cowbird parasitism might have for host birds involves some new ideas based on just a handful of observations. In several cases, researchers using video cameras to record nesting activities have observed a female cowbird come to a nest and kill all the young. It has been suggested that a female that couldn't find an appropriate host nest might increase her chances of success by killing the young in existing nests, thereby forcing the host parents to renest, which would provide the cowbird a chance to lay an egg. Circumstantial evidence for this behavior comes from a long-term study on Song Sparrows on Mandarte Island, British Columbia, where the researchers found a large increase in nest predation shortly after female cowbirds arrived on the island to breed (Arcese et al. 1996). This study did not have cameras watching nests, but other researchers with such equipment have picked up the occasional cowbird predation of nestlings. Although it is unlikely that further studies will find this to be a widespread phenomenon, it still is an intriguing behavior that adds to the costs of parasitism for resident host species.

How Frequent Can Parasitism Be?   We have seen that a pair of breeding birds can be negatively affected by cowbird parasitism in a variety of ways (and we haven't even mentioned such possible long-term costs to the hosts as reductions in survival rate after going through all the effort that it takes to raise a cowbird). For cowbirds to be a major cause of Neotropical migrant population declines, we should be able to show that cowbird parasitism is having strong negative effects for a large number of species across a large area. That is harder to do.

Certainly, there are situations where cowbird parasitism is pathological in its nature. The Shawnee National Forest study sites of Scott Robinson in southeastern Illinois must be cowbird heaven. Scott has found as many as 75% of all nests parasitized, with the average parasitized nest holding more than 2 cowbird eggs (Robinson 1992). For the Wood Thrush, as many as 92% of the nests might be parasitized, and he has found Wood Thrush nests with as many as 11 cowbird eggs. The remarkable thing is that Shawnee National Forest is the largest woodland in Illinois. Some of the smaller forest fragments studied by Scott and his students had even higher rates of parasitism.

Certain species of host have also shown remarkably high levels of parasitism. The classic example is the Kirtland's Warbler, a breeding species confined to the lower peninsula of Michigan. This species did not have to deal with cowbirds until this century, when changing land-use practices allowed the cowbird to expand its range eastward. During the late 1950s and 1960s, 75% of all Kirtland's Warbler nests were parasitized, and these nests produced 40% fewer young than nonparasitized nests. Populations of the warbler dropped by more than half before cowbird control activities reduced the parasitism rates, apparently helping the Kirtland's Warbler population to increase again (Walkinshaw 1983).

In recent years, this scenario has also occurred with several other populations or species. For those with restricted ranges, such as the Black-capped Vireo in the Texas-Oklahoma area or several subspecies in California (Bell's Vireo, California Gnatcatcher [*Polioptila californica*]), parasitism by the cowbird might have been strong enough to cause local if not total extinction without control of cowbird populations. For most species, though, it appears that cowbird parasitism might be a factor in population declines but is probably not a strong enough factor to cause regional or total extinction. As we shall see below, host species often can raise at least some offspring even when their nests are parasitized, and even in severe infestations, cowbirds do not find all nests. Finally, for some of the species that produce several nests, the last nest of the year may occur after the Brown-headed Cowbird has ceased laying. In Missouri, most cowbirds are done with laying by early July, but many other species (e.g., Indigo Bunting and Bell's Vireo) are still producing nests after this time.

Why Are Cowbirds So Abundant? Although cowbirds may not be causing host population extinction, it is obvious that they are a major problem in parts of the United States and Canada. What is it about the cowbird that has allowed it to become so numerous that it can exert such strong pressures on bird populations? And does this phenomenon occur elsewhere in the world?

As was noted earlier, we have good evidence from Christmas Bird Count data that cowbird numbers have been increasing throughout this century (see Fig. 3.1). This can be explained by a couple of factors, chief among them that cowbirds feed on seeds during the winter. With the general increase in agriculture and the development of mechanical harvesters during this century, the amount of waste grain available in fields during the winter has increased dramatically. Certainly, there is currently more food for cowbirds in the winter than there ever has been.

Food might also be more abundant during the breeding season now than it was in the past. Because males are not producing eggs, they can feed on grain even through the summer, and they are common residents in cattle and horse feedlots. In fact, as cowbirds have expanded their range into the mountains of the western United States, they have often followed the distribution of horses and large riding stables. While breeding, females require a diet that includes more insects as food; they achieve this by foraging in shorter grasses, preferably in situations where cattle are keeping the grass short and the birds can catch insects stirred up by cows, but female cowbirds do not hesitate to forage in mowed lawns (Morris and Thompson 1998). In Shawnee National Forest, mowing the campgrounds and picnic areas may be making things better for cowbirds. Females will also join the males in feeding on grain in feedlots, so food during the breeding season apparently also is little problem for cowbirds.

Finally, as a generalized parasite, the cowbird can turn to many potential hosts during the breeding season to raise its eggs. Here is where the idea of edge effects pops up, for it appears that cowbirds prefer to look for hosts that nest in or near the edge of the forest. Several studies have shown either that cowbird abundance declines as one goes into a large forest or that parasitism rates decline along the same gradient (O'Conner and Faaborg 1993). As we humans have fragmented habitats, we may have made conditions better and better for cowbirds to find hosts.

Studies using radiotelemetry on cowbirds have shown that an individual bird will travel as much as 7 km daily between feeding and breeding areas (Thompson 1994). Thus, one good feedlot or cattle pasture could help sustain a large cowbird population that in turn might affect a large breeding area. In this regard, we might be able to explain why Shawnee National Forest might be cowbird heaven, because it is a heterogeneous mix of pastures, feedlots, and forests, with lots of forest edge for nest searching.

We can see that cowbirds have responded positively to human activities and are now certainly a pest, if not a plague. This phenomenon has not occurred in other parts of the world where other brood parasites live. These other host-parasite systems are much more sophisticated than the cowbird system; species or even populations of a species lay eggs that perfectly mimic the egg of the single host species they parasitize, and they display the host nestling ejection behavior discussed earlier. In contrast to cowbirds, the adults of the main parasites in Europe, the cuckoos, are large insectivores whose populations cannot be artificially increased by human activities. In Africa, the other parasite is the honeyguide, which is undoubtedly limited in population by its feeding on bee larvae, which often are provided by native peoples who are shown to the hive by the honeyguide and who leave food for their mutualist. Both the limited foods available to these brood parasites as adults and their specialization to a single or small set of host species suggest that these parasites will never become abundant enough to cause the problems that cowbirds do in parts of the United States.

Where Are the Cowbirds?   We have seen that cowbirds can be a severe problem for some species or even communities of birds in the Midwest, and we know that cowbirds have expanded their range both to the east and into the western mountains. Are cowbird populations a problem or potential problem everywhere?

Frank Thompson and colleagues of the U.S. Forest Service have analyzed the distribution and abundance of cowbirds, using Breeding Bird Survey data (Thompson et al. 2000). Basically, they found the Brownheaded Cowbird to be most abundant through the center of its range, from western Texas up through the Dakotas and into the prairies of Canada (Fig. 5.1). Its abundance declined in both directions away from the core area, such that states well east or west of this region had fewer cowbirds. By using data on regional forest cover, the authors also were able to show that this factor helped explain cowbird abundance on a more local scale. Basically, all other things being equal, as an area has more and more forest, it has fewer cowbirds. The probable reason is that cowbirds require the mix of forests for finding nests and fields for feeding, and as forest cover gets higher, there just isn't enough feeding area to support large populations. We will look at this pattern a bit more in Chapter 6 when we consider landscape effects on migrant bird reproduction.

From these analyses, it is apparent that cowbird parasitism pressures can vary on several spatial scales. They will probably always be high in the interior of the United States, which is the historic center of the cowbird's range, and they might be locally high in other areas where the proper mix of forest and feeding areas is found. But in general, away from the vast hordes of cowbirds in the interior, cowbirds are just not as big a problem as studies in the Midwest have shown. Several studies of nesting success in the East have documented much lower rates of parasitism in that re-

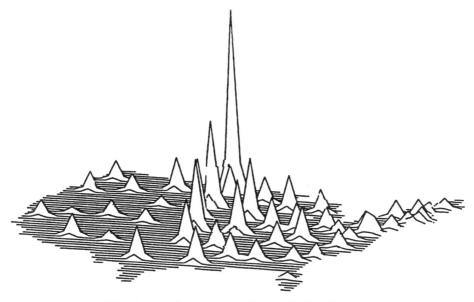

FIGURE 5.1. *Distribution of the Brown-headed Cowbird in the United States, using BBS data. Reproduced from F. R. Thompson III, S. K. Robinson, T. M. Donovan, J. Faaborg, and D. R. Whitehead, 2000, "Biogeographic, Landscape, and Local Factors Affecting Cowbird Abundance and Host Parasitism Levels," in* Ecology and Management of Cowbirds and Their Hosts, *ed. J. N. M. Smith, T. L. Cook, S. I. Rothstein, S. K. Robinson, and S. G. Sealy, pp. 271–279, by permission of the University of Texas Press.*

gion, such that the cowbird is not the major problem or really a problem at all (Hoover and Brittingham 1993).

What about Two or Three Cowbird Species? Although there is evidence that cowbird parasitism may be the major problem for Neotropical migrant birds only in some circumstances, the high rates of parasitism found across some large areas are still not a good thing. If cowbird populations continue to rise as they have through most of this century, cowbird parasitism may become more of a limiting factor in larger areas of the United States and Canada.

An additional potentially scary situation is offered by the expansion of the ranges of two other cowbird species into the United States in recent years. The Bronzed Cowbird has always occurred in extreme southern Texas, but in recent years its populations have increased there and it has expanded its range northward. The Shiny Cowbird (*Molothrus bonari-*

ensis) was originally found in South America, but it has moved through the West Indies and has recently invaded Florida. On several West Indian islands, the Shiny Cowbird has been a major factor in causing the endangerment of local bird populations. In Puerto Rico alone it is the chief factor in the decline of the Yellow-shouldered Blackbird (*Agelaius xanthomus*) and the Black-cowled Oriole (*Icterus dominicensis*), and it has been implicated in the recent declines of the Puerto Rican Vireo (*Vireo latimeri*) (Woodworth 1999). Like some of the Californian subspecies or species discussed earlier, island endemics are particularly vulnerable to new brood parasites, because the endemics are naive about parasitism and occur in small populations over restricted areas. Only with cowbird eradication in key areas have wildlife managers been able to save the Yellow-shouldered Blackbird in southwestern Puerto Rico.

We do not know what the addition of one or two more cowbird species to an area will do. Cowbirds have never occurred in parts of Florida, so many species will have to deal with this new problem. When two cowbird species begin to overlap in range, we will see if they accentuate the parasitism problem by using different hosts or feeding areas or if they just divide it up among themselves, such that the total problem will be the same but two species will be involved. Of course, if ranges expand enough, an area might have three species of cowbird, which will present an interesting ecological phenomenon even if it is a frightening conservation scenario.

NEST PREDATION

Most humans find eggs to be a tasty and nutritious food; even some folks who do not eat meat include this food item in their diet. The same is true for the animal world; few predators will hesitate to eat eggs when they are lucky enough to find a nest, and a large group of animals that we think of as primarily vegetarians (squirrels and mice, for example) seem to look for eggs to eat when they are in season. Interestingly enough, many of these same animals also will eat nestlings without hesitating, including the aforementioned rodents that lack canine teeth.

The possibility that nest predation might be an important component of Neotropical migrant bird declines arose well before the evidence for declines. Many of the early studies of habitat fragmentation noted that long-distance migrants were more sensitive to fragmentation than short-distance migrants or residents. Those studies suggested that this might reflect two general facts about the long-distance migrants: (1) they almost always had open cup nests, which are more vulnerable to predators than the cavity nests used by many resident birds, and many of these open nests were on or near the ground; and (2) many Neotropical migrants are single-brooded, which means that if they lose part of their brood to nest predation (or through parasitism, as discussed above), they don't have any further chances to make up for the loss, as would be the case for multiple-brooded species. Part of the reason that so many migrants are single-brooded may be their migratory strategy, which often gets them to the breeding grounds when residents and short-distance migrants are already well into breeding. Thus, Neotropical migrants have fewer opportunities to attempt to renest following a predation event, because they also need enough time to raise the young (around 4–5 days for egg laying, 10 days for incubation, 10 days in the nest, and 2–3 weeks of postfledging care) and still have time to molt and fatten up for fall migration.

How Bad Can Predation Be?   Given that the standard Neotropical migratory bird nest has eggs or young in it for 3 to 4 weeks and that so many creatures love to eat the contents of these nests, it is not surprising that even in natural situations more nests may fail because of predation than are successful. For example, in a huge forested area such as the Missouri Ozarks, nests are nearly immune from cowbird parasitism, but if even half the nests are successful, the birds are probably doing really well. Predation is a natural part of the system, and most migrants will renest rather quickly following loss of eggs or young. With a 50% chance of the loss of each nest, a pair of birds that nests twice will have a 75% chance of being successful through the season; with three attempts, the probability of success goes to nearly 90%. Given that predation often occurs early in the nesting cycle with eggs or recently hatched young, many temperate situations easily provide enough time for three such nesting attempts, even for Neotropical migrants.

Of course, if the predation rate goes up, the number of attempts needed for one successful nest through the summer also goes up. Studies have found nest predation rates in Illinois forest fragments as high as 99% (although 80–90% nest loss is more typical). Using data from a variety of forest fragments, Scott Robinson and Jeff Brawn from the Illinois Natural History Survey showed that the average migrant female in Illinois (lumping all species) produced only 0.17 female young per nest attempt (Brawn and Robinson 1996). Just to replace the number of adult females that will die each year would require 7 nesting attempts during the season, something for which there probably just isn't enough time. For the Wood Thrush, things were so bad that it would take 20 attempts to balance adult mortality, something that certainly is impossible.

As was noted earlier, a factor in these high predation rates may be cowbird parasitism, but even nonparasitized nests are lost to predators at higher rates in fragmented situations than in large contiguous forests. In regions such as the eastern United States, where parasitism is not a major problem, fragmentation is still generally associated with higher predation rates of nests. Only a few fairly recent studies from such spots as southern Ontario have shown fragments where predation rates might not be as catastrophic as those found in much of the Midwest, but even in the Canadian studies nest predation rates on fragments were shown to be higher than in larger or contiguous forests (Friesen et al. 1999).

Is Higher Nest Predation on Fragments an Edge Effect? A fairly intense scientific controversy has developed in recent years about whether or not predation rates are related to amount of area per se or are an edge effect. Many studies have looked at where predation occurred to attempt to come up with some sort of general truth about nest predation.

Most of these studies involved artificial nests, which is part of the controversy. Finding real bird nests while they are active is a difficult chore; to find enough nests to have strong statistical power for scientific analyses takes a lot of manpower, which costs a lot of money. Additionally, to make strong statements about the occurrence of edge effects, one should have, in addition to large sample sizes, equal samples of nests of the same species at all distances from the edge. This is not always possible, so many scientists have used artificial nests as an approximation of what happens to real nests around edges.

The standard situation for artificial nest studies involves using wicker nests such as the ones that can be bought at a pet store to put in a canary cage. These make the nest structure consistent and, because they are fairly cheap, allow for large sample sizes. Some researchers have gathered old nests, cleaned them out some, and then reused them, while others have even made artificial nests of their own, usually to match the species under study. Real eggs are used as bait for the predators. Different studies have used Japanese Quail (*Coturnix coturnix japonica*) eggs, Northern Bobwhite (*Colinus virginianus*) eggs, and plain old hen's eggs. Recent studies have shown that the size of the egg chosen can affect the measured predation rates, because small egg predators such as mice cannot break through the large eggs (Haskell 1995). A few researchers have even recorded the scratches on their large eggs as a measure of attempted predation. Although most researchers attempted to guess at what the predator was by observing how the egg was taken or eaten, such attempts were very much an art rather than a science. Several recent researchers have used a clay egg in with the natural egg; this gives the predator a reward, but when the predator bites into the clay egg, it leaves a tooth or bill imprint that allows the researcher to identify the predator in many cases.

David Wilcove was among the first to use artificial nests to study predation on fragments, and his 1985 paper from the journal *Ecology* has been cited widely. By the early 1990s, numerous experiments using artificial nests had been published, all with some similarity of technique but each a bit different from the others. Many showed strong edge effects with regard to predation rates, but a few did not. Peter Paton (1994) tried to resolve the controversy by reanalyzing all of the published studies of nest predation and edge; he found that edge effects were a common component of these studies and that 50 m (about 150 feet) seemed often to be the distance into the forest that this edge effect extended.

Obviously, if predation is related to edge, and most studies show that it is, then the shape of the fragment is almost as important as its size. In addition, if internal edges such as wildlife plantings or clear-cuts also increase edge effects, they should be avoided. Although the general consensus is that predation rates are higher around edge, we will look at this phenomenon a little more when we consider regional effects in Chapter 6.

Which Animals Are the Predators? Obviously, if we want to understand why such high levels of nest predation take place and then attempt to control the situation, we need to know both which animals the predators are and what their proportional contributions to overall predation rates are. The first part of this is easy; the second part is pretty hard.

As noted earlier, lots of animals like to eat eggs. Not surprisingly, small to mid-sized predators such as raccoons, opossums, skunks, and foxes are major nest predators, for these species are adapted to search for these types of foods, they are large enough to patrol a fairly large area for nests (and thus have an impact over a large area), and they are small enough that a typical songbird nest makes a decent meal or at least a good snack. Predatory birds such as hawks and owls are also rather obvious nest predators, although most of these predators do not spend a lot of time searching for nests. Rather, some mid-sized to large avian omnivores, especially crows and jays from the family Corvidae, constitute major avian nest predators. To these can be added a few other large

FIGURE 5.2. *A rat snake eating a baby bird. Photo courtesy of Frank R. Thompson III and Dirk Burhans.*

birds, such as the Common Grackle (*Quiscalus quiscula*) and some of its relatives. Finally, many species of snakes finish out the list of expected nest predators, at least in parts of the world. In Missouri, several snake species have been observed depredating nests, and the common black rat snake is a renowned nest predator (Fig. 5.2). Obviously, as one goes north, snakes become fewer and are probably a relatively small problem. In areas with human occupation, or locations with feral animals, dogs and cats can be nest predators.

Although the list of expected nest predators can easily become an imposing one for most areas of the Temperate Zone, the situation is accentuated by the recent observation that many other species that we do not think of as predators will eat eggs or nestlings. Squirrels, chipmunks, and mice will all readily feed on these foods when given the chance, and it appears that predation from these species is common enough in some situations that it must involve these species actually going out and searching for nests, rather than just finding the occasional opportunistic snack.

Perhaps the most unusual "predator" of bird nests was one discovered by one of my students, Therese Donovan, while taking photographs at artificial nests. On at least two occasions, her cameras caught white-tailed deer feeding on the eggs in her artificial nests (Fig. 5.3). Although her photos don't show the lips of the deer actually sucking down the eggs, the sequence of photos (taken with fairly long intervals between shots so that a whole roll of film was not used on a single visit by a predator) showed the deer reaching for the nest in one shot, then the nest without eggs in the next. A friend who bands birds in this same region has seen deer trying to pull birds from his mist nets, particularly during the time of year when the does have fawns and are probably protein-starved.

As the dozens of students who are attempting to understand nest predation complete their studies, the list of nest predators will probably increase to include virtually everything. Although I have yet to see a deer attempt to eat a bird from one of my mist nets, I have had netted birds attacked by such "nonpredators" as iguanas and even box turtles. Obviously, birds that build open nests, where the eggs and young are very vulnerable, must deal with a large number of potential predators.

Determining Which Are the Important Predators Obviously, the list of potential predators for any location can be impressive. If one finds that nest predation is potentially a limiting factor for the birds of an area, the best thing would be to determine which predator or predators are the chief culprits. With this knowledge, one could potentially insti-

FIGURE 5.3. *A deer about to eat bird eggs at an artificial nest. Although this photo does not record the deer eating the eggs, other researchers have observed this behavior. Photograph courtesy of Therese Donovan.*

tute predator control programs for these important predatory species and thereby increase the success of the breeding birds.

Until recently, rather indirect means were used to try to determine the species involved in nest predation. Examining the nest for a Blue Jay feather or some snakeskin, for example, could provide clues. Some researchers were convinced that the manner in which a nest was damaged could tell us something about what the predator was. In many cases, though, the nest was either destroyed with no clues or seemed untouched but lacked the eggs or nestlings that once were there.

As was noted above, some of the artificial nest studies have attempted to determine the predator by putting an artificial egg made of clay in the nest. The predator bites, pecks, or gums this egg a bit, hopefully enough to leave a distinctive imprint, then gives up on it. The researcher, armed with mammal skulls, Blue Jay beaks, and other predator parts, then tries to match marks in clay with the predator harvesting apparatus. In many cases this has provided quite a bit of information, including evidence of eggs eaten by rabbits, although the method doesn't always work, especially with snakes.

Another indirect measure of predator identity has involved putting out either artificial nests or scented posts surrounded by a substrate that records the imprints of the predator. In some studies this has involved a piece of sheet metal that has been covered with soot; other studies have put the bait in the middle of a bed of sand. These have provided some good information, but once again they have biases and don't get everything. For example, flying predators are easily missed.

The most reliable information on what the nest predators are has come from camera and, most recently, video camera studies. The more primitive camera studies used a simple box camera set a few feet from the nest and some sort of tripping mechanism (see Fig. 5.3). When the predator visited the nest, a picture or set of pictures was taken. In today's world of high technology, the thing to have to study nest predation is a miniature infrared video camera. This tiny camera can be placed near the nest with little disturbance to the nesting birds, requires relatively little power (e.g., car batteries), and, because it uses infrared light, can take pictures all night long. The camera can be programmed to take a video "picture" every second or so, such that one gets a continuous record of activities at the nest, including predation.

My colleague Frank Thompson and his associates have been using several of these cameras in Missouri for the past three summers, with interesting results (see Fig. 5.2; Thompson et al. 1999). For example, they have found that snakes are the most common predator in second-growth, shrubby habitats where avian predation has been a fairly small factor. These snakes seem to be much more sophisticated predators than one might expect. For example, the researchers have one sequence of tape in which a snake attacks an Indigo Bunting nest with three nestlings, taking one nestling with its first lunge. The snake falls to the base of the bush to swallow this young, then attacks again. While the snake is involved in grabbing the second nestling, the oldest nestling flutters from the nest. The snake proceeds to drop below the nest to swallow its second bite. After a bit, it returns to the nest for the last young, which of course is not there. The snake not only looks around for this young bird for a few moments but also sits around the nest for more than 20 minutes, periodically returning to the nest that it is convinced still has part of its meal. It almost makes you think that snakes can count.

Some of the other evidence that Thompson and his associates have gathered with these video cameras makes one wonder about some of the assumptions we have made in earlier studies of nesting success. For example, their data suggest that snakes are really good at depredating nests just as the young are about to fledge. Although this would make good sense in terms of snake optimal foraging (by providing the biggest meal possible rather than eating the eggs or young nestlings), it suggests the snakes are smarter than we generally want to give them credit for. Additionally, if snake predation is responsible for a burst of predation just before fledging, then studies that visit nests only at 3-day intervals may be overestimating nest success. This study has also been able to correlate the predator with the condition of the nest following predation. The findings suggest that nest conditions provide little evidence about the predator. Some snakes pulled the young from the nests without causing any damage to it, whereas other snakes came up through the bottom of the nest, tearing it apart. The data suggest that we need to be careful about some of the assumptions we are making about what is causing nest predation.

Numerous other studies have been done or are under way to determine the local predators of bird nests. Such studies may be valuable on a local scale, but with the wide variety of potential nest predators that can occur in a location, it is unlikely that any single study will be able to make sweeping generalizations about what the nest predators are and how they should be managed.

Meso-predator Release: Why Are There So Many Predators?

With such an impressive list of potential nest predators, we could spend a lot of time examining how human land-use practices or other factors have affected species distribution and abundance. Rather than do that, we will discuss three major factors that are widespread and probably favor these predator populations no matter what species is involved or where the populations are.

All of these factors are related to human activities in one way or another, but we first must look at direct subsidization of predator populations through human activities. The most obvious factor here involves human pets, both those fed by their owners and feral dogs and cats. Recent work has suggested that feral cats may eat billions of adult birds. This study did not document nest loss, but that undoubtedly is substantial too. Human trash has been implicated in the range expansion and increased density of the raccoon, which is generally regarded as the ultimate bird nest predator. Limits on the amount of harvest in a hunt, particularly with species such as deer, has often resulted in unusually high populations of these species, at least in some locations or habitats. Finally, human feeding of such species as Blue Jays during the winter may have greatly increased their numbers, with negative consequences in the breeding season.

The increased amount of edge is also a major factor in the increased abundance of many of these predators. Crows, jays, raccoons, and other predators seem to prefer edge habitats for nesting and/or foraging. Certainly, to the extent that edges attract both forest and edge species, they may have higher nest densities, which makes them optimal foraging habitat for these predators. With more edge, we simply get more predators.

A final factor that works in accord with increasing food or increased amounts of prime edge habitat is the demise of those predators that ate the predators of bird nests and thereby regulated the abundance of these middle-sized predators. The absence of wolves, bear, puma, and even coyote in some areas means that the smaller predators can be more abundant, a phenomenon that ecologists call meso-predator release. Even with human effects and increased edge, the predators that eat bird nests would probably be less abundant if some of these big predators were around.

Good evidence that large predators can have such an effect comes from studies on waterfowl nest success in the northern prairies. In some regions, foxes were a major duck nest predator; certainly, a batch of duck eggs was a great meal or two for a fox. As coyotes extended their range into some of this waterfowl habitat, fox populations crashed (as the fox helped feed the baby coyotes), and waterfowl nest success increased dramatically. Although coyotes will occasionally eat a duck nest, they generally are after bigger things. Other stories from the Tropics show how the absence of predators such as jaguar or Harpy Eagles (*Harpia harpyja*) can increase monkey populations and decrease nesting success of small birds.

What Can We Do? Because the increase in predators of bird nests is so related to human activities, it seems that there ought to be something a person can do to help out. Certainly, one can keep the household cats and dogs under control so that they do not eat birds or bird nests, and one can keep the trash covered so that raccoons do not have access to it. Maybe we should put out bird feeders that exclude Blue Jays. Beyond that it gets a bit more difficult, though. Perhaps all of us who care about migrant birds should become hunters and include more deer and mid-sized predators in our diets (when I was being raised in Iowa, I was told that Missourians eat a lot more possum than they actually do, as I found out when I moved here). In general, though, it is not a problem that is easily rectified.

CHANGES IN FOOD SUPPLY ON FRAGMENTS

Studies by plant ecologists on the effects of forest fragmentation have focused on two major factors: the effects of microclimatic changes that accompany fragmentation of forest, and changes in seed dispersal patterns associated with fragmentation. Most of these studies have occurred in the Tropics, and it is not surprising that the edges of tropical moist forest show a variety of changes when the forest is fragmented. In general, these forest edges are drier than similar pieces of contiguous forest or than the forest was before fragmentation. This difference is caused by increased light and wind from the neighboring, nonforest habitat. Similar results have been shown for temperate forests but are not as serious in temperate climates as they are in the Tropics.

With the occurrence of such microclimatic changes, we might expect to find other changes along edge, including changes in food supply or other factors that are important to breeding birds. No one had discovered such changes until recently, when work by Burke and Noll (1998) in forest fragments in Ontario showed that insect densities were lower in small fragments and along the edges of larger fragments. The authors were convinced that this difference helped explain lower densities of Ovenbirds in these fragments.

Other studies may expand our knowledge of the effects of edge on food supply in the future, but I would be surprised if these studies did not find both increases and decreases in foods, depending upon what the foods are. Certainly, some fruit-bearing plants such as raspberries, buckbrush, and the like are thicker around forest edge, so these resources may be more abundant in edge situations. On the other hand, insects sensitive to desiccation would be expected to decline in most situations.

BEHAVIORAL RESPONSES TO EDGE

Although human activities have increased the amount of edge in many situations, edge habitats occurred before humans dominated the earth. These edge habitats probably displayed the higher parasitism and nest predation rates we see today, although perhaps at somewhat less extreme levels. Given that birds have had to deal with these negative effects for thousands of years, it is not surprising that some species appear to have evolved behavioral adaptations to reduce the impact of negative edge effects.

The first adaptation that has been observed in migrant birds is simple avoidance of forest edge; it has been suggested that many forest-breeding species simply do not set up territories near the edge of the forest. This would minimize their vulnerability to the negative impacts discussed earlier, if the territories were far enough from the forest edge. This "edge avoidance" has become a fixed part of the dogma about migrant bird ecology, although a recent commentary by Marc-Andre Villard (1998) suggested that many of the studies that purport to show this phenomenon really did not test it properly. Nonetheless, some good studies have shown that some species regularly avoid putting their territories close to the edge of the forest.

An associated behavioral response whose occurrence may provide a mechanism for the evolution of edge avoidance behavior in territorial male migrant birds revolves around studies of pairing success in fragmented habitats. After a few years of studying Ovenbirds and Kentucky Warblers on fragments of varying size in central Missouri, we found that the sites had differing levels of birdsong later in the breeding season and that we had trouble finding nests on those sites with the most song.

One of my students, James Gibbs, decided to take a closer look at this and started examining singing behavior in these two species (Gibbs and Faaborg 1990). He would find a territorial male and follow it for 90 minutes, noting each time it sang, what it was doing at the time, and so forth.

During this period he also watched for contact between the singing male and his mate. He found that birds with mates made contact with their mates regularly, such that for birds that were paired, it rarely took more than 15 minutes of the 90-minute period to get evidence that a singing male had a mate. For many males, though, the whole 90-minute period would elapse with no evidence of a mate. These unpaired males also were distinctive because they sang at a much higher frequency than the paired males. For Ovenbirds, Gibbs discovered that by counting songs for a 5-minute period, one could predictably distinguish between paired and unpaired males. In Kentucky Warblers, paired birds rarely sang the *cheri cheri-cheri* song but did nearly all their communication with chirps and squeaks.

After determining the pairing status of numerous Ovenbirds and Kentucky Warblers on two fragmented and two less-fragmented study sites in central Missouri, Gibbs discovered that the smaller sites had many more unpaired Ovenbirds than did the larger sites. Kentucky Warblers did not differ with regard to pairing success in these sites. The domination of unpaired Ovenbirds in these fragments helped explain why they were easier to spot-map late in the breeding season and why nests were so hard to find.

Two other students did follow-up studies on pairing success rates in Ovenbirds in the same region (Van Horn et al. 1995). Robert Gentry surveyed all the Ovenbirds he could find in fragments in Boone and neighboring counties. When he found a small population, he would visit it regularly, searching for nests, following males to see if they had mates, and recording song rates. Bob found a linear relationship between both area of the fragment and total population size of Ovenbirds and pairing success of the Ovenbirds. As fragments got smaller, the chance of a male's having a mate went down, to the point that a couple of 5-male populations apparently never attracted a female mate.

Mia Van Horn returned to our largest fragments and plotted Ovenbird territories from the edge of the forest to the interior. She then followed males, recording singing rates and looking for mates. When she found a nest, she described the habitat of the territory in detail. Not surprisingly, Mia found that few Ovenbird males with territories within 300 m of the edge of the forest attracted mates, whereas nearly all the males more than 300 m from the edge had mates. Those few males near the edge with mates had territories with vegetation characteristics associated with high-quality territories (at least by Ovenbird standards), whereas several males well within the forest on lower-quality territories also had mates.

By combining the patterns of the Gentry and Van Horn studies, we could see that the small populations with few or no paired males all occurred on fragments that had little or no forest habitat more than 300 m from the edge. It appears that Ovenbird females, which bear most of the costs of reproduction, are more selective than males, and natural selection has favored those that choose mates away from the undesirable things associated with forest edge. Several other studies have found similar patterns in other species and other situations, such that reduced pairing success is a regular pattern associated with fragmentation.

These small fragments with unpaired males are an interesting phenomenon. They possess males that are singing like crazy, in contrast to larger forests where breeding males may be relatively quiet as they help raise young. Without knowledge of these patterns of pairing success, a researcher roaming through the countryside would be more likely to find one of these nonpaired populations, especially later in the breeding season, and the researcher certainly would suggest it had higher densities than found in larger fragments. This reinforces why modern studies of migrant birds cannot just go around measuring densities or relative abundances; we have to have these data, but they must be accompanied by good data on pairing and nesting success rates.

FRAGMENTS AS ISLANDS: WHY ISN'T EXTINCTION MORE COMMON?

Small habitat fragments are generally horrible places for migrant birds to attempt to breed. As shown above, nests in fragments face higher chances of brood parasitism and higher nest predation rates. In the most extreme cases, only 5–20% of all nests are successful, which we are pretty sure is not a high enough success rate to replace the natural mortality of the breeding birds (this will be discussed more in Chapter 6). With little reproduction on an annual basis and mortality rates on the order of 50% annually, one would expect the bird populations of small fragments to go extinct quite often — the numbers needed to maintain a population just are not there.

Yet, most of us studying populations on fragments find that they seem to persist from year to year at a fairly constant level, a level that seems independent of the level of reproduction observed in prior years. In the extreme cases where reproduction approaches zero, populations still persist. What gives?

Two possibilities present themselves to explain this conundrum. First, maybe we just aren't that good in the field, and the birds are reproducing more young than we can find. Perhaps the nests we biologists find are also the nests that predators can find more easily. Problems with keeping track of survival rates or dispersal may mean that we just don't understand what is really going on in these small fragments. That's possible, but I doubt it. I have seen results from too many excellent field-workers to believe we are missing things this much.

The second possibility is that a lot of birds are being produced somewhere else that immigrate to these fragments and decide to settle down. We know that most young birds disperse to a breeding site that is some distance away from where they were raised, so this is not a new revelation. The problem is that we don't understand how far these young birds may disperse, which greatly affects our understanding of local demography. If a species lives only in a fragmented situation, then one would expect this sort of exchange of birds to lead to local extinction fairly quickly, because local populations that were underproducing young would not be able to subsidize other such populations for long. But many of our fragmented populations seem to be doing just fine. This suggests that there might be places somewhere out there that are producing enough young to effectively subsidize the populations of smaller fragments. As we shall see, this observation fits in well with some new ideas about how and where populations are regulated, ideas that forced many of us to change our basic perceptions about avian demography.

REGIONAL VARIATION IN PATTERNS: CAN WE GENERALIZE?

Nearly all fragmentation studies confirm the patterns in species densities, edge effects, and reproductive success that we have outlined above. Yet, as was already noted, there is a lot of variation in these patterns. Some of this variation is related to the details of human fragmentation—how much original habitat was left, what type of habitat lies between the remaining habitat, and whether there are cattle feedlots in the area. Other variation is due to larger-scale features; for example, snakes are more common as nest predators in the south than the north, and cowbirds are more abundant in the central Great Plains.

With all this variation in pattern, can we come up with a clear picture of what is going on? For a while I didn't think it was possible, but as fragmentation studies in many different situations accumulated, we could start doing comparisons. In addition, the field of ecology provided some new approaches to doing this analysis, approaches that were critical to making sense of all this variation. These new approaches allow us to understand much better not only what goes on as habitats are fragmented but also why and how this occurs. With this knowledge, we are much better able to design effective management schemes. These breakthroughs are examined in Chapter 6.

6 | RETHINKING AVIAN DEMOGRAPHY

Understanding Landscapes, Sources, Sinks, and Dispersal

As was noted at the end of the previous chapter, the patterns associated with edges and habitat islands are pretty consistent, but not perfectly so. Although species-area curves have been found in every habitat fragmentation study I have ever seen, the slopes of these curves are often highly variable, such that similar-sized fragments in different parts of the world can vary greatly in the number of species they support. The same is true with edge effects; most studies show edge effects, but they vary greatly in intensity and in the distance the effect seems to extend.

In some cases, this variation has led to arguments that revolve around which study or studies are correct and which are flawed, in an effort to come up with the "true" generalization about this phenomenon. In a couple of cases, review papers have attempted to summarize these studies with the goal of finding this truth by something akin to keeping a baseball score (i.e., if there are 12 papers that show edge effects and only 9 that don't, then edge effects "wins"). Obviously, such an approach may reflect where or who did the most studies of this phenomenon, not what the true patterns are.

Fortunately, as those of us trained in more classical ecology struggled with this variation, two major changes were occurring in the field of ecology that would turn out to be lots of help. First, the field that is known as landscape ecology was rapidly developing. In part because of the development of computer mapping systems such as geographical information systems (GIS), ecologists were able to look at patterns on a much larger scale than they could in the past. Rather than confining measurements of birds and their habitat to the study area alone, GIS allowed one to look at how the study area was positioned relative to other habitats in the region. GIS allowed one to measure rather easily the amount of forest, grassland, or edge within any given distance of the study site. As the technology to make these measurements advanced, landscape ecologists also began developing theories about how the traits of a particular study site might be affected by the patterns that occur around that study site.

The second breakthrough that was of great help occurred in studies of demography, a completely different area of ecology that deals with the quantitative variation in the size of populations. Classical ecology had always considered local population size to be a function of births and deaths, immigration and emigration, but the models almost always assumed that the latter two traits balanced each other out. The old MacArthur-Wilson equilibrium model dealt with the idea of populations at equilibrium, but the assumption was always that once equilibrium had been reached, colonization and extinction were both rare events. New models dealing with "metapopulations" or "source-sink" population dynamics took into account that immigration and emigration could be important aspects of demography and provided a quick explanation for all those fragments with poor reproductive success but stable populations. Interestingly enough, some of these early models were inspired by the dynamic equilibrium model of MacArthur and Wilson, even though the details of the MacArthur-Wilson model were shown to be incorrect with respect to patterns of demography on habitat fragments.

These new ideas provided many explanations for the variation in patterns seen across North America; they have completely changed the way conservationists must look at the options they have, particularly with regard to migratory birds. Before we explain how the new management works (in Chapter 7), let's look more closely at these two major changes and how they help us understand the general patterns related to fragmentation and demography.

Landscape Ecology: Understanding Islands without Oceans

We have already discussed how important the ideas developed within island biogeographic theory became in understanding avian responses to habitat fragmentation. Everyone who considered using the island biogeographic model in terrestrial situations immediately knew there would be some differences between habitat islands and true oceanic islands. The biggest of these differences quite simply had to do with the "matrix" between the islands. For real oceanic islands, this matrix was the ocean, which didn't support any species of bird or any other animal that had any effect on the island birds except perhaps in sites where oceanic birds nested. Island bird populations were constrained by these oceans, and the coastline simply was a barrier to movements and population expansion.

In contrast, the matrix between habitat islands is a terrestrial habitat itself, and this habitat may support species that may affect those of the habitat island in many ways. Some species could be competitors, living primarily in the matrix but occasionally penetrating the habitat island enough to remove resources useful to the birds of the fragment. Other species of the matrix could be brood parasites, which enter the habitat island to lay eggs. Finally, the matrix may be preferred habitat for nest predators, which also may enter the habitat island to feed on eggs or nestlings.

Of course, none of this is new—edge effects and their role in determining the loss of species on habitat fragments and the reproductive problems of those species attempting to survive there have already been discussed. The new, simple, and quite logical revelation is the idea that the amount of matrix relative to habitat fragment might actually alter the number of organisms potentially affecting those species living in the remnant. If there are lots of predators and parasites in the area, the birds of the forest fragment might be in big trouble. If the region doesn't support many of these detrimental species, then the birds of the fragment might be better off. And the beauty is that the modern landscape approaches have allowed us to rather easily make measures of regional habitat characteristics and correlate them with what we were finding on the fragments.

These modern approaches are termed regional or landscape approaches, because they measure traits of habitat beyond those that were measured in the past. Until recently, researchers usually performed a variety of habitat measures in a study site to describe it quantitatively. They might go so far as to note how big the study site was (fragmentation studies obviously put a lot of weight on this measure, drawing from the relationship between species number and island size), but many other studies just described their immediate study site. After regional maps of forest or grassland cover had been made and put into GIS, researchers could rather easily measure habitat traits around study sites, often using circles of varying diameter. They could then look for how regional and landscape habitat patterns might explain some of the variation seen in the study sites. In many cases, researchers might use circles of varying size around the study area in an attempt to see which area of landscape actually was most revealing about what was going on in their study. As we shall see, different factors or different habitats may respond to landscape effects at different scales (i.e., with different-sized circles), but this is to be expected because the organisms involved should have different movement patterns and other biological traits.

Landscape-Level Patterns of Parasitism   If landscape-level patterns are ever going to be clear, one might expect them to be clearest with patterns of parasitism in most of North America, because these patterns would be measuring the response of a single species (the Brown-headed Cowbird) to habitat distribution at this scale. In contrast, trying to explain patterns of nest predation will be confounded by the fact that many predator species are involved.

Before using landscape approaches, researchers had seen that parasitism rates generally declined with increasing fragment size, but there was a lot of scatter among the points in plots of this phenomenon. In addition, other studies of fragmentation had often found similar trends but sometimes very different intensities of parasitism. Therese Donovan did the first studies that I know of that attempted to explain variation among parasitism rates in fragmented environments by looking at landscape measures of habitat around the study sites. Basically, she compared two measures. First, she took the recorded rates of nest parasitism from a number of study sites. Then, for each of these, she made a series of nested measures of habitat, starting with the size of the forest fragment (the old "island size" approach) and then making circles of increasing radius centered around the study site, using 1, 3, 5, and 10 km distances. For each circle she measured amount of forest, amount of forest edge, mean patch size, and an index of amount of "core" (forest more than 100 m from an edge, a measure of amount of forest in pretty big pieces). Obviously, heavily forested environments had lots of forest cover with little edge, whereas in fragmented environments the reverse occurred (Fig. 6.1).

What Donovan found was that cowbird densities and parasitism rates were better correlated with habitat measures at the larger spatial scales than they were for fragment size. The best correlations were between cowbird measures and forest cover in circles of 3 and 5 km, but the 10 km circles did a better job of explaining parasitism rates than the size of fragment. This can be rather easily explained, because cowbirds require both

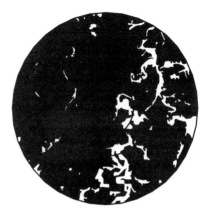

FIGURE 6.1. *How landscape measures around a study site may be computed. Each circle is centered on a forested (dark) study site, with 1, 3, 5, and 10 km circles around the center of the study site. The amount of forest, forest edge, average size of forest, and many other measures at the various spatial scales (circle sizes) can be computed. Here, obviously, one study site is heavily forested, and the other highly fragmented. Reproduced from T. M. Donovan, F. R. Thompson, and J. Faaborg, 2000, "Cowbird Distribution at Different Scales of Fragmentation: Trade-offs between Breeding and Feeding Opportunities,"* in Ecology and Management of Cowbirds and Their Hosts, *ed. J. N. M. Smith, T. L. Cook, S. I. Rothstein, S. K. Robinson, and S. G. Sealy, pp. 255–264, by permission of the University of Texas Press.*

feeding areas and breeding areas. The preferred areas for parasitizing nests in Missouri seem to be forest edges, whereas for feeding they need short-grass pastures, preferably with cattle (Morris and Thompson 1998; Thompson and Dijak 2000). Highly fragmented areas may contain lots of feeding habitat, such that the large populations of cowbirds intensively search the relatively few forest fragments for host nests. The result may be high parasitism rates. In contrast, in heavily forested regions, cowbirds are most likely limited by feeding areas, resulting in generally low regional populations and, because of the high host densities, low parasitism rates. Although cowbirds will regularly move up to 7 km between feeding and breeding areas (Thompson 1994), an area with just a few feeding sites cannot support many cowbirds.

A number of my colleagues (Scott Robinson, Frank Thompson, Therese Donovan, and Don Whitehead) and I used a similar approach to examine parasitism and predation rates across a 5-state region (Robinson et al. 1995). This study combined our data from 9 study sites, 5 field seasons, and more than 5,000 nests. We knew that our highly fragmented study areas had high parasitism rates and that our large Ozark sites rarely saw any parasitism, but we didn't know if there was a clear pattern of change as the amount of forest cover changed in a landscape. We used 10 km circles around these study sites and correlated the amount of forest cover with cowbird parasitism rates; the results were extremely clear, with all species showing lower parasitism rates in more forested environments.

Although our data strongly suggested that landscape-level measures of forest cover were highly correlated with cowbird parasitism rates in the Midwest, there was concern about how applicable the model was to other parts of the United States. For example, it has already been noted that cowbird abundance declines as one goes east from the Great Plains. In addition, cowbirds are not as abundant in much of the western United States, and in some regions they are fairly new colonists. Did one dare make the same assumptions about cowbirds and forest cover away from the Midwest?

An attempt to see if the Midwest patterns worked nationally was made by using data gathered from the Breeding Biology Research and Monitoring Database (BBIRD) of the Cooperative Wildlife Research Unit Program of the U.S. government (currently the Biological Resources Division of the U.S. Geological Survey). Under the guidance of Tom Martin, BBIRD involved more than two dozen cooperators who used standardized methodology of counting birds, monitoring bird nests, and measuring vegetation in study sites across the United States. The BBIRD statistician, Wes Hochachka, combined landscape data and cowbird parasitism rates from more than 23,000 nests from 26 study sites and 366 study plots (Hochachka et al. 1999). Although one analysis showed little relationship between the amount of forest cover and the presence of cowbird parasitism, if one included just those studies where cowbirds actually occurred, a pattern of decreasing parasitism rates with increasing forest cover in 10 km circles was evident across the United States. However, the patterns from such an enormous, wide-ranging data set were pretty ugly, despite their statistical significance, and an analysis using forest cover in a 50 km radius suggested that parasitism rates in the western United States went up with forest cover at that level.

Given the observation that a cowbird will commonly move as far as 7 km between a feeding site and a potential host nest, we believed that a 10 km circle was not a bad estimate of how a cowbird might perceive its landscape. I think that the validity of a 50 km circle in predicting cowbird parasitism is less clear, but perhaps cowbirds in the West move differently from those in Missouri or the relationship between forest cover and cowbirds is different when there are vast areas with few if any trees. Certainly, in nearly all the United States, it appears that to truly understand cowbird parasitism rates within a particular site, it is necessary to understand both the characteristics of that site (size, amount of edge, habitat, etc.) and the amount and type of cowbird feeding habitat around that site (Thompson et al. 2000).

Predation Rates and Landscape Measures As was noted above, similar logic can be used to try to understand how the matrix between habitat islands can affect the amount and intensity of predation from animals living within that matrix and how far these predators might go within the habitat fragments. In addition, to understand nest predation rates, one must also know the type and abundance of predators within the habitat, some of which might be responding to habitat fragmentation themselves. Thus, we have both edge and interior predators of a variety of forms, including many species of mammals, birds, and, in some parts of the world, snakes. Even in habitats with "natural" conditions and high nest success, we expect that nest predation rates often approach 50%. We know that forest fragments may have nest loss rates greater than 90%, but with a range of values from fragments to large forests with only a 40% difference (relatively small when compared with the nearly 90% difference for parasitism rates) and so many organisms involved, we would not expect the variation in predation rates across landscapes and regions to be as easy to understand as parasitism rates.

If predation pressures change with landscape, we also might expect that the intensity of edge effects might change with landscape. We already have mentioned how contentious the discussion of the occurrence and/or intensity of these effects has been in recent years. Landscape ecology offers the possibility that all the variation in edge effect studies might make sense if these effects are mediated by factors of the regional landscape (i.e., different landscapes support different types and densities of predators that affect nest predation rates).

For example, the multistate Midwest study mentioned earlier (5,000 nests in 9 study sites) showed a number of species with highly significant correlations between daily nest predation rates (the measure used to determine predation intensity) and the amount of forest cover in the 10 km circle around the study site. Although a number of other species showed nonsignificant patterns, the general relationship for nearly all species was one of reduced predation with increasing amounts of regional forest cover. Although these patterns fit a hypothesis of regional control of edge effects, the data of this study were not gathered in a fashion that allowed this idea to be tested.

Two excellent studies have been able to test the variation of edge effects with landscape variables more directly, using different techniques. Hartley and Hunter (1998) used meta-analysis to look at the roles of forest cover and edge on predation rates of artificial nests. Meta-analysis is a new statistical method that allows one to combine the similar parts of a variety of studies to test hypotheses by using measurements common to these studies. The authors used artificial nests because so many studies have used such nests to try to measure edge effects (in part because it is so hard to find natural nests around edges and to get the sort of numbers of nests that it takes to get strong statistical significance). In this case, Hartley and Hunter found 13 studies from the United States to use, and they compared predation rates to forest cover at three scales (5 km, 10 km, and 25 km circles). With all the data combined, they found significant correlations between predation and landscape measures at all three scales. When two somewhat questionable points were excluded from the analysis, the relationships at the 5 and 10 km scales were still significant, but the one at 25 km was no longer significant. The authors also found a tendency for studies in highly fragmented environments to show strong edge effects, whereas those in more forested landscapes did not, although the significance value for this comparison was only .095 (with .05 or less usually needed to have statistical significance). Once again, though, the addition of landscape measures of forest cover helped explain the variation in the results from a variety of studies nationwide.

The clinching evidence on the effect of landscape-level factors on local edge effects came from a field experiment done by Therese Donovan, Frank Thompson, and their coworkers (Donovan et al. 1997). Using maps of forest cover from the Midwest, they had a computer randomly select 18 study sites with three different landscape designations (highly fragmented landscapes [<15% forest cover], moderately fragmented landscapes [45–55% forest cover], and unfragmented landscapes [>90% forest cover]). At each site they did artificial nest experiments (plus a number of other measurements not relevant here). Their results were exceptionally clear with regard to the role of landscape on edge effects: edge effects were not pronounced in landscapes with either high fragmentation or little fragmentation, because predation rates were either uniformly high (fragmented sites) or relatively low (unfragmented sites). In moderately fragmented sites, edge effects were pronounced. In other words, in highly fragmented sites the effects of the many predators living around the forest fragments pretty much ruin all nesting attempts, no matter how far away from edge the nests may be. In heavily forested environments, predator numbers are relatively low, and this is probably especially true for predators relying on the disturbed habitat, such that little edge effect occurs and nests in all locations do pretty much the same. Only when there is the proper (or improper) mix between the number of predators living in the matrix and the number of birds nesting in the forests do we see really major edge effects.

Although these studies provide a lot of evidence in favor of the role of landscape-level factors in determining the strength of local edge effects, some researchers don't want to make the jump to accepting such an important role for landscape effects. They argue that most of the studies are from the Midwest or the eastern United States, which may not represent the rest of the country or the world. They also argue that using these large-scale studies may cause us to lose sight of local factors that may be important. For example, Josh Tewksbury et al. (1998) found that nest predation increased in riparian forest fragments in Montana, primarily because it took a fragment of a moderate size to support squirrels, which were major nest predators. The birds on tiny forest fragments without squirrels did better than those on somewhat larger fragments with squirrels. Although I realize that these specific data are correct, the numerous studies supporting landscape effects makes it difficult for me not to feel comfortable in accepting a hypothesis that landscape-level effects are critical to understanding what is going on in any particular habitat fragment. It is clear that by adding measures of habitat at the landscape level we have greatly increased our ability to understand individual habitat fragments and to make the appropriate conservation suggestions, given this situation.

AVIAN DEMOGRAPHY: IT'S NOT LOCAL ANYMORE

The scenario we have just presented could be visualized as one in which some landscapes support large numbers of cowbirds and predators that make daily forays into the remaining natural habitat fragments, pillaging, plundering, and dumping eggs in any nest they can find. Here the force of the attack is determined primarily from factors outside the habitat fragment, factors that often vary with the structure of this landscape. Obviously, forest birds in highly fragmented landscapes may face high nest predation and parasitism rates, whereas those in more pristine situations do not have to deal with these extra problems.

As was mentioned earlier, many early studies of birds living in frag-mented situations showed that they were producing few if any of their own young (and actually not that many cowbirds). Nesting success rates were abysmal, and it was easy to look at this factor and believe that bird populations should be declining. The dilemma for some of us was that, despite these awful rates of nest success, many of our study populations seemed to be able to maintain the same local measures of abundance. In a world where one looks at births and deaths to understand local popula-tion dynamics and assumes that emigration and immigration cancel out, the equations weren't working. Most study sites had virtually no births to add to the equation; the only way to keep local populations steady was for death rates to be much lower than we thought or for the immigration-emigration factor to be much more important than we had previously thought.

Metapopulations, Sources, and Sinks Fortunately, theoretical ecologists had been working for several decades with models for popula-tions that lived in isolated groups, and by the late 1980s they had even con-nected some of these theoretical models to real-world situations with frag-mented populations. Richard Levins (1968), a colleague of MacArthur and Wilson's, developed the first metapopulation models after being in-spired by the book on equilibrium island populations by MacArthur and Wilson (1967). A species with a metapopulation is one in which a lot of local, isolated populations occur across a region, with dispersal possible among populations and with the local extinction of a population also a possibility (Fig. 6.2). One could envision this kind of metapopulation occurring on a system of islands like the West Indies or perhaps with populations occupying distinctly fragmented habitats like caves or moun-taintops. As long as there is a reasonable probability for movement from one population to another, the metapopulation concept applies. Levins examined how the demographics of these small, isolated populations would vary, given different patterns of both local extinction and disper-sal among populations. Like those of Levins, most early metapopulation models showed how important dispersal could be in keeping small popu-lations from avoiding extinction and in allowing a larger total population than isolated populations without such exchange of individuals would.

Much of the early work on metapopulations was highly theoretical. One of the first conservation applications of any form of a metapopula-tion model was that of Jim Brown and Astrid Kodric-Brown (1977), who combined both metapopulation ideas and the equilibrium model and

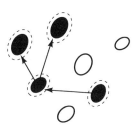
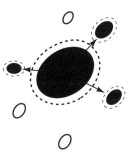

FIGURE 6.2. *Representation of two metapopulation models. The model on the left has several small populations that may move from site to site, and the one on the right has a large population that feeds the smaller sites (as in a source-sink situation).*

showed how important dispersal could be in keeping small populations alive. They termed this the rescue effect, suggesting that dispersal from other populations may be an important component in understanding the demography of isolated local populations.

Metapopulation models really came to the forefront (and made the shift from primarily theory to having important applications) with some modifications done to the basic model by Ronald Pulliam (1988). Pulliam recognized that for many populations, the metapopulation was composed of subpopulations of varying size, with the small populations having a higher chance of going extinct than the large ones. He also noted that small populations, particularly in fragmented situations, might have to deal with pressures that the larger populations did not have, also resulting in local extinction. He developed what he called a source-sink model (see Fig. 6.2), in which large, stable populations (the sources) would rarely go locally extinct and might regularly produce more young than are needed to replace the breeders that die on the source. These excess young might disperse to the smaller habitats, where they would subsidize the local populations; because these populations had low reproductive rates, though, the local population was considered a sink, for it would draw in dispersers from elsewhere but would provide few dispersers of its own because of low reproductive rates.

Evaluating the Source-Sink Model: Problems with Survival and Dispersal Pulliam's source-sink model quickly became important to those of us studying fragmented systems because it provided a possible explanation for how we could find low reproductive success without declining populations on the habitat fragments we studied. When we found areas with large amounts of habitat and high reproductive success, we had potential source habitats.

Unfortunately, although the model is extremely attractive and actually may be the appropriate model for us to use, we are still a long way from providing the data needed to show that bird populations actually work in a source-sink fashion. The major weakness of the model has to do with our lack of good measures of most of its components; this problem is compounded by having no strong evidence to date that shows the kind of movement patterns needed to prove a source-sink scenario at work.

The equation used to determine if a local population is a source or a sink is a simple one:

1 – adult survival = mean number of female young per female per year – juvenile survival

Female young are used as a baseline because females are necessary to produce more young in the future (and are more limiting than males in most cases). If a location produces enough female young per female per year that survive to the next breeding season to have a larger number on the right side of the equation than on the left side of the equation, then you have a source population. If the value on the left is larger than that on the right (i.e., adult mortality exceeds production of female young), then you have a sink population. All we need to measure in the field to compute this important population value is adult survival, juvenile survival, and the reproductive rate of each breeding female in our study sites. Unfortunately, in most cases we do not have good measurements of any of these values, let alone good measurements of all three taken from a single local study population.

Production of Young   We often have good measures of female production of female young, or at least good estimates of total production, with the assumption that half the offspring produced are female. A tremendous number of studies in recent years have looked at reproduction in rigorous fashion, with lots of natural nests found, visited every 2 or 3 days, and observed as well as one can at the time of fledging. Most of these data are excellent, and they are generally analyzed by the Mayfield method (Mayfield 1975), which is a technique that is used to avoid overestimating nest success by finding nests only near the end of the breeding cycle, when they have a higher chance of fledging. The Mayfield method gives us measures of daily nest mortality, which can then be extrapolated through the nesting period of each species to determine overall nesting success.

Although the Mayfield system is the best system available, it is not without its possible biases. For example, if one does not mark individuals but just tries to find nests, one could find several nests of a pair, all but one of which is found to be destroyed by predators. Depending upon how the numbers fall out, one might get values suggesting that this pair of birds did not produce young at an adequate rate, but if this pair is single-brooded (produces only one brood each year), it may actually have achieved maximum productivity. The inclusion of failed nests into a larger sample may reduce the measured nest success over that actually occurring, given that many birds of single-brooded species will renest quite readily after predation events. Thus, for a Puerto Rican Vireo or Black-capped Vireo that finally raises a brood on its sixth try, we have to record success rate as 1.0 rather than 0.17 (1 in 6) or perhaps less, depending upon what sort of Mayfield numbers one got.

Unfortunately, finding and monitoring nests is hard enough work by itself, without adding the new chores of marking and monitoring individual breeders. It is important to keep the incredible persistence of some of these birds in mind, though, when trying to determine source-sink status. I have seen Indigo Buntings fledging in September, and a number of studies have implied that many species may do quite well late in summer, when cowbirds are no longer active and predation rates may decline.

Adult Survival   How long does a bird live? As critical as that information is to a variety of ornithological questions, not just source-sink equations, you would expect that researchers would be able to provide a crisp, clean answer. Unfortunately, as of yet we cannot.

Ecologists are still arguing about whether or not tropical birds live longer than temperate birds, even though there have been a bunch of theories about life history evolution in recent years, all of them resting on the assumption that tropical birds are longer-lived. For example, nearly all tropical birds raise a single brood a year, with clutch size of 2 or sometimes 3 eggs. Temperate birds raise at least one brood of usually 4 or 5 eggs and sometimes more, and some species are multibrooded. Even Neotropical migrants that may get to their breeding grounds later than permanent residents are generally thought to produce more young than their tropical counterparts. Since populations of all species tend to be relatively constant, the logic used is that species with smaller clutches live longer, whereas those with larger clutches spend the winter in cold places or do things like migrate that lead to higher mortality rates.

A few studies have appeared in recent years with actual data to help with these arguments. Most studies have suggested that temperate birds have survival rates in the 0.50 to 0.65 range, meaning that most adult birds have a better than 50–50 chance of seeing next year, once they have made it to adulthood. A couple of studies have shown that tropical birds have somewhat higher rates of survival, with mean survival rates in the 0.65–0.70 range for Peru, Puerto Rico, and Trinidad (Faaborg and Arendt 1995; Johnston et al. 1998; Francis et al. 1999). In contrast, Jim Karr et al. (1990) found that a group of birds living in Panama had survival rates more in the 0.55–0.60 range.

Although it is not important to our arguments here if North American Neotropical migrants live longer than their tropical cousins, the existence of this controversy shows how little we know about actual survival rates. Further confounding the situation is a recent study from Finland that found survival rates of the Siberian Tit (*Parus cinctus*) to be around 0.79 (Orell et al. 1999). We do not understand the survival rates of Neotropical migrants very well, and certainly we must be careful before we start computing source-sink equations using the data we currently have. For example, my former student Paul Porneluzi studied the Ovenbird in both fragmented and contiguous forest in Missouri (Porneluzi and Faaborg 1999). He spent hours and hours trying to catch and color-band every male with a territory in his study sites, and he spent equal effort in subsequent years trying to resight them to see if they had returned to their former territories. By intensively following each male every few days through the summer, he also had a strong measure of whether or not they had produced any young, because males help out extensively after the young fledge. The annual survival rate he got for all of his banded males was 0.52, but he noticed that only 2 of 22 of these males returned the next summer after being unsuccessful throughout a breeding season, which suggests some sort of dispersal event in these unsuccessful birds, rather than higher mortality. When he excluded these males from his calculations, he got an annual survival rate of 0.61, which is probably more realistic.

Without an understanding of how factors such as adult dispersal affect survival rate estimates, we are not going to have good numbers to plug into source-sink equations. Unfortunately, studying survival rates is a difficult job that takes a long time. For a Neotropical migrant, one ideally needs to mark 50 or more adult breeders each year for at least a 4-year period. Ideally, one should understand the breeding status of each and its annual success. For tropical birds, which often live 10 years or more, studies of survival may require 8 to 10 years or more for reliable estimates. All of these periods are relatively long for students trying to gain degrees or faculty seeking tenure, but these data are urgently needed.

Juvenile Survival   If you think the situation is bad with regard to our knowledge of adult survival rates for migrant birds, it is 1,000 times worse for juvenile survival. In nearly all migrants, young birds disperse away from their natal area. Since nearly all survival rate estimation is done using capture-recapture models, and juvenile birds are almost never re-captured, we are often without any sort of estimate. (This juvenile behavior also messes up the dispersal estimates, as discussed below.) What do we do?

Early attempts to develop source-sink models often took what researchers considered were reasonable estimates of adult survival and halved those figures to estimate juvenile survival. For example, Temple and Cary (1988) used 0.31 for juvenile survival of Wood Thrush, which was one-half their estimate of adult survival. One cannot fault them too much for doing this, since they needed some value to solve the equation, but numerous subsequent authors have used the 0.31 value solely on the basis of its having been used before.

Given the great importance of good estimates of juvenile survival, one would think that the scientific community would be working tirelessly trying to solve this problem. The problem is simply that these birds sometimes move great distances and are hard to follow (as discussed below). Most are too small for radio transmitters, but even these transmitters would last only a few weeks, and mortality rates need to be measured until the birds return to their first breeding area. Angela Anders from the University of Missouri put radios on Wood Thrushes, in part because they are the only Missouri forest migrant large enough to carry a decent-sized radio transmitter (Fig. 6.3). Anders found that the average annual survival rate for her birds by the time the radios ran out of battery was about 0.43. If the estimate of 0.31 for annual juvenile survival in this species is correct, the birds Angela followed had to fly to their wintering grounds, spend the winter, and return to their first breeding site with losses of only 12 birds per 100. That seems like a stretch to me.

Obviously, we need better information on juvenile survival of migrant birds if we want to understand source-sink dynamics. Although any

FIGURE 6.3. *A juvenile Wood Thrush with radio transmitter (which is not visible). Because this species is large enough to carry radios, it has been well studied with regard to dispersal. Most migrants are too small to carry radios. Photograph courtesy of Mark Fink.*

sort of species-specific estimate would be useful, it would be ideal if we understood how being raised in different landscapes, at different times of the breeding season, or with cowbirds affected juvenile survival. As has already been noted, some species will attempt several nests until they eventually produce young late in the season. Do these young have as good a chance of getting to the wintering grounds and surviving the winter as their brethren who were fledged in early June?

Understanding Dispersal Even if we had good measures of all the components of the source-sink equation for a site (adult survival, juvenile survival, production of female offspring), we still would need evidence of exchange of individuals from sources to sinks to prove that such a scenario actually exists. Although it is nice if the demographics of various study sites match a source-sink model (as those of the Midwest do), without some proof of exchange, we still must be careful about believing that such a model is at work.

The problems with understanding dispersal are similar to those with trying to measure juvenile survival. Juveniles can be marked on their natal sites, but their role in life is generally to disperse somewhere else. For Neotropical migrants, this dispersal may not be until the next spring, after a trip to the Tropics. Once a marked bird leaves the boundaries of a study site, it might as well be 1,000 miles away. If it actually flies a few thousand miles to its wintering grounds, then the thought of it ending up 1,000 miles from its birth site doesn't seem too farfetched. Of course, the above assumes that only juveniles are the dispersers, which may not be the case. But certainly the role of most juveniles is to disperse.

Although banding programs have been in place most of this century, they have provided little information about actual juvenile dispersal, especially for Neotropical migrants. Two factors are at work here. First, not many birds are banded as juveniles on their natal sites. Banding birds is hard work, and sample sizes are often small. Even if you have an abundant species, you might be lucky to band 100 juvenile birds, but the chances of anyone else finding the ones that make it through the winter (maybe only 30 or so) are incredibly small. Some banding stations capture large numbers of migrants that can be aged as juvenile birds, but these stations do not know where these birds actually came from, so the captures provide only general data.

As was already discussed, all migrants are too small to carry a radio transmitter that could last for nearly a year and have a powerful enough signal that someone could find the bird. Are there any technological breakthroughs that don't require batteries? Two different approaches are being tried that hold some hope of supporting source-sink concepts, although both of these approaches will probably be more general in their support than banding would be. Dick Holmes and his colleagues have attempted to use geochemistry to understand dispersal, although their immediate goal was to match wintering and breeding areas (Hobson and Wassenaar 1997; Marra et al. 1998). As a bird grows its feathers in an area, the feathers acquire a distinctive signature with regard to the chemical compounds found in that area. Different compounds (isotopes of carbon, nitrogen, etc.) have distinctive regional patterns with regard to the proportions of the isotopes they have. Thus, a Wood Thrush with a certain chemical composition would come from a particular region of North America; by using the gradients of several different compounds, these researchers hope to be able to determine within a relatively small distance where a feather was formed.

How does this help with understanding dispersal? Since juveniles form their tail feathers where they were raised but keep them through their first breeding season, one could go out and catch birds that are known to be less than a year old (using plumage and other traits) and just pull a tail feather for analysis. You know where the bird is breeding now, and with its tail feather you can figure out where it came from.

A similar approach is being used with measures of DNA structure. Interbreeding populations will have very similar DNA, whereas those with little interbreeding will have different DNA. If the DNA structure is distinctive for a region, as it appears to be, then one could go out and catch birds that are known to be less than a year old and analyze their DNA to see if it reveals their home location.

Currently both these techniques are in preliminary stages, and even if they work, a lot more work will have be done to see how precise they can be. Until then, though, we have to remember that these source-sink models seem to be highly compatible with what we believe is going on with regard to avian demography, but they still need a lot of support before they are actually proven to exist.

Does "Landscape Size" Vary by Habitat?

As was already noted, some of the previously mentioned studies have varied in the measures used as the "landscape" around the study site and in recording how different birds responded differently to various landscape measures. In the Midwest, 10 km circles worked well, while the national meta-analysis of predation studies suggested that both 5 and 10 km circles were effective. For cowbird parasitism, a 10 km circle seemed appropriate because it contained the 7 km distance that cowbirds were observed using to move between feeding and breeding areas. For predators, it seems that the landscape measures must reflect local population sizes in some fashion, because no mammals or snakes and even few predatory birds will move much more than 1 km during a day or two. Of course, depending upon a species' dispersal abilities, different landscapes may provide bigger or smaller barriers. Given all the things going on, there seems to be no reason why a 10 km circle is always going to be the correct landscape measure, and I would expect that different habitats or different problems (parasites or predators, or different types of predators) will show different patterns with regard to landscape effects.

With this in mind, it is interesting to note that recent work on grassland birds has suggested that they show similar qualitative responses with regard to nesting success and the amount of regional landscape covered by their habitat, but the relationship seems to peak with circles of just 2 or 3 km. This has been shown to be true both for birds using Conservation Reserve Program non-native grasslands (McCoy 2000) and for birds living on native grassland fragments (Winter 1998). The general patterns shown by these grassland birds are similar to those of forest birds, but once the landscape measures reach just a few kilometers, avian responses to fragmentation seem to have peaked.

Several reasons for this difference between grassland and forest birds may exist, looking both at the outside pressures provided by different landscapes and the way that different birds react to habitat distributions. We have already suggested that matrices that support higher predator densities may lead to higher nest predation rates in woodlands, but once the distance from woodland edge becomes 2 to 3 km, it probably is farther than any small mammalian predator or predatory bird would fly to look for a small meal. Cowbirds will easily fly these distances (2–3 km), but cowbirds actually are not important parasites to many grassland birds (Dickcissels excepted). Both of these landscape traits may dissipate as one gets far from woodland, which is what various studies suggest. In addition, grassland birds seem to be much more mobile than forest birds, often colonizing new sites each year. Return rates of individual grassland birds are often very low, perhaps because grasslands are dynamic systems, changing in structure each year in such a way that a site may be great for a species one year but awful the next. For example, Henslow's Sparrows (*Ammodramus henslowii*) may use a prairie in great numbers one year, but if the prairie is burned during the next winter, they will not return for a period of time. On the other hand, after 3 to 4 years without fire, Henslow's Sparrows also do not prefer a site (Zimmerman 1988). Thus, the birds living on a grassland habitat fragment in any given year may be an assemblage of birds that have chosen that site individually for that year only. Source-sink dynamics in this situation may be relatively meaningless except on some relatively large scale, although the components of the source-sink model are still important.

In contrast, forest bird communities are composed of individuals that are homing to a particular site each year. Long-term dynamics are at work, both for the birds and for the sites, which, as relatively mature forests, do not change much from one year to the next. Even with low reproductive success, some young are produced each year, many birds return, and new birds arrive that are dispersing from other sites. As these new birds assess the regional habitat, they may key in to relatively large forest fragments or highly forested landscapes. Notably, although many grassland migrant birds are not found on small grassland tracts, once these reach 160–200 acres in size, most species will occur (except really large species like prairie grouse). In contrast, many forest species in the Midwest do not occur on forests smaller than 500–600 acres, perhaps because landscapes with smaller tracts are too risky for nesting.

Given that the source-sink model is new and needs lots of verification, it also is silly to think that there will ever be one set of criteria for the best way to manage any natural habitat for birds. We will always need to calibrate the general principles we are discovering to the patterns of each local region. For example, recent work in southern Ontario showed much higher nesting success rates in small forest fragments than were found in the Midwest, even though the general patterns of predation with regard to fragmentation were still there (Friesen et al. 1999). Nevertheless, the recent work described here allows us to come up with some general guidelines for managing migrant birds in all habitats, with some ideas on where the specific constraints may be different.

7 | Modern Management Guidelines for Breeding Migrant Birds

In the previous two chapters, we have seen how recent work in fragmented habitats and differing landscapes has increased our knowledge of how birds respond in these different situations, at the same time as new ideas about regional demographics have changed our understanding about how bird populations might be regulated. Although some of the management implications of these findings are pretty obvious (e.g., do not leave fragments smaller than the minimum area on which a target species occurs), there is still a lot we do not know, particularly with regard to the specific constraints needed in each region or landscape. As we proceed, I will present some general truths that I believe must be incorporated into all migrant management schemes, but I will also gloss over some of the details, in large part because we generally don't know all the details. Some of these truths have been around a long time, but many of them are quite recent in origin, and some of the new ideas put some interesting constraints on the old knowledge. These concepts sometimes overlap, but here we go.

Habitat Quality Is Always Important

Birds have specific needs with regard to habitat structure, and these needs cannot be ignored. A great deal of work has been done on some species, with habitat suitability index (HSI) models and the like. Many studies have determined the optimal habitat situations for species in some quantitative fashion. If a nature reserve does not offer the proper habitat for a target species, it is unlikely that the target species will occur. I think that too many studies have focused on determining the optimal habitat for a species, when in fact what we may want to find is the range of conditions that a species will use, so that we can perhaps manipulate vegetation in such a way that it attracts the greatest number of species. But we always have to remember that the needs of particular species must be met, and the occurrence of these required habitats most likely determines the real extent of fragmentation that the species is dealing with.

Obviously, manipulating habitats is something that can be done easily with some habitats and not so easily with others. The successional process in Midwestern forests takes decades, with slow changes in forest structure once it has become a closed canopy forest at 15–20 years of age. Earlier successional stages, though, change more rapidly; shrub-scrub birds enter second-growth forests within a year or two of cutting, increase for several years, and then decline as the forest gets tall. For these bird species, a window of 5–10 years may exist before some sort of manipulation is needed to provide new habitat for these species (Annand and Thompson 1997). In native grasslands, although the general composition may not change dramatically with time, we know that even annual changes following haying or burning can change the way birds perceive and respond to the habitat. Obviously, in these more dynamic situations, management will have to be much more active in order to provide the proper habitats.

HABITAT QUANTITY IS EQUALLY IMPORTANT

With the occurrence of such patterns as minimum area requirements or source-sink dynamics, some important constraints are evident with regard to how much of a particular habitat is necessary to support a viable population of a species over time. Certainly, habitat needs to be provided in chunks that are large enough at least to attract the species, and ideally they should be large enough that the local population has a fighting chance to replace itself when breeding (see below). The main lesson from all of the many fragmentation studies has been that nature reserves that are large will support more species than those that are small, all other things being equal. Although I am implying that these ideas are new, they can be summarized by suggestions presented first in 1974 by John Terborgh and in 1975 by Jared Diamond in separate papers (Fig. 7.1). Although there was a fairly heated debate about whether or not several small refuges

BETTER   WORSE

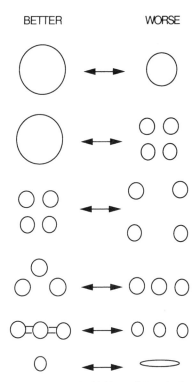

FIGURE 7.1. *Guidelines of "applied biogeography" suggested in the 1970s. Various versions of these suggestions were found in Diamond (1975), Terborgh (1974), and many more recent publications.*

were better than a single large refuge, all of the data for North American migratory breeding birds show the advantages of large areas over small. Small refuges might be advantageous for other reasons (such as saving a specific nesting site), but the odds are high that for migrant birds they will simply support sink populations.

We must remember that the data have shown that many so-called area-sensitive species do not occur in blocks of habitat that are large enough to support dozens of breeding territories. Many minimum area requirements were of 300–1,000 ha (750–2,500 acres), and some were even higher. Many of these blocks might have the perfect forest structure for a target species, but the species won't be there. When HSI models were most popular and landscape ecology was not so accepted, I used to complain to my colleagues who were working on such models that they weren't much good if they didn't take into account at least minimum areas of occurrence, if not actual source-sink dynamics.

LANDSCAPE COMPOSITION IS IMPORTANT

Although the general pattern that bigger is better is almost always true, we have already shown that this pattern can be ameliorated by habitat that occurs in the general vicinity of the nature reserve. Landscapes with lots of habitat tend to have lower levels of stress from predators or parasites, such that a patch of habitat of a given size might support birds better than one of larger size that occurs in a landscape with less remaining habitat.

Recent work by Maiken Winter on the effects of prairie fragmentation on grassland birds in southwestern Missouri showed clearly the effects of landscape on the abundance and success of grassland birds (Winter 1998). Small prairie fragments that were surrounded by non-grassland habitats supported fewer species, which did less well reproductively, whereas a small fragment in a grassland landscape acted as though it were much larger. Managers who are involved in the purchase of nature reserves should keep this phenomenon in mind when making decisions about what to buy. Once a fragment is under management, one should consider the landscape in which it occurs before making any changes in the site. In a highly forested landscape, putting some wildlife openings or having other disturbance within the nature reserve may not be a problem, but in an isolated reserve, any loss of the native habitat may have more severe consequences.

Several of my students and I recently analyzed 6 years' worth of point count data on both fragmented and unfragmented forest sites in Missouri (Howell et al. 2000). One of the things we could do was examine how habitat and landscape factors affected species abundances. As expected, we found that many species were more abundant in forests that had better microhabitat conditions for those species. Interestingly, we also found that the abundance of some species was most highly correlated with landscape measures such as amount of edge or amount of forest cover. In some cases these were species that preferred edge or core area, but it points out that one must examine the region in which a managed area exists before making decisions about how to manage it.

SOURCE AREAS MUST BE PROTECTED

It is pretty widely accepted these days that many populations exist under a source-sink scenario of population dynamics. As noted earlier, we do not understand all of the details of how this dynamic works, but we have lots of evidence that supports this model. Very large, relatively undisturbed blocks of habitat may be critical to maintaining the populations of a species across a large geographic zone. To maintain these populations, these large source areas must be protected and preserved. It is possible that known source locations like the Missouri Ozarks and the forests of northern Wisconsin and Minnesota support the populations of species attempting to live in the fragmented habitats that make up most of the Midwest. Areas as large as Shawnee National Forest in southwestern Illinois may still not be large enough to serve as a population source; Hoosier National Forest in southern Indiana may be a source for some species but not others.

Obviously, without these source populations, the whole source-sink scenario would break down and species would disappear from fragments and, eventually, perhaps even the source area. Therese Donovan et al. (1995) modeled how sources can support sink populations and how declines would appear first in these sinks, should the source population diminish in size. Given that some of those species showing declining trends on Breeding Bird Survey routes show declines only at the periphery of their range, perhaps this type of effect is already taking place. Most certainly, source areas are critical to the long-term maintenance of many migrant bird species.

SINKS HAVE VALUE TOO

In the development of our understanding of what is going on with regard to avian demography in habitats of different size, it is important to recognize the differences between source populations and sink populations. Without this knowledge, one could possibly suggest that habitat areas large enough to support a large number of territories were large enough to serve as a management unit, when in fact this unit was still a sink population. If the whole range of the species in question was managed with units no larger than this, the species could possibly disappear. Proper management requires the recognition of which areas support source populations and how regional populations might be maintained with the proper mix of source and sink habitats.

It is important to remember, though, that just because the reproductive rate at a local site may fall below that needed to balance adult mortality, this does not make the site worthless. Sink populations have a variety of positive traits. First, they may not be sinks by much, which means that they help maintain regional populations, but just not enough to match adult mortality. In some cases, annual variation may be such that in some years a site is a source, and in others it is a sink. Even if the average is below replacement level, it is worth keeping the population going. In some species, sink populations may constitute a large proportion of the total population. Without this habitat, where would these birds go to exist? It has been suggested that these sinks might even serve as reservoirs where birds could live before moving back into source locations to breed (Howe et al. 1991). Certainly, there might be lots of birds living in sinks that could not exist elsewhere. And although many studies suggest that their reproductive rates are low, it appears that survival rates of birds in fragments may be the same as those in contiguous forests (Porneluzi and Faaborg 1999). Finally, sink populations may often occur in smaller parks or nature areas that are popular birding locations. Without these sink populations, birders might have to work much harder to find many of their favorite species.

Another reason to protect sink populations is that we scientists may be wrong. As mentioned earlier, we may be underestimating reproductive success for some species, which might turn a sink into a source, or at least make it close to a source.

SOME CLEAR-CUTS MAY BE VALUABLE

As researchers examined how loss of habitat and edge effects reduced the distributions and reproductive success of birds in fragmented environments, some wanted to apply these findings to the effects of timber harvest in forests. Cutting down trees in what was a contiguous forested environment has some similarities with the standard situation in fragmented habitats, although if the landscape remains forested, the situation is not really fragmentation so much as just making the environment more heterogeneous.

Obviously, though, if timber is removed with clear-cuts (large areas where all trees are removed; Fig. 7.2), then the forest birds that used to

FIGURE 7.2. *A clear-cut in the Missouri Ozarks.*

live in those areas will no longer stay there, and it is possible that there will be detrimental edge effects extending into the forest around the clear-cut. Because of the many negative traits associated with some types of clear-cutting (soil erosion, vast areas with timber removed), alternative methods have been developed for removing trees. Some of these are considered uneven-aged management, because they remove single or small groups of trees from a larger area of the forest, leaving the forest itself with a diverse distribution of tree ages. (In contrast, a clear-cut is even-aged management, because all of the trees that replace those in the clear-cut are of about the same age.) Uneven-aged management has been favored by some because it does not leave a large area denuded of trees, although the effects of this type of management on birds have not been studied until recently.

The general comparison between these two forms of timber harvest concerns not so much how many trees are cut but how concentrated the cutting is. Let's assume we are managing a forest for timber with a 100-year rotation age and timber harvests of 10% of all trees every 10 years. In even-aged management, the trees will be removed from one to several clear-cuts whose total area reaches 10% of the forest area. The other

90% of the forest is not affected by this harvest, other than roads for hauling trees out and the noise involved in the harvest process. In contrast, uneven-aged management will remove just as many trees, but it will do this either as single-tree selection (where single trees are removed) or group selection (where up to half an acre of trees might be removed from a small clearing). For example, imagine two forests with 10,000 trees. In the most extreme case of even-aged management, we would cut down 1,000 neighboring trees every 10 years, with the other 90% of the area not disturbed during that harvest sequence. In the most extreme form of uneven-aged management, we would select the 1,000 trees to be cut from the whole population of trees, such that 100% of the forest has some tree removal nearby.

How do these two techniques affect bird populations? We would expect that clear-cuts do not support forest birds and may have some effect on bird numbers around the clear-cuts, but that most of the forest is not changed for forest birds. The clear-cuts themselves rapidly revegetate and provide habitat for second-growth species. In uneven-aged management, the habitat for forest birds has been altered by the trees removed, but has it been changed enough to negatively affect the forest birds? Do the little openings from the removal of single trees or groups of trees provide enough habitat for second-growth birds?

Since 1991, I have been involved in a giant project in Missouri sponsored by the Missouri Department of Conservation and called the Missouri Ozark Forest Ecosystem Project (MOFEP). It is a massive effort to understand the effects of forest management on all aspects of forest ecology, with components looking at timber harvest effects on birds, mammals, reptiles, amphibians, herbaceous plants, insects, soft mast (such as blackberries), hard mast (such as acorns and hickory nuts), forest genetics, soils, and more. It was begun as an experiment, with 9 approximately 1,000-acre study sites with similar forest selected, treatments assigned at random (with 3 sites clear-cut, 3 cut with uneven-aged management, and 3 kept as controls), and with up to 5 years of baseline data collected before the forest was cut. Initially, the bird work focused on forest birds and the possible negative effects of cutting on their abundance and reproduction. As the cuts develop more vegetation following timber removal, the focus will shift to how second-growth birds respond positively to the new habitats being created.

We used a crew of 27 undergraduate interns each summer from 1991 through 1995 to gather the pretreatment data on bird distributions. For our focal species, we generally found stable populations during this period and relatively high rates of production of young. Timber was harvested in 1996, and no fieldwork was done then. Since 1997, we have been trying to assess the effects of timber harvest on forest birds, and we have been getting some information about how the creation of new habitats affects second-growth bird species. With such a massive experimental design and 5 years of baseline data, we had hoped that we could make pretty simple comparisons between the densities of birds we had on the disturbed sites before and after treatments, while the controls stayed pretty much the same. Unfortunately, for whatever reason, all bird populations were low in 1997 (Fig. 7.3), even those of the control sites. Thus, our comparisons of overall abundance before and after treatment are not as clear as we would like. We are currently looking at the actual distribution of territories to try to clear up our understanding of the situation.

Even with these problems, we can see some general effects of timber harvest. Removing trees negatively affects most forest birds. Ovenbird populations went down in both treatment types, with greater losses in even-aged management, perhaps because some breeding area (the clear-cuts) was totally lost (see Fig. 7.3). Ovenbird populations in uneven-aged management seemed able to adapt better to the small clearings in what had formerly been uniformly forested territories, although densities were lower than pretreatment and controls. Other forest birds — Acadian Flycatcher, Wood Thrush, and Worm-eating Warbler — showed similar patterns of abundance. Although we are still analyzing the data, no major differences seem to have occurred since treatment with regard to nest predation or cowbird parasitism rates. Thus, for forest birds, uneven-aged management seems somewhat less detrimental to populations than even-aged management, but the differences are not large.

Although we are just getting started with our second-growth bird studies, it appears that the two treatments are very different with regard to how they affect these species (see Fig. 7.3). The small clearings that occur after single-tree or group selection cuts (uneven-aged management) are quite attractive to Hooded Warblers and Indigo Buntings; Yellow-breasted Chats sometimes occur on particularly large group selection cuts. Few other second-growth birds are seen in these forests. In contrast, the clear-cut areas are becoming incredible nurseries for a large group of second-growth bird species. Although few birds nested in these clear-cuts in 1997, when the areas contained mostly piles of branches and wood slash, by 1998 the many trunk sprouts, shrubs, and vines attracted many birds. Indigo Buntings seem to swarm to these young clear-cuts, along with large numbers of chats, White-eyed Vireos, Prairie Warblers, East-

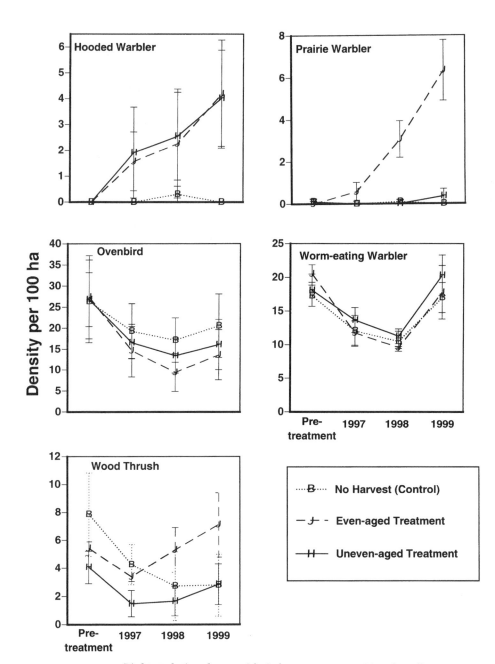

FIGURE 7.3. *Bird population change with timber management. Note that all forest birds declined with loss of timber, whereas second-growth birds that were rare in contiguous forest became abundant soon after harvest.*

ern Towhees, Northern Cardinals, and a few other species. So far, all of these species seem to be highly productive, with little predation or parasitism.

Some of the MOFEP results had been predicted by survey work done earlier in this region. These counts showed similar patterns in these and some other forest management types. To date, it appears that clear-cutting has its costs to forest birds but provides a tremendous benefit to second-growth species. Some of these second-growth species are more abundant and widespread in more fragmented regions, but there they often have high parasitism rates and low reproductive success. Also, many of these species are declining on eastern BBS routes. The possibility exists that these Ozark clear-cuts are major source areas for these species, although this needs to be confirmed. Certainly, clear-cutting has some obvious costs and benefits, but one must look at all the species involved in order to calculate them. In contrast, uneven-aged timber management has costs to forest birds, but little benefit to second-growth birds, with the exception of the Hooded Warbler. Because preliminary data suggest that some of these second-growth species require clearings of a minimum size, there actually may be advantages to clear-cuts that are reasonably large.

As an avian conservationist, I must be pretty careful when I express my favorable view toward clear-cutting. Clear-cuts are great for second-growth birds, but this clear-cutting must be done with reasonable rotation ages (100 years or more in the Ozarks), long cutting intervals (say, every 10 years), small incremental losses (10% per cutting sequence), and limits to clear-cut size (no bigger than 25 acres). Clear-cuts that involve giant regions and that have major impacts on watersheds or future forest growth are not what I am advocating here. Small (but not too small) clear-cuts are favorable because they limit the extent that forest birds are negatively affected by timber loss and they provide excellent conditions for second-growth species. In general, other forest management techniques may not be as hard on forest birds, but they do not provide the benefits to second-growth species.

A final caveat about timber harvest involves the landscape in which this harvest occurs. Our study in the Missouri Ozarks is situated in a heavily forested landscape. Cowbird parasitism is low there, clear-cuts do not provide cowbird foraging habitat, and any differences in parasitism rates since the treatments probably involve cowbird responses to preferred host species or attraction to the host densities found in clear-cuts. We doubt that overall parasitism has changed much. Nest predators have changed some, but since these clear-cuts are still a forested habitat

(just not a tall one), they do not attract the abundant meso-predators that seem to thrive in fragmented, human-dominated environments. As long as forest harvest is done in a forested environment, species abundances and habitats are shifted, but the harvest probably has little effect on parasitism or predation rates. In a fragmented environment, a clear-cut may attract much parasitism or predation, although if the landscape is already saturated with parasites and predators, it may just be shifting the focus of an already severe problem.

SOME SPECIES MAY NEED POSTBREEDING HABITAT

Most researchers, myself included until recently, have concerned themselves with studies of optimal breeding habitat for a species. Although this may include both habitat quality and quantity/dispersion, the assumption always was that this sort of habitat was the potential limiting factor for a breeding species. Two things happened to make me change my mind on this. First, some of my students did projects that included mist-netting birds in clear-cuts in the Ozarks. Mist nets in these cuts in late July caught not just lots of second-growth birds but also lots of birds we associate with mature forest (Wood Thrush, Worm-eating Warbler, Ovenbird, Northern Parula, Red-eyed Vireo). Then we started the radio-tracking study of Wood Thrush in the Ozarks (Anders et al. 1998), which provided some amazing insights.

Wood Thrush in the Ozarks nest in mature oak-hickory forest, usually within a dark, damp ravine with lots of dogwood in the understory. In fragmented regions Wood Thrush require fairly large forest tracts, although they sometimes occur in smaller fragments. The radio-tracking study showed that after fledging, young birds were fed by their parents for about 3 weeks, and the family stayed generally in the vicinity of the nest and its mature forest. At this point, young Wood Thrush left their family and dispersed out on their own. After a day or two of wandering around, they settled into a site where they often stayed until either they migrated or their radios died. To our surprise, though, the sites where they stayed were not mature forest but clear-cuts, thickets, thick riparian brush, and other habitats with a large second-growth component to it. These sites were almost the opposite of what we would expect for a Wood Thrush, yet they made sense. They were thick, so predators would have a hard time catching the young thrushes, and they were full of berries for food. None of the birds that got settled into one of these patches was ever known to die there. Similar studies in Virginia have shown similar results (Vega Rivera et al. 1998), plus these workers found that adults did the same thing later in the season. In some cases, these adults would go through a wing molt that was so rapid that they were flightless for a period of time.

These findings suggest that we might need to be concerned about a second type of habitat for some species to use after breeding. In parts of North America, this may not seem important, because birds of the north barely have time to breed before turning back south for the winter. But in Missouri and regions like it, a young Wood Thrush may become independent by mid- to late June and have 3–4 months during which it needs to find a safe place to stay. Breeding adults also may need these sites for as rapid a molt as possible following the breeding season.

Obviously, we need to learn more about how critical these sites are to what we think of as mature forest birds, but the use of these thickets and clear-cuts by Wood Thrush with radios and the capture rates of forest birds in clear-cuts in late summer suggest that they are favored environments. If forest birds need some second-growth habitats for late-summer activities, that is another reason why clear-cuts may have their advantages.

FRAGMENTS MIGHT MAKE GOOD STOPOVER HABITAT

Although we have not yet looked at problems with migration habitat and stopover ecology (we will in Chapter 10), it should be pointed out here that habitat fragments that are too small to be good breeding sites might still be important, if not critical, as stopover sites for migrants traveling through a fragmented region. Forest birds that cannot feed or find cover in cornfields or other croplands probably do well in small fragments; certainly these small habitats are better than no habitat at all for these travelers.

WE MUST CONSIDER WHAT "OLD-GROWTH" VEGETATION REALLY WAS

Long-term management plans often involve some component of protected areas that are currently considered or slated for future designation as "old growth." These are usually suggested to represent the original habitat conditions, or at least the original conditions as we think they existed at the time that Europeans settled North America. In some cases, what we get if we leave a site protected now might be very different from the vegetation types the site supported 300 years ago. Bob Askins (2000) discussed how our conception of "natural vegetation" is often quite wrong, given that such natural disturbance forces as fires are not allowed to proceed as they did in the past. Too much protection without natural disturbances may result in something very different from the original vegetation.

MIGRANT BIRD MANAGEMENT MUST HAVE A REGIONAL COMPONENT

I hope that I have shown how avian conservationists have changed in the way they look at how bird populations are regulated. Obviously, managers need to recognize these changes and how they affect what managers can do with the locations they are attempting to manage. First, one must look at how the reserve fits within the local landscape. Is it an isolate, or is it part of a contiguous habitat? Is it probably a source or a sink for the most important bird populations? Depending upon the answers to these questions, the manager can put into perspective possible changes to habitats, development of edge, and other manipulations. For example, many managers have to serve the needs of groups such as hunters, who might like more quail, turkey, or deer, which do well in conditions with lots of edge. Management for these species often may work against Neotropical migrants, but this depends a lot upon the situation in which the reserve exists. In some cases, if parasitism and nest predation are prevalent everywhere anyway, managing for quail may not really change conditions. In heavily forested regions, new edge has little effect. But a manager must look at where the managed area sits in the regional landscape before making decisions.

Ideally, someone is also analyzing goals and management plans at a state or other large regional level. This person should be cognizant of areas that are undoubtedly important source populations to be sure that these are being protected. This analyst should inform local managers of species of concern and how local management practices might affect them. This person also should be active in Partners in Flight management activities (see Chapter 12) to keep up with how our ideas about sources and sinks and regional demography change. Someone has to keep the big picture of population exchange and regulation in view at all times, to ensure that the most critical sites are managed properly and protected adequately.

BIRD CONSERVATION AREAS: MODERN MANAGEMENT IN ACTION

We will talk about the many positive things that have come out of the Partners in Flight (PIF) program later, but one of the best things the organization is doing fits into the discussion right now. PIF has done an excellent job of having researchers and managers interact and communicate. The result is minimal lag time between the development of new ideas about how migrant birds should be managed and the transfer of these ideas to managers.

Although I have just described to you a set of management ideals that are required for adequate migratory bird management on the breeding grounds, most of these ideas are already being applied with the concept of Bird Conservation Areas (BCAs), and researchers are out in the field, testing to see if these concepts work.

The basic concept behind a BCA is an attempt to provide both large areas of target habitat and landscapes dominated by the target habitat. Ideally, there should be enough habitat to support a large population, with good reproductive conditions such that the local population will have long-term stability and, ideally, be a source for a region. Of course, the need for large areas of habitat must be balanced by the costs involved in purchasing such areas, so BCAs also attempt to involve private landowners in the development of the area, using interests of the landowners or financial rewards as leverage.

Thus, a BCA ideally has a large area of core habitat. This area should be big enough that parasitism or predation rates are minimized within it and that it supports relatively large, source populations of the target bird species. This is primarily the "bigger is better" principle at work and should follow the guidelines shown in Figure 7.4. Around this core habitat is a zone where nontarget habitat is allowed, but an attempt is made to make the landscape as hospitable to the target bird species as possible. This zone may have higher parasitism or predation levels than the core,

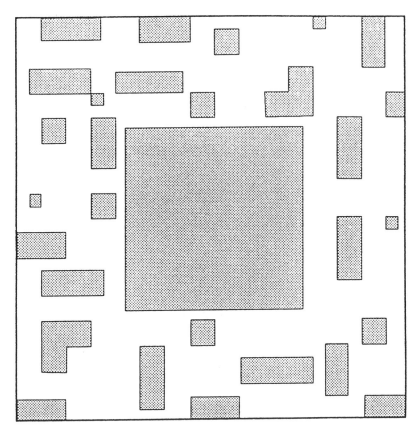

FIGURE 7.4. *Sample design that implements Bird Conservation Area guidelines. For grassland birds, this design included a 2,000-acre block of permanent grassland at the core within a 10,000-acre matrix with 25% grassland. From Fitzgerald et al. (1998).*

but it is hoped that they will not be too high. Beyond this is a second zone where the landscape parameters are relaxed even more but ideally provide a situation of benefit to the target species.

A proposed BCA plan for grassland birds has been developed and is currently being tested in Minnesota and North Dakota. Obviously, we will need to have different parameters with regard to size of core area, landscape levels around the core, and number of BCAs required for different habitats and target bird species, but the BCA is an exciting application of the most up-to-date ideas in migrant bird management.

8 | MIGRANT WINTERING ECOLOGY
Characteristics and Constraints

Neotropical migrants share the common characteristic of spending their nonbreeding season in the Tropics or subtropics of Central America, South America, or the West Indies. For a few species, individuals have been recorded on the wintering grounds for up to 8 months of the year, although 5 to 7 months is probably a more common amount of time spent on the wintering grounds. Since many of these same species spend only 2 to 4 months on their breeding grounds, it is easy to see how the site where a bird spends the most time is of great importance. (Of course, we must not fall into the trap of automatically saying that the site where a bird spends the most time is the most important site.)

With lots of recent news about loss of habitat in the Tropics, including the New World Tropics, it was easy for concern to develop about the state of Neotropical bird populations when declines were reported during the 1980s. The connection between Neotropical migrant declines and tropical habitat loss is a logical one; it doesn't take a rocket scientist to observe Neotropical migrant population declines and tropical habitat loss and suggest cause and effect. Unfortunately, like most everything else with Neotropical migrant birds, the situation is not that simple. About the only thing that these species share with one another is the general location of their wintering grounds. Otherwise, we need to look at each species with regard to its winter needs and how recent changes in habitats may or may not have affected that species. In this chapter, you will be introduced to some of the variation shown by Neotropical migrants to see the extent to which one can or cannot make generalizations about Neotropical migrants as a group.

What Does a Neotropical Migrant
Need for the Winter?

The goals of a typical Neotropical migrant bird during the nonbreeding season are pretty simple: it wants to find a place where it can find enough food and protection from predators that it can stay alive, with enough food at the end of this period that it can fatten up enough to start its migration northward. Survival is the only goal, and because few of our migrants are social in any fashion (that is, they don't run around in family groups in which a parent bird might have to consider making sacrifices to protect its young), it is very much just a matter of each individual's looking out for itself.

The extent that predation on adult birds affects how a bird selects habitat is not known. Certainly there are types of hawks that live in the wintering grounds and specialize on birds as prey. Many North American breeding *Accipiter* species (Cooper's and Sharp-shinned hawks, for example) are Neotropical migrants themselves. From northern Mexico throughout the Neotropics there also exists a set of *Micrastur* falcons that are *Accipiter*-like in their food habits. The possible effects of such predation on populations is even harder to track. Nonetheless, we assume that wintering birds use predation as one of the factors that they evaluate when choosing a wintering site. Additionally, these winter residents often are part of the common tropical mixed-species foraging flocks that occur in most habitats, flocks that exist at least in part to minimize predation risk.

If predation is a small part of habitat selection, then food supply is the dominant force. The wintering bird needs enough food to keep it healthy and happy during the nonbreeding season, plus a little extra at the end of that season when it is time to head north. Trying to figure out how a bird actually determines whether a site has enough food for this 6- to 8-month period is more problematic. We assume it involves some sort of assessment of several factors, including how much food there actually is and what else is around that wants to eat the same food.

Actual Resource Abundance   We assume that a bird roaming through appropriate habitats has the ability to assess the quality of the habitat either directly by seeing how much food there is or indirectly by observing vegetation structure and correlating that in some fashion with expected food abundance. Studies about habitat selection during the breeding season suggest that most birds have a genetic program that tells them which habitats they should choose, and we can easily assume that such an ability should also evolve in birds that choose winter habitat.

We assume that some sort of general habitat selection behavior has evolved because such behavior would be able to take into account seasonal changes in food supply that might occur in different habitats. Although the amount of food presently occurring in a site might be a good index to food supply at that time, it might not predict future food supply. To the extent that a bird wants to stay in that site for a long period of time, it wants to select a site that will provide food over that long period of time. On the other hand, a site that looks like good habitat for the long run but has no food currently is not a good choice. So both long-term expectations and current food supply may be used in assessing a wintering site.

Long-term expectations must take into account any seasonality of climate that might occur in the site being chosen. Most of the Neotropical migrants winter in Mexico, Central America, or the Caribbean (discussed below), an area that is characterized by its wettest conditions in September to November, the period when migrants arrive. In contrast, a dry season begins in late November or December and extends until mid- to late April, the time when most of these migrants are leaving or have already left. In moist habitats, this dry season has little effect on forest structure, despite the reduction in rainfall. But in drier habitats, the dry season is associated with several months with little or no rainfall. In these drier habitats, many trees are deciduous and lose their leaves, resulting in a barren environment where only the large cacti may be green for several months of the year. This lack of leaves undoubtedly affects food availability. Quite obviously, a bird needs to evolve habitat selection behavior that takes such seasonality into account or else it may find itself trying to survive in a site without food.

Competition with Other Species   Most folks with any knowledge about tropical ecology know that the Tropics are famous for their diversity. A single tropical site may have more species breeding in it than have been recorded in whole states in the Temperate Zone. A Neotropical migrant trying to choose a wintering site must evolve the ability to assess not only how much food a habitat might support over the winter but also how much food might be available to that migrant once all the other birds (and perhaps bats, monkeys, and other possible competitors) living in that habitat have taken their share.

If we confine ourselves to possible avian competitors, the evidence is impressive. For example, El Cielo Biosphere Reserve in northeastern Mexico (just 300 miles from Texas) has around 150 breeding species in the various habitats it contains. Diversity of resident species goes up as one goes south from El Cielo, such that the tiny countries of Costa Rica and Panama have bird lists much larger than the list for the United States and Canada. By the time one enters South America, one is confronted with almost unbelievable diversity. Colombia supports nearly 1,700 species. A single location in Amazonian Peru (Cocha Cashu Biological Station) has a bird list of nearly 600 species for a few square miles and is known to have more than 300 resident species whose breeding territories overlap. Obviously, all of these species have to eat, so a migrant must be able to deal with competition with resident birds as it chooses where to spend the winter.

Finally, we also have to be aware that there are many Neotropical migrant species all trying to find a spot for the winter. Some of these are very similar in their requirements for foods or habitats, such that having two migrant species trying to winter in the same spot might not work. Certainly, a migrant trying to choose a wintering site has to figure out not just how much food there is but also how much food there might be left after everyone has had lunch.

Competition with Conspecifics   If all of the potential interactions with other species weren't enough, we have to remember that there might be hundreds of thousands or even millions of individuals of a particular species headed for the wintering grounds. If they all end up in the same place, it is quite obvious that most won't survive. Because these individuals are of the same species, they are nearly identical in their food habits, behavior, and body size, which means that two conspecific individuals are after exactly the same sort of food when they are foraging. Thus, avoidance of overlap with conspecifics may be the most important behavior that a winter resident bird develops.

As we shall see in more detail later, this avoidance of conspecifics is a critical issue to most Neotropical migrants. Some species show extreme territorial behavior, with each individual having its own little wintering territory. In most cases, these are defended by that individual from intrusion by other individuals of the same species. In some cases, individuals of different sexes defend territories against one another, while in others the sexes seem to specialize in different habitats and in a few cases use somewhat different wintering ranges. Other species do not seem to be territorial, although most of these are widely dispersed across the habitat.

Only a few Neotropical migrants occur in single-species flocks during the winter, although this behavior is common among birds that winter in the United States.

Habitat Selection Is Constrained by Morphology   Although we are assuming that a bird assesses its winter habitat by looking at foods, habitat, and competitors, we also must remember that the availability of foods for each species will be limited by the way that the species is built and how it can forage. Grassland birds have a variety of adaptations that make them successful in open habitats with short vegetation; they cannot simply enter a rain forest and start hopping around in the trees or even in the leaf litter. Food habits are also constrained by both bill and digestive morphology. A warbler cannot do a good job of either handling seeds with its bill or digesting them once they are swallowed. A large-billed sparrow or grosbeak may not be very good at gleaning small insects off of leaf surfaces. Obviously, if a bird is adapted to living in a forest to breed, it most likely will live in some sort of forest during the winter (or vice versa, as is discussed later).

Although most birds are constrained in their habitat and/or food selection by morphology, some of them are also remarkably flexible in what they do during the nonbreeding season. Many birds that we think of as insectivorous are primarily frugivorous during the winter. It doesn't take any great morphological adaptations to swallow or digest a soft fruit, and the fruit may provide a lot of sugar, which is one of the chief requirements for staying alive during the nonbreeding season when no eggs need to be laid and no molting needs to be done. A few other species have morphological adaptations for their winter foods, adaptations that they simply don't use during the breeding season. Some of these will be discussed in more detail later, but it is important to remember here that a migrant is constrained in its habitat choices by the way it is built and what it can eat.

Migrants Must Reach Wintering Grounds in a Timely Fashion
The final factor that we must remind ourselves about when thinking about the evolution of wintering grounds is quite simply that the migrant needs to be able to find its wintering site the first time and then be able to get back to it in subsequent years. The trip between breeding and wintering sites should also not take so long or burn up so much energy that the migration is not worth it. Ideally, the wintering site should be as close as possible to the breeding site, or at least it should be a place that the bird

has a decent probability of getting to or from during each migration. We will next look at some of the factors that constrain migration in this way, for it is a major factor in the evolution of a wintering range.

NEW WORLD GEOGRAPHY AND MIGRATION

To get a feel for the options and constraints that must have occurred as winter ranges were evolving for migrant birds, we need to take a look at the basic patterns of geography found in the main breeding range of these birds (the United States and Canada) and the wintering range (Mexico, Central and South America, and the West Indies). This look should involve simple comparisons of the area available for wintering and breeding, how different habitat types are distributed between these two regions, and the distances between possible breeding and wintering sites.

One way to get an idea about how breeding and wintering habitat is distributed is to compare equal-area projections of the Western Hemisphere after a little cutting and pasting (Fig. 8.1). Taking into account that the breeding grounds are the United States and Canada in North America, while the wintering grounds exclude the southern third of South America, the simple comparison of areas of breeding grounds and wintering grounds suggests that these areas are fairly similar, but only because of the large size of northern South America, particularly the Amazon basin. If we subtract all of boreal North America (the region of tundra that covers much of the upper quarter of the map shown in Fig. 8.1) from the breeding range of Neotropical migrants, then the amount of breeding area is closer to being equal to that of potential wintering grounds.

Unfortunately, the location of the wintering grounds in reality makes our comparison a bit more complex for a migrant bird. As Neotropical migrants evolved their wintering behavior, they were faced with the fact that the nearby wintering areas (Mexico, Central America, and the West Indies) were relatively small and became smaller as one went farther south. The vast area of South America that could be used for wintering was a long way away to both the south and the east. To get to this large area, a migrant would either have to take the long trip down the Isthmus of Panama or have to do some ocean and/or island hopping across the Caribbean or Atlantic. The reality is that nearby wintering habitat for North American breeders is limited in area; only by traveling long distances is the amount of wintering habitat equivalent to that of breeding habitat.

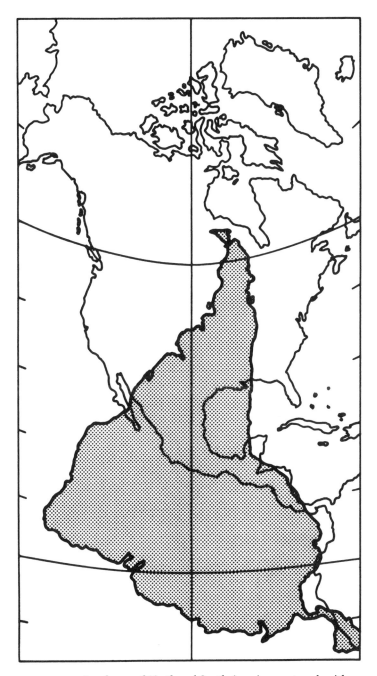

FIGURE 8.1. *Land area of North and South America compared, with South America rotated for comparison of tropical and temperate areas of the continents. Note that fairly similar amounts of land area occur in both the Tropics and the temperate zones, but the tropical area of South America is distant from North America and separated by ocean.*

Comparisons between the amount and location of breeding and wintering habitats are further confounded when we take into account the habitats that occur in both locations. Assuming that a grassland breeding bird must have grasslands for the winter and a forest breeding bird must winter in some form of forest, the distribution of breeding and wintering areas becomes less balanced at any spatial scale. This is particularly true for grassland birds. Vast grasslands of various types occur throughout much of the central United States and Canada, with extensions into Mexico. Yet, natural grasslands in the rest of Mexico, Central America, much of northern South America, or the West Indies are limited to some coastal areas and savannahs. A grassland bird has to travel all the way to northern South America to find any grassland area at all (the llanos of southern Colombia and Venezuela); to find large areas of such habitat, it must cross the Amazon basin to the pampas of Argentina or associated grassland habitats. Although the amount of breeding and wintering habitat overall is not that different, obvious problems are associated with trying to get from the grasslands of North America to those of South America.

The limitations faced by forest birds are not as severe as those faced by grassland birds, provided these forest birds can be flexible in the types of forest they use. Such flexibility is undoubtedly a requirement for forest birds; for example, species that breed in the coniferous boreal forests of the United States and Canada will have very limited wintering habitat if they insist on using coniferous forest during the winter, because these habitats are confined to upper-elevation forests in Mexico, Central America, and a couple of islands in the Greater Antilles. In general, though, forest habitats stretch continuously from the temperate breeding grounds to the tropical wintering grounds, except for some oceanic barriers.

WHERE ARE THE MIGRANTS IN WINTER?

Given the constraints on the distribution of habitats that we have just examined, it is not too surprising that most Neotropical migrants winter in Mexico, Central America, and the Caribbean. Rappole et al. (1983) summarized the winter distribution of Neotropical migrant species and suggested that only 6% of migrants wintered primarily in South America. With taxonomic groups, the pattern is equally clear; both warblers (Parulidae) and flycatchers (Tyrannidae) have winter distributions with the

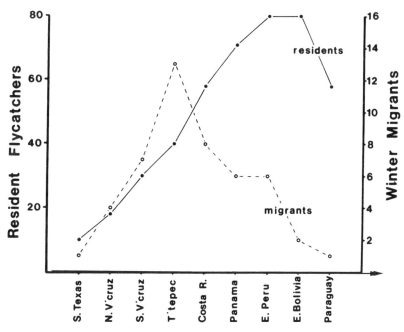

FIGURE 8.2. *Distribution of wintering flycatcher species in the Western Hemisphere in relation to diversity of resident flycatchers. Note that most migrants do not go as far as South America. Reproduced from John W. Fitzpatrick, 1980, "Wintering of North American Tyrant Flycatchers in the Neotropics," in* Migrant Birds in the Neotropics, *ed. A. Keast and E. S. Morton, pp. 67–78 (Smithsonian Institution Press, Washington, D.C.), by permission of the author.*

greatest density of species in southern Mexico around the Isthmus of Tehuantepec (Fig. 8.2). In contrast, most grassland birds winter in North America, limiting their movement to the grasslands found in the southern United States and northern Mexico. Although a few species make the spectacular move to southern South America (e.g., Upland Sandpiper and Swainson's Hawk), most do not.

Evolutionary theory would suggest that these species have evolved strategies of migration that balance such factors as distance and amount of competition in making their "decision" on where to winter. For example, as a migrant travels farther into southern Central America or South America, it not only is increasing the distance it must travel but also is moving into habitats with more and more resident species. Although the Amazon basin might be a great big habitat in which to spend the winter, it also is a habitat with 300 bird species or more living in it in any site. Although even northern Mexico has greater resident bird diversity than anywhere in the United States, this Mexican diversity is still usually far less than 100 species in a habitat, which must be easier to deal with than the incredible diversity of tropical South America. Of course, many species do travel all the way to South America and deal with this diversity, but they amount to only 6% or so of all the migrant species, suggesting how difficult a strategy this might be.

Given these patterns of migrant distribution on the wintering grounds, we are faced with the fact that most North American migrants attempt to squeeze into a relatively small area for the winter. Terborgh (1980) suggested that the ratio of breeding area to wintering area for most species was about 8:1. To the extent that this ratio is correct (and obviously Terborgh's estimate was a generalization), loss of an acre of habitat on the wintering grounds could have much more effect on a population than loss of an acre on the breeding grounds. These patterns also make it clear that what is happening north of South America is key to the future of most Neotropical migrants.

PATTERNS OF WINTER ECOLOGY

Although the patterns of habitat distribution and land area allow us to make some generalizations about the evolution of distributions among wintering Neotropical migrants, as we attempt to look at the details of winter ecology, we have to be careful about making generalizations. Each of the Neotropical migrant species has its own characteristics with regard to such factors as habitat selection, diet, and winter distribution. To successfully understand the extent that a species faces problems in the future, we must be able to understand where potential limiting factors occur for it, rather than trying to make sweeping generalizations about migrants. As our knowledge of how winter residents live increases, perhaps we will be able to find groups of species with similar enough traits that we can try to manage them as a group (as suggested by Petit et al. 1993), but the safest way to approach such decisions is by understanding the ecological and behavioral traits of each species and then grouping species with similar traits, rather than trying to group species before we really understand what they are doing.

Habitat Selection   Each migrant species has a set of habitat criteria that it uses to select its wintering habitat. This can be described from vegetation measurements just as one can do for the breeding season, and for most species there seem to be strong similarities between the critical components of the habitat selected in both seasons. For example, the Common Yellowthroat likes short, scrubby vegetation in both seasons, and the Wood Thrush is found mostly in more mature forests with a canopy and understory in both winter and summer. To understand how a bird selects habitat, though, one must try to figure out the critical components required by a species for a habitat to adequately serve as wintering or breeding habitat. For example, the Ovenbird in winter can be found in all sorts of vegetation types, from cloud forest at upper elevations to tropical rain forest or very arid deciduous scrub with tall, arboreal cacti (Fig. 8.3). The one commonality in all these sites is that there is an understory with leaf litter in which the Ovenbird can hop around and forage.

Determining which habitats are critical for each species can be a problem in part because these migrants are able to roam around so much that it is often difficult to be sure which species actually are relying on which habitats. In long-term studies at the Guánica Forest in southwestern Puerto Rico, my colleagues and I have netted 16 different species of potential winter-resident warblers and more than 20 species of potential winter residents in all. Some of these we have caught only once or twice in 26 years; others we catch once or twice a year in a massive netting effort. Only 3 species in this forest are caught every year in nearly every net line. For which species should we realistically consider that the Guánica Forest is serving as an appropriate wintering habitat?

Habitat selection may also vary by age or sex within a species. The Guánica Forest winter-resident community is dominated by female birds in all the common species. Other studies have shown habitats that are male-dominated, although these studies usually look at just a single species. In some cases, which will be discussed in more detail below, this habitat difference by sex seems to be a result of male exclusion of females from certain habitats, including those that are apparently better in terms of food supply. In other cases, including the Black-throated Blue Warbler, it appears that the male and female select different habitat characteristics. In habitats with a certain structure, a researcher might find all males, while other habitats might support all females. In some cases, when habitat conditions are just right, males and females might each defend a territory against other members of their sex, but individual territories of a male and a female might overlap (Wunderle 1992).

There is some evidence that habitat preferences for a species may

FIGURE 8.3. *Ovenbird habitat at Guánica Forest, Puerto Rico. This habitat does not resemble the lush oak-hickory forests in which this species usually breeds.*

vary across its winter range. For example, Black-throated Blue Warblers never occur in lowland dry scrub habitat in Puerto Rico or Hispaniola, but this species is common in similar habitat in Cuba. Why this sort of shift occurs, and why sex ratios vary from habitat to habitat, have not been explained, partly because we have only recently gotten good data about winter-resident distributions in Cuba. In temperate-wintering species that show patterns of habitat or range segregation by the sexes, usually it is the males that occur farther to the north, with females to the south. Three mechanisms have been suggested to explain these patterns (Ketterson and Nolan 1983):

1   Males dominate females in habitat selection or at feeding sites, forcing females to move away from males in winter to survive. This would be at work in species where males force females into dry scrub habitats (as in Puerto Rico), but we need to see that males also dominate in moister habitats to know that this mechanism is functioning.

2   Males need to winter closer to the breeding grounds than females because males need to get to the breeding grounds first in order to set up territories. Because females can afford to arrive on the breeding sites a week or so after males, they can afford to go farther south in winter. In the West Indies, this mechanism could be used to explain the dominance of females at Guánica, but one would expect that all habitats in Puerto Rico should be female-dominated, since it is the island farthest away from the breeding grounds. In contrast, Cuba should in general be male-dominated.

3   Males are larger than females, so for energetic reasons they can more easily stay to the north and deal with cold temperatures. In Neotropical migrants, this explanation is pretty irrelevant.

Obviously, we need more good data that record sex ratios and habitat preferences of wintering birds across their wintering ranges. Unfortunately, many of the Neotropical migrants are not sexually dimorphic in plumage or size, so figuring out if they have sexual differences in winter habitat selection will be particularly difficult for those species.

Social Structure   How are Neotropical migrants dispersed across the wintering habitats that they choose? Although some researchers would like to generalize, once again we must be careful about doing so, because it appears that migrants show a wide range of different dispersion patterns, ranging from rigid individual territories to nomadism.

The classic model for territorial behavior among Neotropical migrants has come from the work of Dick Holmes and Tom Sherry (Holmes et al. 1989) in Jamaica. They have studied the American Redstart in two major habitat types—mangroves and dry scrub. Redstarts have individual territories that do not overlap and are defended from other redstarts aggressively. Should a bird die, its territory will be taken over by another, either by movement from a different territory or by movement of a nonterritorial floater into the territory. This classic territoriality is reminiscent of breeding territories in the Temperate Zone.

In the case of Jamaican redstarts, territories in moister habitats (mangrove) are almost completely occupied by males, whereas drier habitats are used by females. Males take over territories through dominance interactions, with males always dominant over females, and older members of a sex always dominant over younger members. In many cases, females may arrive on the wintering grounds first, establish territories in the mangroves, and then get chased out by males when they arrive. In these systems, a certain amount of habitat can support only a certain number of birds; if habitat is limited, it appears that females (especially young females) will be the birds that cannot find a place to winter.

Other species defend individual territories, but they are not always tied into male-female dominance systems in the same fashion as redstarts. As was noted earlier, Black-throated Blue Warblers seem to have individual territories, but the sexes are keying in on different habitat conditions and may even overlap in sites that contain all of the habitat components required by the sexes. In cases like this, males and females may have differing chances of finding good wintering habitat, but differences between sexes in survival will be a function of the amount of remaining habitat, not of interactions between the sexes.

Recent work with Prairie Warblers in Puerto Rico and Hispaniola has shown variation in the social system of this species (Latta 2000; Baltz 2000). In old pastures in southwestern Puerto Rico, Prairie Warblers are known to roost communally (which is discussed more later in this chapter). These birds then wander around during the day, perhaps in the same general area each day, but with no evidence of any sort of defended territory. In dry habitats in the Dominican Republic, this species does have territories, although they are fairly large and do not appear to be as rigidly defended as those of redstarts on Jamaica. In this case, the territories at any particular site seem to be occupied by a mix of ages and sexes, such that no habitat separation by age or sex class is readily apparent.

In general, showing territorial behavior in a species is pretty easy.

One observes marked birds while mapping their territories over time and notes the lack of overlap in individual distributions. It is harder to show that a species is not territorial, particularly if the area each individual uses is fairly large. Black-and-white Warblers in Puerto Rico seem to be spaced in their distribution, but they also seem to overlap in their foraging areas, and my students and I have never seen them defending a territory. It is possible that they do defend territories, but we cannot see it where we do our research. It is possible that they did actively defend these territories earlier in the winter and that, because we do most of our work in Puerto Rico in January, we have missed the important interactions. On the other hand, most rigid territorial behavior involves relatively small areas, because of constraints with regard to resource protection and the cost of territory defense. The areas used by Black-and-whites seem large enough that active defense of the area from the one or two other conspecifics that might wander through probably isn't worth it.

In sharp contrast to the species with rigid territories are those that seem to be fairly nomadic throughout the nonbreeding season. Morton (1980) showed how several species that spent the winter in the Panama Canal area changed habitats repeatedly through this period. In species such as the Bay-breasted Warbler and Chestnut-sided Warbler, such habitat shifts were also associated with shifts from eating insects to fruit (discussed below). In at least one species, social behavior may span the range from territorial to nomadic; the Northern Waterthrush is thought to be territorial throughout the winter in much of its range, but in mangroves in northern Venezuela, individual birds seem to move in and out throughout the nonbreeding season, with an individual bird staying in a site and defending a territory for only a few weeks before moving on (Lefebvre et al. 1994).

Only a small number of wintering species have been studied in depth with regard to their social system in winter, so we cannot generalize much about these traits. Although the work on redstarts in Jamaica is meticulously done, we must be careful about assuming that this sort of dispersion system is common in migrants until we get more data from species elsewhere.

Foods and Foraging   Most of the migrants familiar to those of us living in the Temperate Zone are insectivorous during the breeding season. The dominant migrants are warblers, vireos, flycatchers, blackbirds, swallows, and the like, all of which we associate with a diet of insects. Even such groups as tanagers and finches, whose large bills are associated with a fruit or seed diet, eat many insects during the breeding season and are known to feed insects to their young. This is not surprising, because the insect resource in the Temperate Zone is highly seasonal; the assumption in most models of the evolution of bird migration is either that migrants must leave their breeding grounds because they would starve if they didn't or that they leave the Tropics to take advantage of the seasonal glut of food in the Temperate Zone during the breeding season. The only birds that can winter in really cold areas and still eat insects are species such as chickadees and titmice, which have heavy bills to dig at larvae and dormant insects in bark and also eat lots of seeds, and woodpeckers, which search for dormant insects beneath tree bark (and also eat lots of seeds).

Do these temperate-breeding species eat mostly insects during the nonbreeding season? Certainly, those species adapted for fruits and seeds tend to focus on these foods during the nonbreeding season, which is understandable, given their adaptations for such foods. The surprising thing is the extent that species we think of as extremely insectivorous will shift their diets during the winter. We have already mentioned that Bay-breasted and Chestnut-sided warblers shift their diets to include much fruit in winter, but many flycatchers also do this. The Eastern Kingbird, which we tend to think of as such an extreme insectivore during its breeding season, eats primarily fruits during its winter sojourn in Amazon basin rain forests (Fitzpatrick 1980). Similarly, White-eyed Vireos in Mexico are considered to be a critical fruit disperser for several plant species. Although few studies have been done that document in detail the extent to which warblers and vireos rely on fruit, all one has to do is sit and watch the avian visitors to a tropical fruit tree to see that many wintering species include fruit in their diets. Given that the chief goal in winter is simply to stay alive, and fruit provides lots of easily harvested energy even if the fruit is not highly nutritious, why not?

Speaking of easy energy, we know that all Temperate Zone hummingbirds must leave their breeding grounds and go south at least far enough to have flowers available through the winter. The Ruby-throated Hummingbird of eastern North America heads for southern Mexico (flying across the Gulf of Mexico) to winter, where it can count on enough flowers for nectar and survival. Some of the hummers of the western United States can get away with staying in southern Arizona or coastal California, where conditions are not so severe, but most of these also head for Mexico. A couple of species that are widespread in Mexico can live in the Rio Grande Valley of Texas all winter. Otherwise, nectar is not a resource to count on in most of the United States and Canada during winter.

Some other migrants also take advantage of nectar during the non-breeding season, although their adaptations for doing so are less obvious. The Cape May Warbler winters in the West Indies and feeds heavily at flowers. It even has a brushy-tipped tongue, an adaptation for lapping up nectar that is usually associated with honeycreepers and other nectar specialists. Many temperate-breeding oriole species also spend a lot of time in the winter at flowers, as do their tropical-resident relatives.

As is so often the case, we do not have good information on the nonbreeding-season diets of most Neotropical migrants. We know enough to be careful about characterizing them based on their breeding-season diets, but that is about all we know.

Flock Foraging during Winter   Flocks are common to Temperate Zone birdwatchers during winter. Blackbirds, robins, bluebirds, finches, waxwings, and many other species wander around in large, often single-species flocks during winter. In most cases, these species are feeding on fruit or seeds during this time of the year, and flock foraging is adaptive both as a means of finding and efficiently harvesting these patchily distributed foods and as a means of protection from predators in open habitats (and most temperate habitats are relatively open when the leaves are on the ground).

Few winter-resident birds occur in large single-species flocks on the wintering grounds. The most distinctive of those that do is the Eastern Kingbird, which we have already noted shifts its diet to fruit during the winter. Eastern Kingbirds roam around in sometimes huge flocks (200 or more individuals) at this time of year, wandering from one fruit tree to the next to find easy food. I had heard about this before a recent trip to rain forests in Peru, but I was very impressed in late September when these huge flocks of kingbirds showed up doing what they were supposed to be doing. Nothing else in the Amazonian rain forest occurs in flocks like this; other wintering kingbirds or large flycatchers may eat some fruit, but they also eat many insects and are widely spaced. Even those warblers or orioles that eat fruit and move around a lot during winter do not occur in such large groups.

Temperate birders also are aware of mixed-species flocks during the winter. These flocks are often composed of chickadees, titmice, nuthatches, and perhaps a few woodpeckers that travel together as a group, gathering food and gaining some protection from predation. Mixed-species flocks are generally explained as an adaptation that allows species that need to be widely dispersed and usually territorial—because their food supply is widely dispersed—to garner the advantages of group foraging in regard to predator protection. Such mixed-species flocks are a dominant factor in the social system of many tropical birds; they may include 15 to 25 species that forage together at a similar rate on similar foods. A single tropical rain forest may have several flocks with overlapping distributions: an understory flock of insectivores that works the leaf litter, herbaceous plants, and smaller trees, and midstory and canopy flocks feeding on insects in the zones above. One or two layers of flocks adapted to finding fruit may overlap with these insectivorous flocks. In recent years, researchers found that many of these flocks are composed of a single pair of each participating resident species, with the flock members sharing territorial boundaries (Munn 1985).

It is not surprising that during their time in the Tropics many winter-resident species join these tropical mixed-species flocks. In northern Mexico, migrants constitute up to half of the species of the large mixed-species flocks found there (an average of 18 species per flock [Gram 1998]). Generally, one individual of a species was found in each flock. In cases like this, where flock membership may be a limiting factor (that is, there can only be one individual of a species per flock and the flock is rigidly territorial), flock participation will restrict wintering densities of migratory birds. In other cases, several individuals of a species may participate in the flock, so that flock membership characterizes the species' winter ecology but may not be as potentially limiting to populations.

Other interesting social factors affect migrant birds. A distinctive trait of tropical birds is their following of army ants. These army ant swarms wander through the forests, chasing and catching insects and other live prey. As they move, the insects and other potential prey items run for their lives, at which time they are quite vulnerable to predation from birds. Although many species will visit such ant swarms when they get the chance (such as when a swarm moves through their territory), a few species show this behavior quite regularly and several are what we call obligate ant followers (they do this behavior all the time). Many migrants have been observed at army ant swarms, and it has been suggested that the Kentucky Warbler may regularly search for army ants as part of its wintering ecology, at least in that part of its range where such swarms occur regularly.

Flock Roosting During the second symposium on migrant birds, Cynthia Staicer described a situation in Puerto Rico where winter resident warblers were congregating in large numbers at a small grove of thick trees for the night (Staicer 1992). Such group roosts had never been observed for species like this before. Recently, other researchers have observed similar behavior in several locations. With such limited data, it is hard to understand why this occurs, but the sites where it has been observed seem to be open, with relatively small, shrubby trees that provide little cover from rain. Of course, it also is possible that many more winter residents show this behavior, but we can see it only in small, open habitats, where the movements of dozens of birds at dusk are more easy to observe than they would be in thick, uniform habitats. Certainly, the extent to which such roosting trees may be needed for high winter survival remains another mystery that requires investigation.

ADJUSTING TO HUMAN HABITAT DISTURBANCE

As we try to understand all of the factors at work in determining the winter habitat requirements of Neotropical migrants in enough detail to know whether habitat limitation could be at work on migrant populations, we must understand both what we consider the "natural" requirements of these species and the ability of each species to adapt to manmade alterations in their habitats. Most migrant studies have occurred in the past few decades, whereas aspects of habitat alteration such as loss and fragmentation have been around for hundreds of years. Thus, we are not always sure what "natural" conditions are. A good understanding of how habitat distributions have changed over long periods of time is handy here. As Douglas Morse (1980) pointed out in the first migrant bird symposium, much of the region of southern Mexico and Guatemala that we considered as forested in recent times, but about which we were concerned because of deforestation during the past 50 years, was much more open and unforested during the height of the Aztec and Mayan civilizations. At those times, winter habitat for Neotropical migrants may have been less widespread than it is even now, and at other times (such as the 1800s) it may have been more abundant than it currently is.

How has human alteration of habitats during the past 500 years altered the conditions under which migrant habitat selection evolved? Once again, we can expect that some species are affected negatively by habitat change and others may actually benefit. For example, conversion of some tropical forest habitats to grasslands may have made life easier for grassland migrants trying to make the jump between continents. Increases in the amount of second-growth vegetation in the Tropics due to agricultural practices also may have increased the amount of habitat for these species. I have seen lots of Indigo Buntings as I've walked along the edges of sugarcane fields but few of them in nearby undisturbed tropical deciduous forests. Are buntings better off now that humans have wiped out much of the original vegetation? The Red-eyed Vireo winters in the Amazon basin and seems to be most abundant in second-growth forests there. Is the increase in forest cutting in that region actually of benefit to this species? We must recognize that the wide array of Neotropical migrant species with differing habitat requirements means that any given habitat change will probably have both a plus and a minus side to it for different species. Of course, if you pave paradise and put in a parking lot, every bird species suffers, and conversion of primary forest to agriculture undoubtedly reduces the number of species and individuals of Neotropical migrants that can survive in a site, but nevertheless a few species may actually benefit from this conversion.

Those species requiring primary forest types are undoubtedly facing less habitat, which is more fragmented and isolated in its distribution, than they have in centuries. For these species, we must be concerned about loss of habitat, and to the extent that these are rain forest birds, the early generalizations about tropical rain forest destruction and Neotropical migrant declines may be appropriate. But we must also recognize which species truly require these habitats and that other migrants may prefer these sites after they are modified.

We have already seen that habitat fragmentation has some fairly severe consequences on Neotropical migrants on their breeding grounds. Do migrant species that require native vegetation types that are less abundant, in smaller pieces, and more isolated from other such pieces of habitat suffer during the winter? Early observations suggest that fragmentation does not have much if any effect on Neotropical migrant abundances (Robbins et al. 1987). Most species seem to occur in fragments at the same density with which they occur in contiguous habitats of the same type. In some cases, perhaps because of their dispersal ability, migrants seem to be more abundant in fragments than in the larger habitat blocks.

Before it appears that researchers are suggesting that fragmentation in the Tropics is not a problem, a couple of disclaimers are in order. First, we have to be careful about equating bird abundance and habitat quality. We have reason for this caution on the breeding grounds, and we must accept the fact that fragments might attract migrants in high numbers but not be supporting them through the winter as well as more contiguous habitats do. Although Robbins et al. (1987, 1992a) looked at a few sites for 2 years and found some birds returning to fragments, extensive work is required to determine that the quality of these fragments is equal to that of larger pieces of habitat.

Second, and most important, we have to remember that Neotropical migrants are only a portion of the avifauna of tropical forests; habitat fragmentation has tremendous negative effects on the distribution and abundance of most tropical resident species. Because tropical communities are so diverse and the resident birds are fairly sedentary, the effects of habitat loss in the Tropics are much worse than we see in the Temperate Zone, even though we have shown that temperate fragmentation is fairly severe in its effects on breeding. We must be exceedingly careful in actively or even tacitly supporting activities that might promote fragmentation because of minimal effects on migrants when we know these activities might be devastating to residents.

SUMMARY

Can we make any generalizations about "the winter ecology" of Neotropical migrants? Not if we want to make any sense. There is too much we do not understand about what is going on with these species during the majority of their annual cycle. Many species that breed in the Temperate Zone spend the rest of their year as integral parts of the amazingly diverse tropical bird communities we find in the Neotropics. If we studied these communities for only 6 months a year, it would be hard to predict which were the migrants and which bred on the sites where we were studying them. For some of these species, generalizations about loss of tropical forest and population declines may be valid. On the other hand, some migrants seem to avoid diverse tropical habitats and specialize in disturbed sites with low resident diversity; these species actually may have more habitat than they ever had in the past and, perhaps, more wintering habitat than they need. Even if we had detailed knowledge of the winter requirements of all migrant species, we would need to be careful about making generalizations based on the number of species that do this behavior or choose that habitat. Rather, we would need to be continually aware of the diversity of wintering strategies that occurs among the species we call Neotropical migrants.

9 | POPULATION LIMITATION
IN WINTER
Theory and Evidence

Around 1990 the apparent declines in the populations of many bird species that wintered in the Tropics were quickly explained as being the result of loss of tropical habitats, particularly rain forest. This was certainly one of the take-home points from John Terborgh's *Where Have All the Birds Gone?* and numerous other articles written for popular audiences with titles like "Future Shock for Birders" and "Silent Spring Revisited." The link between temperate declines and tropical habitat loss helped push Partners in Flight into existence.

The tight link between tropical habitats and migrant populations that is required for a logical conclusion that the former can limit the latter was something relatively new. Before the first meeting on migrants in the late 1970s, the general consensus about the ecology of birds that wintered in the Tropics was that they used parks, gardens, and other disturbed sites. If that were true, there was lots of habitat available for them; the talks during the first symposium had little to say about conservation. (However, it is interesting to note that this is where John Terborgh [1980] first noted that the discrepancy between the areas of wintering grounds and breeding grounds might be a future problem.)

The symposium volume from that first meeting changed how we thought about Neotropical migrants (Keast and Morton 1980). Suddenly, they were part of the tropical avifauna, as tightly tied into tropical habitats as any resident species. As such, if tropical habitats were lost to human development, there was no reason to assume that migrant species would not suffer.

This shift to possible limitation of wintering grounds was a major one. Now that we know a little bit about the ecology of wintering migrants from Chapter 8, we need to think about what it takes to show that habitat loss in the Tropics can actually limit population size and possibly cause the declines seen in migratory bird populations.

WHAT IS POPULATION LIMITATION OR REGULATION?

A basic principle of ecology is that most natural populations tend to have relatively constant density within a particular site over time. Even those that might show annual or longer-term variation tend to have consistency in the size of the population at various stages of the cycle (Fig. 9.1). We know that populations have an incredible ability to increase if given the chance, but this rarely occurs. The cases in which populations do seem to grow without limit, at least for a while, usually involve species that have been introduced into new habitats where the natural controlling factors do not occur. Good examples of this in the bird world include the House Sparrow (*Passer domesticus*) and the European Starling (*Sturnus vulgaris*), which were introduced into North America and expanded across it in less than 100 years. Some of the most severe problems facing conservationists today involve trying to control exotic species, particularly, but not exclusively, plant species that are taking over natural habitats in many locations because their natural regulators are not present.

This consistency of population size over time is generally taken as good evidence that natural systems have mechanisms that limit or regulate the populations of their component species. The occurrence of this population limitation or regulation is central to nearly all of ecology; for most species, we need to understand limiting factors to understand how the system works. For conservationists, understanding population limitation may be critical to saving endangered species. For wildlife biologists, understanding population regulation is at the foundation of determining harvest limits so that something close to an optimum yield can be recorded on a long-term basis. The recent best-selling book *Population Limitation in Birds* by Ian Newton (1998) attests to the importance of this concept; it is at the root of much of what is done in ecology and conservation.

Although it is easy to accept that population regulation occurs in natural systems, it is much harder to understand the exact way in which populations are limited. The Newton book is more than 500 pages long,

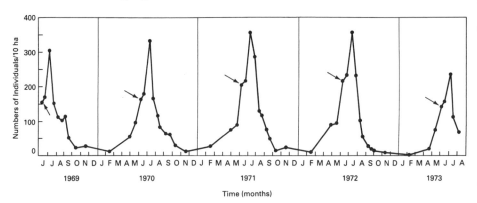

FIGURE 9.1. *Population fluctuations in Hubbard Brook birds. Despite the great annual fluctuation, peaks and valleys are quite consistent. Reproduced from R. Holmes and F. W. Sturges, 1975, "Bird Community Dynamics and Energetics in a Northern Hardwoods Ecosystem,"* Journal of Animal Ecology *44:175–200, by permission of Blackwell Science.*

with 16 chapters, and it could be considered a simple survey of the subject. One section deals with what are considered natural limiting factors, with chapters on food supply, nest sites, predation, parasites and pathogens, weather, and interspecific competition. Another section looks at how species have evolved behavioral mechanisms to deal with limiting factors, including such mechanisms as social systems (flock foraging, for example), habitat selection, territorial behavior, density dependence, and various dispersal behaviors. A final section looks at human impacts on populations, with chapters on hunting and pest control, pesticides and pollutants, and human-caused extinction.

Studies of population limitation have regularly been able to show how a particular factor works to limit a population in a particular situation. In some cases, experimental studies have been quite helpful. If one suspects that the number of acceptable nest sites is limiting a population, one might provide nest boxes and see if the population gets larger. This has been done in many studies, with the common conclusion that nest sites were the limiting factor. The hypothesis that territorial behavior was keeping some birds from breeding was shown by removal experiments, which found that the removal of territorial males resulted in new males moving into the territories almost immediately. Particularly wet or dry climatic conditions have often provided researchers the opportunity to see how these factors affected populations.

These studies of the effects of single factors on populations have been valuable in showing us how factors may influence populations, but one has to be careful in taking the step from showing an influence to suggesting that that influence totally regulates the population. For example, a study might show that providing nest boxes increased the local population, but a subsequent study might show that the birds in that higher density did not raise young as well because food became limiting. Is our measure of the population the density of breeding pairs, or is it the success of these breeding pairs? Is the population here being limited by breeding density or breeding success, and if so, which factor is more important? It seems logical to think that one cannot increase the density of nest boxes without at some point reaching food limitation, but what is that point? A final chapter of the Newton book points out that various factors might interact to limit populations in such a way that a researcher might see one factor at work but not realize that a separate factor was also important.

The reality of most natural situations is that a number of limiting factors are potentially at work in any given situation; we can see any one of them at work only under certain, often unusual situations (say, a harsh winter). To the extent that the naturally occurring limiting factors are predictable (e.g., winter conditions are fairly consistent, food supply is predictable, cavities occur with a certain regularity), we also expect the species dealing with these factors to evolve behaviors (e.g., flock foraging, territoriality) that may effectively limit their populations while increasing the chances of an individual's survival through the limiting period. Population limitation is an exceedingly complex subject even for such species as deer, which are relatively easy to count and remain in a small area throughout the year. To understand population limitation in a Neotropical migrant, one has to deal with multiple factors on the breeding grounds, on the wintering grounds, and while in migration. That's a tough row for population biologists to hoe.

HOW MIGHT WINTER EVENTS AFFECT FITNESS?

Ecologists believe that each species responds to the whole set of potential limiting factors by evolution through the process of natural selection (survival of the fittest). The basic idea is that those individual birds that have a set of genes that help them make the proper decisions about where to go, what to eat, when to migrate, and so forth survive and produce offspring that inherit these same genes for success. Individuals that have genes that lead them to making decisions that result in fewer offspring do not pass along as many of their genes as the more successful individuals do, so gene frequencies in the population change and we have evolution. The ability for any individual bird to pass on its genes to subsequent generations is termed its fitness. It is easy to see how breeding-season factors affect fitness, because so many of these factors are directly related to the production of offspring. How might winter population limitation affect the fitness of the birds trying to survive through the winter?

Winter habitat limitation may detrimentally affect birds in two ways, one direct and one indirect. As has already been noted, the key factor for wintering migrants is survival; they need a place to stay alive through the nonbreeding season. If they don't find a place to do this, they die. Dead organisms do not pass on their genes anymore, so their direct lifetime fitness ends with their death. (Of course, their offspring may still be alive and reproducing, but the most direct way to put a limit on one's fitness is through death.)

Winter limitation also could have less direct effects on fitness. If a wintering bird ends up in a spot where it can just barely survive, it may be in lousy physical condition at the end of the winter. This may cause it to migrate late, get to the breeding grounds late, lay fewer eggs, not have as much energy to feed young, and so forth. All of these factors may reduce the number of young the bird raises, which will, of course, reduce its potential fitness.

Obviously, understanding a Neotropical migrant bird's fitness during the nonbreeding season is a daunting task. Fitness in winter certainly involves survival rates, particularly because a dead bird has no further direct fitness. Making these survival measures requires that we know that a bird is dead, which can be difficult if it moves around within or between winters (see below). Measuring fitness also might involve subtle variation in physical attributes that can have effects on breeding success, reducing the fitness of the bird during another season at another site. We have little real data showing how these effects might occur, although some recent work provides a possible breakthrough in this area. Population regulation is a difficult concept, but one that is crucial to gaining credible knowledge about winter limitation.

MODELS OF WINTER DISTRIBUTION
THAT MAY AFFECT LIMITATION

We know from Chapter 8 that migrant birds have habitat preferences that involve selecting certain habitat types and sometimes involve social interactions with other members of the same species. We also know that every member of a population cannot survive in the same location. How does an individual migrant choose where to spend the winter, given constraints on habitat?

Most of the studies on winter habitat distributions were built on a model developed by Stephen Fretwell (1972) while he was a graduate student studying wintering Field Sparrows (*Spizella pusilla*). In a world where Field Sparrow wintering habitat varied in quality, Fretwell suggested that the first sparrow would move to what it perceived as the best-quality site with regard to ensuring its fitness. Subsequent sparrows would also probably cue in on this same site, and at some point the density of sparrows would result in a reduction of food at this best site, such that the next sparrow that chose a site would actually be as well off moving to a site that was somewhat lower in terms of observed quality but was just as good as the best site in terms of fitness, because the value of the best site had been reduced by the high density of birds trying to live there. Birds making choices late in this process might end up in habitats that were initially considered low quality, but because there might be few birds in these sites, the fitness value for all birds in all habitats would be pretty much the same. Fretwell labeled this an "ideal free" distribution, because the birds were able to make individual decisions about where to go, but they did so by looking at both the quality of the habitat and the number of other birds already there.

Of course, Fretwell recognized that birds are often territorial, so he also designed a model that took this behavior into account. In this case, the first birds into the highest-quality habitat would defend territories that excluded other individuals of the same species from using that site. As more birds entered the habitat, they would select territories on the sites with the best-quality habitat available. Because this behavior undoubtedly involved the territorial birds' exclusion of intruders, Fretwell called this the "ideal despotic" distribution. In this system, territory size might vary, with birds in high-quality territories having smaller territories than those in poor habitat.

These two models serve as alternative end points of the strategies that winter residents might employ in selecting habitats, assuming the birds are trying to select a single location for a long period of time. If more birds are present than the habitat can support, we might see very different situations in the two models. Under an ideal free distribution, if too many birds are scattered through the habitat, all the birds may not get enough food, at least until some of them starved. In the ideal despotic situation, though, birds might be able to defend territories that ensured adequate food supplies. The "extra" birds are excluded from this system by being chased away; they survive only if they can find enough food by foraging in other habitats or, perhaps, by sneaking around in the large territories that probably occur in poorer-quality habitats. In this case, birds in good habitats have high fitness, whereas those in lousy habitats suffer fitness losses in some fashion.

With the strong advantages to having a good territory in an ideal despotic situation, one would expect lots of competition for the best locations. We have already shown that those species with winter territories often have systems in which old birds dominate younger birds and/or males dominate females. These interactions could potentially be important in affecting the overall fitness levels of these age or sex groups (as is discussed below).

Although it is true that the Fretwell models are a bit simplistic, they are good ecological models in that they provide alternative responses to a set of ecological conditions and they allow us to make predictions about how the birds involved might respond to these conditions. This is particularly true with regard to how population limitation might occur in wintering species with different spatial distributions. As someone who was exposed to the Fretwell models as a graduate student in the early 1970s and then saw them disappear, I find it fun to see these "old" models become so important again.

MEASURING HABITAT QUALITY BY LEVELS OF FITNESS

Using the above concepts, measuring the quality of different habitats in terms of the wintering bird's fitness should be relatively easy. One just marks a number of wintering birds in different habitats at the start of the study (probably soon after arrival on the wintering grounds) and then follows them through the winter to see how they survive. Obviously, those habitats in which lots of birds either die or have to leave in order to survive are not as high-quality as those where the birds can make it until the time for migration north. Any effects that habitat quality might have on the ability for the bird to initiate migration would also enter into the equation, but at some point after the bird had left the wintering area, the measure of the effects of winter habitat quality on survival would have to end.

In addition, one would like to measure the physical condition of the birds in the various habitats and how this condition affects anything related to fitness. In this case, one would need to follow the birds through their breeding process to see how variation in winter condition might affect fitness through reproduction. Finally, one would probably want to follow these birds back to their wintering grounds (if they are still alive) to see the extent that they return to the place where they were the winter before. We certainly might expect that habitats that show high return rates are favored over those where birds live for a winter but do not seem to prefer to return.

Of course, in the real world it is not this easy. Let's look at how the various components of fitness have been studied in recent years to see what we know and where the gaps in our knowledge occur.

Persistence, Return, and Survival Rates   One of the basic ways to understand habitat quality is to make direct measures of how well birds survive in different habitats. This is the most direct measure of fitness, because if we can see that a bird is still alive in a habitat, and that it returns to the habitat year after year, we have measured both that the bird has survived and that it has made a choice to stay in that spot over a long period of time.

Persistence rates generally refer to measures of the rate at which individuals are found in the same site throughout a winter. We assume that if the same birds can be counted in high numbers in both October and March in some sites, but few birds occur in both October and March in others, the latter sites are of lower quality. Persistence rates are handy because they can be done in a single winter; of course, if the study incorporates only a single winter, the rates can only be generalized to the conditions found that year. Additionally, such measures of persistence are confounded if researchers are unable to mark all the birds in the first sampling period, do not record some of the previously marked birds in the final sampling period, or have birds that wander through the study site during any of the sampling periods. Such "floaters" are apparently wandering around trying to find an open territory, and they are a common component of most wintering bird communities. So as simple as it may seem, measuring persistence within a winter has its problems. Yet, in many cases one can factor out birds recorded only once and get solid measures of site persistence for a site.

Return rates refer to the extent that the same birds return to a wintering site from one winter to the next. As was noted above, we assume that if the bird was comfortable enough in a site to return to it, it must be a preferred site. If another area had low return rates, we assume either that the birds it supported the year before are dead or that they chose to go elsewhere. In either case, it appears that it is not a preferred habitat. Of course, to study return rates requires at least two field seasons, one in which the birds are marked and another in which the return rate is measured.

Return rate measures can be confounded by a number of factors. Of course, the sampling and floater problems mentioned for persistence studies would occur here; if a bird is missed in year 1 and seen in year 2, a significant return event would be missed. In addition, if a bird from the first year is missed in the second year of the study, a researcher would have to assume either that the bird was dead or had dispersed somewhere else. Although the dispersal might indicate that the habitat that the bird chose not to return to was not of high quality, it also is possible that the habitat was adequate but not as good as another habitat the bird was able to obtain in year 2. So although return rates are a decent measure of habitat quality, we have to keep their limitations in mind, recognizing that birds may disperse because they chose to move to better habitats, not just because a habitat is of inherently lousy quality.

If one has enough return rate information over a long enough period, one can compute real survival rate estimates for a habitat or study site. If done properly over a number of years, this method allows one to come up with measures of survival rates for a site that incorporate a number of different individuals in that site. The modern way to compute survival rates is with highly sophisticated Cormack-Jolly-Seber (CJS) models (Pollock et al. 1990). These are complex ways to analyze quite simple capture-recapture data. For example, if one marked 20 birds in year 1, recaptured or resighted 10 of these in year 2, 5 in year 3, and so on, one would be able to estimate that the birds had a 50% annual survival rate (since half the birds returned each year).

Because these survival rate estimators are based on the same sort of data used to measure return rates, they suffer from the same problems with regard to marking all the birds in year 1 and finding them all in subsequent years. The CJS models are several models that analyze the same data in different ways, with most of the variation in analysis related to dealing with variation in sampling parameters. The extent that one recaptures a high proportion of birds from year to year (recapture probability) is important to determining how well the models work. As with return rate measures, CJS models treat an unsampled bird as a death, even though it is possible that the bird just moved outside the sampling area.

CJS survival rate estimates are of great value, but to get them, one needs a fairly large sample of marked birds over a period of several years. As many as 50 birds sampled over a 4-year period is a pretty small sample for CJS; simpler statistical tests exist for those sorts of data. As a result, few studies of Neotropical migrants have gotten to the point of computing CJS survival estimates. Wayne Arendt, Katie Dugger, and I have a long-term project in the Guánica Forest of southwestern Puerto Rico that has involved banding birds at a single net line since 1973 and 8 additional net lines since 1989. Each net line involves 16 nets, each 12 m long, that are operated from dawn to dark for 3 consecutive days (Fig. 9.2). All birds are banded, or the band number is recorded if the bird had been banded previously. Using CJS models and data from the original net line over an 18-year period, we were able to calculate survival rate estimates for three winter-resident species in this forest. The Black-and-white Warbler showed an estimated annual survival rate of 0.59, indicating that 59 out of every 100 Black-and-whites that wintered in Guánica in a given winter were alive and wintered there the next winter. The American Redstart showed a survival estimate of 0.56; both Black-and-white and redstart populations at Guánica are nearly completely female, which is quite interesting because most breeding-season studies do not capture many females. Our Guánica estimate for the Ovenbird involved a smaller number of individuals and gave only a 0.43 annual survival rate. For this site, we could get results for only these 3 species, because the other 12 wintering species that had been sampled at that site were recaptured rarely.

We have recently been working on survival rate estimates for wintering species by using the much larger data set we have accumulated by operating 9 net lines over a 10-year period. This has been a good-news, bad-news story. We have banded many more individuals of all the species, but we also have discovered that the abundance of winter residents varies a lot through the forest. Some sites may have several birds in some years, none in others, and never any recaptures. This provides noise to the models, giving us estimates that don't fit the models well. Thus, despite larger sample sizes, we feel comfortable in making only two

FIGURE 9.2. *A net line in Guánica Forest. The short, scrubby vegetation ensures that most birds using the forest are catchable.*

survival rate estimates from this expanded data set. We estimated annual survival of the Black-and white Warbler at 0.49 and the Ovenbird at 0.44. We could make estimates for other species, but the variance is so great that the estimates don't really mean much.

As was noted earlier, as we expanded our Guánica study, we found variation within this forest type in the density of these winter residents. Some sites had birds only in years when that species was very abundant; in other years no birds were found in that site, and over the years no re-captures occurred in that location. Although this messes up our forest-wide estimates of survival, it will allow us to compare these microhabitats within the Guánica Forest, because it appears that the sites with high re-turn rates are of better quality than those with no returns. We might be able to compute survival rates using subsets of our data from these "good" sites, but we have not done that yet.

Obviously, it is critical to understand which habitats support win-ter residents throughout the winter and which do not, but it is not that easy to do so. In particular, when we have age-related dominance sys-tems, many birds may be shifting their wintering location between their first winter and later winters. This may particularly be true for females or young males. Such movements either within a winter or between winters make it difficult to take the sort of detailed measurements one would like to have to determine winter habitat requirements for Neotropical migrant species.

Body Condition   The measures of persistence or survival revolve around one simple measurement: Is the bird there? If it is, we know it is alive and we assume that it has made a decision to stay. If it is not, it may be because the bird is dead, but it also may be because the bird has decided to go elsewhere. Of course, we also need to deal with the fact that the bird may be there but we missed it in our censuses.

If one has good data on persistence or survival in different habitat types, one undoubtedly has valuable information about how good each habitat is. Certainly, a habitat with high persistence and return rates and survival estimates must be a good habitat that the bird prefers, whereas a habitat with lower persistence and survival rates might be one that is not as preferred, as shown by the amount of either death or movement away from the site.

The component measures of persistence or survival are quantified as either a 1 for a bird that is there for a sampling period or a 0 for a bird that is not. That is also how one sets up tables to compute the appropriate persistence or survival rates. Obviously, in some habitats individual birds may be there, but they may be in better body condition in some places than in others. One would assume that these measures of body condition would correlate in some fashion with the quality of the habitat for the species under study. Thus, one would be able to come up with a scale where an individual occurring in a good habitat (score 1 for persistence/survival measures) would get a higher relative score than an individual occurring in a bad habitat (also score 1 for persistence/survival).

These body condition scores might be reflected in survival/ persistence patterns, because individuals in poor condition might be less prone to return to a site either because of death or dispersal. These body condition measures also might be valuable for giving clues to fitness costs of staying in poor habitats for the winter that are independent of just individual survival. Even if the bird should persist or return to a site, these measures of body condition might give us clues as to such things as late arrival on the breeding grounds, lower nesting success, or other fitness costs of breeding.

Actual measures of body condition vary from simple to complex. Perhaps the easiest way to keep track of body condition of a wintering bird is by measuring body mass (weight) through the winter. A relatively heavy bird is presumed to be in better condition than a light bird, and a bird that keeps the same body mass through the wintering period is considered to be in a better situation than one that loses mass through this period. By weighing birds when they are captured, one can get an idea of mass, but you have to be careful about comparing weights taken at different times of the day, because many migrants put on some body fat as they go through the day, so late-day masses are generally greater than morning masses.

One can make direct measures of fat levels on individual birds as indices of condition. The skin of birds is so thin that one can just blow the body feathers apart and look at the deposits of fat in various locations on a bird (Fig. 9.3). There are methods of scoring these fat deposits, leading to what banders call fat scores. Of course, the absence of fat may or may not tell you that a bird is stressed. Many researchers have measured the size and shape of the breast muscles of birds to get an index to body condition. The breast muscle is the biggest muscle on a bird's body. When the bird is in excellent condition, this muscle is generally large and bulging in shape. If the bird is stressed such that it may have metabolized some muscle in order to stay alive, the breast muscle is smaller and concave in shape. These muscle scores are particularly valuable for birds with little

FIGURE 9.3. *An Ovenbird that has been color-banded at Guánica Forest. The color band allows us to resight the bird later or in other locations, and catching it allows us to check for age, sex, fat levels, and other morphological traits.*

or no fat, because they provide a relative index of body condition within this "fat score" group.

Because birds can accumulate fat or muscle mass quickly (while in migration, these birds can put on several grams of fat a day), all of the above condition scores can vary even on a daily basis. There also is a certain amount of variation in mass or other body measurements related to age or sex. Thus, a researcher has to be rigorous in keeping track of how and when various body condition measures are taken, to ensure that this variance does not confound the goal of measuring body condition in habitats of different quality.

To overcome these problems with measuring body condition, Peter Marra of Dartmouth College started measuring blood hormone levels to record what he hopes are measures of stress in wintering birds that occupy different habitats (Marra and Holberton 1998). He measured levels of the hormone corticosterone, a chemical that reaches high levels when an animal is under stressful conditions. In his study of the American Redstart in Jamaica, Marra first looked at the hormonal response of birds when retained in captivity after capture. He found that in the fall, all birds had low corticosterone levels at capture, but if held in a cage for 30 minutes, these levels would rise dramatically. This is what corticosterone is supposed to do, and the higher levels help make the bird more active and better able to deal with whatever stress has driven the levels upward.

Marra made the same measurements among birds in two different habitats in March, a time when the scrub habitat was well into its dry season and food was becoming less common, whereas the mangrove habitat was not showing any seasonal shifts in food. Birds caught in the mangroves (mostly males) showed patterns similar to those found in the fall, with low corticosterone levels at capture but rapid increases in level with retention. In contrast, birds living in the arid environments (mostly females) had high corticosterone levels at capture; these levels did not go up much over time, because they already were nearly as high as they generally get in these birds.

With these results, Marra concluded that the birds living in arid habitats near the end of the dry season were living under stressful conditions. Although many of these birds returned to these sites for the next winter, it was suggested that the arid sites were not as good for wintering as the mangrove sites, where birds were able to avoid stress and dealing with high corticosterone levels.

LINKING WINTER CONDITION AND BREEDING SEASON EVENTS

When using the results from all the studies of body condition, one has to assume that birds that end the winter in better condition are better off than those that end the winter and begin migration in poorer condition. As was noted earlier, though, we have no studies that are able to follow the same individual birds from wintering grounds to breeding grounds in order to see directly how winter condition might affect fitness during the breeding season. However, we do not have anything but very general information on which breeding birds winter in which area; the generalization from the findings of a dozen or so recaptures of banded American Redstarts is that birds that breed in the east tend to winter in the West Indies, whereas those that breed farther west spend the winter in Mexico or Central America. But that is a vague generality; we need a breakthrough in technology to help us here.

Peter Marra, as a second part of his Ph.D. work, focused on carbon isotope levels in the birds living in the two habitats he and his colleagues were studying (Marra et al. 1998). He could measure these isotope levels from the same blood samples he took to measure corticosterone levels. He measured the levels of the carbon isotope ^{13}C in these samples, with the assumption that the levels reflected conditions in the habitats where the birds lived. The mangrove habitats are dominated by plants with the C3 photosynthetic pathway, so these sites would tend to have relatively low ^{13}C levels in their leaves and in the bodies of insects that ate these leaves. In contrast, arid habitats have lots of plants with C4 or other photosynthetic pathways (CAM plants, for those of you with a biology degree), so the plants and insects of these sites are characterized by high ^{13}C levels. Thus, birds in mangroves (which were mostly male and had low stress as measured by corticosterone levels) could be distinguished from birds of arid habitats (mostly females with high corticosterone levels in the late winter) by the carbon isotope characteristics given to them by their diets.

Marra could not follow these same birds to their breeding grounds, but could sample wintering redstarts at the Hubbard Brook study site where Dick Holmes and his colleagues and students had been studying this species for decades. Most important, though, was that Marra could measure the carbon isotope levels of birds as they arrived on their breeding grounds. He found that birds that arrived earlier on the breeding grounds were those birds with carbon isotope levels that suggested they had spent the winter in higher-quality habitats, whereas late-arriving birds had isotope levels that suggested they had spent the winter in more arid, lower-quality sites. Because several studies have shown that birds that breed later in the season often have reduced reproductive success when compared with those that breed early, Marra believes that his results present a link between winter conditions and breeding success and show a fitness cost for those birds that spend the winter in lower-quality habitats.

This is potentially exciting stuff, because it provides mechanisms both to measure stress and to link wintering events with breeding events. Students in my laboratory are already at work setting up the equipment for making these measurements and picking sites where corticosterone or isotope measures will be most meaningful. Of course, as with any new method for measuring something in the field, we must be careful about taking this technique too far too fast. Many of Marra's graphs show a lot of scatter, suggesting that individuals may have variable sensitivity to these factors. For example, we know that our Guánica Forest study site would show high levels of ^{13}C isotopes for all birds, but we also know that some of the sites within Guánica must be high-quality, as we get very high persistence and survival rates in these sites. Also, much of the effect of lower habitat quality on breeding success is based on the assumption that late-arriving females have lower reproductive success. Although a number of studies show this, most of them are with birds in the North Temperate Zone (for example, the Hubbard Brook study site where Marra worked is in New Hampshire). It is not as obvious to us that being a few days late in arriving on more southerly breeding sites such as the Missouri Ozarks or southern Appalachians is quite as important as it is in New England. This may be particularly true for those species with skewed sex ratios, such that females are the limiting sex (and it appears that many if not most species are skewed in this fashion). Thus, although we have to be careful as we continue studies of this nature in an attempt to link winter habitat quality with summer breeding success, the Marra work provides what may be the first new way of trying to solve this complex problem that we have seen in years.

Do Old World Population Declines Help in Understanding Possible New World Declines?

The material above gives us an idea of how hard it is to measure habitat quality, winter survival, and the other factors that are necessary to document true winter limitation of migrant birds. With virtually no direct evidence of winter limitation in the New World species whose declines were of concern, many decisions have been based on theoretical evidence and some anecdotal field observations.

At the same time as concern for Neotropical migrants was at a peak, there was some quite good evidence of winter limitation coming from studies in Europe, with a focus on the Palearctic-African migration system (this is well covered in a special issue of the *Ibis* edited by Crick and Jones 1992). Populations of several species, including Old World warblers, herons, swallows, and storks, were shown to be generally declining in the period of the 1970s and 1980s, although many of these species showed high reproductive success on the breeding grounds. Investigations of population levels showed that the breeding population levels of most of these species were highly correlated with the amount of rainfall that had occurred the previous winter on their wintering grounds in sub-Saharan Africa (Peach et al. 1991). For several species, long-term trends showed both general declines over long periods of time and year-to-year correlations with winter rainfall. These patterns suggested that the populations of many European breeding birds were limited by food supply on their wintering grounds each winter (which explained the annual variation), plus the amount of wintering habitat was showing a general decline, probably due to habitat loss and the expansion of deserts (which explained the long-term trends).

Much of this evidence from the Old World was convincing, so it was easy to accept the idea that if bird populations in the Old World could be limited by wintering habitat, the same thing could happen in the New World. This generality is certainly true, but one must also be careful when making comparisons between the Palearctic-African and New World migration systems in such a way. The Old World migration system is incredibly different from that of the New World in a number of ways.

For example, the comparison between potential breeding area and potential wintering area in the Palearctic shows much more breeding area than wintering area in Africa. It has been estimated that 5 billion birds once made the migration between breeding areas in Europe and Asia and wintering areas in sub-Saharan Africa (Moreau 1972). Thus, the ratio of potential breeding area to potential wintering area is much larger than for the New World, which makes the potential for winter limitation in this part of the Old World much higher. Much less work has been done on the migration system involving Palearctic birds that winter in India, Southeast Asia, or the New Guinea region. Although there may again be more breeding area than wintering area, we know little about which species use this system, how they might be limited, and how these birds interact with those using Africa for a wintering ground.

The habitats used by these Palearctic-African migrants also differ from those used by most Neotropical migrants. Most Old World migrants winter in savannah and other open habitats; the only heavily forested area in Africa is the region with rain forests in west central Africa, but that area is relatively small. Of course, because these migrants have bred in a region that has been settled by humans for thousands of years, the match between open breeding areas and open wintering areas is a natural. One can only imagine the sort of local extinction or population decline event among forest birds that took place there a few thousand years ago as Europe and Asia were being settled.

These savannahs and open woodlands occur because much of Africa has a fairly arid and highly seasonal climate. Such seasonal climates also often show great variation from year to year, making them prone to drought conditions. Such drought conditions in open habitats undoubtedly have a much stronger effect on habitat and food supply than the variation found in habitats supporting forests. We assume that the birds that deal with this sort of variation have evolved responses to it, including movement patterns during the winter and clutch sizes appropriate to species with fluctuating populations. Certainly, though, the fact that a huge number of birds must spend the winter in habitats that vary greatly from year to year suggests that Old World migrants may be more prone to winter limitation than New World migrants, most of which live in forested habitats and in climates that are not nearly as extreme as those found in sub-Saharan Africa.

Much of sub-Saharan Africa has been suffering from a great deal of habitat loss in recent decades. This is a mixture of habitat loss due directly to human intervention through such activities as farming and grazing, activities that reflect increasing populations in the region, and habitat loss due to the process of desertification. This process is not totally understood, but it may be a function of the reduced rainfall that occurs locally when vegetation is removed from an area. Without plants to move moisture into the air, there is less moisture in the atmosphere and eventually less rainfall. This becomes a cycle, as less rainfall means less vegetation, which means less rainfall, and so on. In addition, some of the expansion of the deserts may be a function of longer-term cycles of rainfall, perhaps natural but also perhaps due to human-induced global climate change. What is clear, though, is that the amount of wintering habitat for Palearctic migrants in sub-Saharan Africa is declining, and migrant bird populations in Europe and Asia may show long-term declines no matter what happens on their breeding grounds.

MODELS INCORPORATING BOTH SUMMER AND WINTER LIMITATION

Although evidence of winter limitation in Neotropical migrant birds is scanty, the Old World examples certainly show us that such an event can occur. We also know that breeding-season events can limit populations. For proper conservation of a species, we would ideally be able to understand where population limitation occurred in that species in order to focus our conservation activities at the point where they would be most effective. Can one design a model that takes into account the possibility of population limitation due to all the various possible limiting factors, including those from both summer and winter?

Richard Holmes and Tom Sherry and their students have attempted to come up with a model that would answer the above questions. Because their fieldwork has included intensive studies of the same species on both their breeding grounds (Hubbard Brook, New Hampshire) and their wintering grounds (Jamaica), these scientists are naturals for making such an attempt (Sherry and Holmes 1995). Their attempt to explain annual population regulation in a migrant species began with a generalized scheme that illustrated the various processes at work in regulating populations (Fig. 9.4). As with most attempts to explain complex ecological processes in an easy fashion, this model is horribly simplistic, with incredibly complex factors such as food and weather reduced to single arrows occurring at various points. Yet a diagram of this sort allows us to see the complexity of the situation and how and where the various separate factors enter in to the total equation.

Of course, the next step is to make this model quantitative. Sherry and Holmes have attempted to do this; a presentation at the American Ornithologists' Union meeting in 1999 developed an equation to match virtually every factor shown in Figure 9.4. In an ideal world, all we would need to do is come up with the numbers required to solve each equation; then we would understand where and when these migrant warblers had their populations limited. Of course, as with the source-sink equations discussed in Chapter 6, in most cases we have either no detailed measures of the factors in question or we have lousy measures. It will be a long time before we have enough information so that we can quantitatively model a Neotropical migrant bird population the way that other wildlife biologists can model some of the species with which they work.

Is There Any Evidence of Population Declines on the Wintering Grounds?

One form of support for the hypothesis of population declines that are due to winter limitation would be evidence of a declining population or populations on the wintering grounds. Of course, such evidence might be explained by any number of other factors, but good evidence of declining populations would be an exciting piece of the story. At least it was for some data that my colleague Wayne Arendt and I had gathered from the Guánica Forest of Puerto Rico. We presented these data both in the journal *American Birds* (Faaborg and Arendt 1989) and at the Manomet-sponsored symposium in 1989 (Faaborg and Arendt 1992), where they were one of the most talked-about pieces of evidence in the symposium.

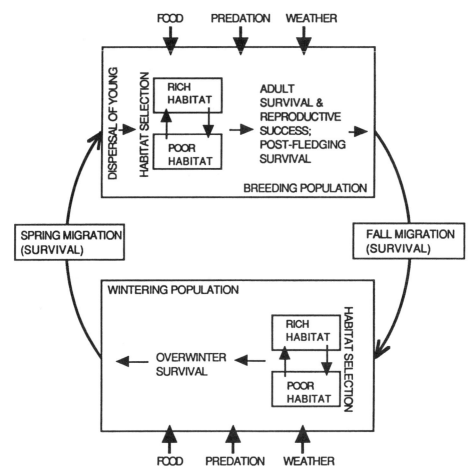

FIGURE 9.4. *The Holmes-Sherry model for population limitation in migratory birds. Note the many interactions involved, most of which are difficult to track over long times or distances. From T. W. Sherry and R. T. Holmes, 1995, "Summer versus Winter Limitation of Populations: What Are the Issues and What Is the Evidence?" in* Ecology and Management of Neotropical Migratory Birds: A Synthesis and Review of Critical Issues, *ed. Thomas E. Martin and Deborah M. Finch, copyright © 1995 by Oxford University Press, Inc. Used by permission of Oxford University Press, Inc.*

Our major figure also appeared in John Terborgh's book *Where Have All the Birds Gone?* Now, with a few more years to the story, does it provide any strong evidence dealing with winter limitation?

One of the reasons it is hard to discuss winter limitation in migrant birds is the paucity of good long-term population measures of these birds on the wintering grounds. Most ornithologists working at sites where Neotropical migrants spend the winter are there to study the resident species; few have methodologies adapted to wintering birds, and fewer used to care that they were missing this element. I know that the reason I went to Puerto Rico and initiated a long-term population monitoring study there was because of its endemic todies and tanagers, not redstarts and ovenbirds.

My friend David Willard and I ran a line of mist nets in the Guánica Forest of Puerto Rico in 1972 and reran that line and added another in 1973. Guánica Forest is a 10,000-acre tract of subtropical deciduous forest on a small mountainous piece of southwestern Puerto Rico. Because it has little soil and is quite hilly, much of the forest was not harvested for timber at all, and the part of it that was grazed reverted back to forest after the Commonwealth of Puerto Rico turned the area into a forest reserve in the 1930s. Guánica is considered one of the best examples of this type of forest remaining in the Caribbean, and it has been well protected now for over 60 years.

Our net line was originally a way for us to get an index to bird populations and to measure the size of the birds we caught (how we used these data for estimating survival rates was discussed above). We run lines of 16 nets, each 12 m long, in a straight line in typical parts of the forest. Each line is run for 3 days from dawn (after the bats go to bed) to dark (before the bats come out); all birds captured are banded, weighed, measured, and released unharmed. We also keep track of all birds banded from one year to the next. Because a visit to Guánica in June 1973 found evidence of a strong drought, I returned to this site in January 1974 to see what had happened to bird populations. Not surprisingly, a major population decline had occurred. I continued visiting the site and running the line of nets annually, with a couple of exceptions, and Wayne Arendt and I published several papers examining the interaction between rainfall patterns at Guánica and bird population changes.

Although we banded and counted the Neotropical migrants we caught, most of our focus for the first 15 years of the study was on resident birds. This changed after year 15, when our analysis showed a striking decline in the total number of winter resident warblers that we had captured over this 15-year period (Fig. 9.5A). Captures of these warblers, which are the only common winter residents at Guánica, had dropped from nearly 30 in 1974 to just 5 in 1989. Since this occurred at the time when so many other researchers were starting to loudly note the decline of migratory birds, our graph showing such striking local declines was quickly incorporated into the evidence that migrants were facing some serious problems.

Although Wayne Arendt and I enjoyed receiving some attention for our work (which doesn't happen often to scientists), I was never comfortable with the thought that the results of this single net line at a single site were all that important. We responded in two ways. First, we expanded our netting effort in an attempt to see if a variety of net lines located throughout the forest would show similar patterns. Second, we examined our original data in more detail to see what stories it really told.

Although the decline in warbler captures on our Guánica net line was real, our analysis suggested that it was the result of two things. First, we had found that the Northern Parula and the Prairie Warbler were pretty common wintering warblers in Guánica Forest during the early 1970s, but they declined in abundance later in the 1970s and were virtually gone from Guánica in the 1980s and 1990s. The three species that were the most abundant wintering warblers at Guánica (Ovenbird, American Redstart, and Black-and-white Warbler) showed fairly constant abundance from 1973 through the mid-1980s but declined by half in the years 1986–1988. These wintering populations increased in 1989 and 1990 and stayed fairly constant in numbers through the 1990s (Fig. 9.5B).

This leaves two questions to consider. What happened to the Northern Parula and the Prairie Warbler in the 1970s? And what happened to the populations of the three common species during 1986–1988? We have no direct measures of what happened to parulas and Prairie Warblers in the 1970s, for all we could record at Guánica was that two once-common species were hardly caught anymore. A few years ago, my student Mike Baltz started work on these species at the Cabo Rojo National Wildlife Refuge, where they are quite common. This refuge is composed mostly of old cattle pastures, where the habitat is a mixture of two species of widely scattered trees that were left to provide shade for the cattle and grass. Although a few new woody plants have started to invade in recent years since the refuge was started, this habitat still dominates. Surprisingly, though, these scattered trees appear to be parula and Prairie Warbler heaven. Mike Baltz (2000) finds high densities of these species on the refuge, and high percentages of these birds return from year to year.

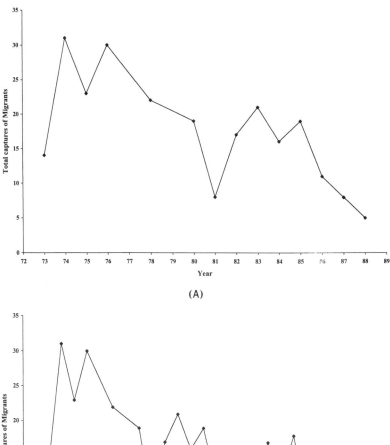

FIGURE 9.5. *Variation in captures of winter resident birds at Guánica Forest. The graph covering 1973–1989* (A) *looked very ominous, but the longer view* (B) *is not as frightening.*

(It is interesting to note that even when we caught significant numbers of these species at Guánica, we almost never got recaptures from year to year.)

It appears that in the late 1970s, the cattle market in Puerto Rico was not doing particularly well, and a significant area of southwestern Puerto Rican pasture had the cattle removed from it. Perhaps the birds that used to winter at Guánica but preferred these old pastures had more habitat in which to spend the winter, leading to the Guánica Forest population declines. We don't know this, but it makes a certain amount of sense.

What about the declines in the late 1980s of the common species? What we do know is that during this period of time, there was a severe drought throughout much of the eastern and Midwestern United States. Several studies showed lower nesting success during this time. Because many migrants have survival rates of just above 50%, a lack of breeding will result in population declines of about 50% a year due to adult mortality. Of course, the drought reduced reproduction but did not stop it completely in all years, as is reflected in our capture totals of 22, 11, 8, 5. For this part of the Guánica decline, we think that breeding-season limitation is the best answer, because nothing else was changing at Guánica at that time to explain these declines.

Obviously, concluding so much from a single study is a mistake. Ideally, attempts to monitor populations on the wintering grounds will adopt good methodologies and larger sample sizes in the future. We have been operating 9 net lines at Guánica (including the one started in 1973) since 1989, with lots of annual variation in total captures but no real long-term patterns. Because winter residents are so quiet in winter at a place like Guánica, we believe that mist netting is about the only good way to monitor their populations, but this is quite time-consuming and I am not sure that even the 9 net lines we have been running are an adequate sample. As best I know, though, it still remains the only long-term, community-level monitoring of migrant birds on their wintering grounds going on.

WHICH SPECIES ARE MOST SENSITIVE TO WINTER LIMITATION?

Although the evidence that winter limitation has occurred in Neotropical migrants is sketchy at best, we have to accept the possibility that it may occur in the future even if it has not occurred to date. Certainly, some species have characteristics that will make them more prone to winter limitation than do others, such that as one tries to explain the occurrence of population declines in these species, winter limitation should be a strong consideration. What are some of these traits?

Small Winter Range   The winter range of many species is enormous. Many species can be found during the nonbreeding season in an area that includes the West Indies, much of Mexico, and even parts of Central and South America. With such a large potential winter range, it is difficult to think that these birds will become winter-limited unless extreme changes occur on the wintering area in the future. In contrast, some migrants have relatively small wintering areas. Terborgh (1989) has suggested that the Bachman's Warbler went extinct because its winter range was limited to parts of Cuba, and these parts have been highly modified by humans in the past few centuries. Certainly, the Kirtland's Warbler is a species of strong concern, partly because its winter range seems to be limited to unknown parts of the Bahamas. Robbins et al. (1992b) suggest that the Cerulean Warbler is suffering some of the largest declines of all, according to BBS data, because of the destruction of habitats on its limited winter range in the northern Andes (Fig. 9.6). The Olive-sided Flycatcher also may suffer from similar problems.

It would be fairly easy to check the winter ranges of Neotropical migrants and note those with small wintering areas, but we must be careful. Remsen (2001) has analyzed data on what we thought was the wintering range of the Veery and suggested that it might be much smaller. It was thought that the Veery had a fairly large winter range in the Amazon basin, but Remsen looked at the dates on museum specimens and suggested that many of these birds were probably migrants. In fact, the winter range of the Veery may be just a small portion of the Amazon, which means this species may be much more susceptible to winter habitat loss than was originally thought.

A Narrow Range of Habitats Used   Species sensitive to winter limitation would also include those that are quite specialized in the habitats that they use in winter. In this case, even a species with a fairly large wintering range could disappear if the habitat on which it depended disappeared. Species that require primary vegetation types are certainly going to be more sensitive to loss of wintering habitat than are species that

FIGURE 9.6. *Devastation of montane forests in the mountains near Cali, Colombia. Obviously, this level of habitat change is detrimental to virtually all wildlife, including migrant birds.*

can use secondary vegetation types. It has been suggested that species such as the Wood Thrush may require undisturbed tropical rain forest; if this is the case, population declines may be attributable to loss of this habitat rather than to the many problems the species faces on the breeding grounds.

Obviously, to predict which species will suffer from this factor requires a better knowledge of what the true habitat requirements of wintering migrants are. Measures of survival or body condition must replace census data in determining what the critical habitats are. In addition, we must quickly find out which species possess both a small winter range and a limited selection of wintering habitat types. These two factors undoubtedly interact, and a species with problems in both regards is headed for problems sooner or later. It is interesting to note that the apparent extinction of the Bachman's Warbler in Cuba may have required both the restriction of the winter range of that species to one island and the almost total loss of preferred habitat on that island. Species with similar breeding habitat problems (such as the Swainson's Warbler) but more flexible wintering behavior seem to have survived better. Both these warbler species, though, are also characterized by specialized breeding habitat, which means they probably had relatively small populations at all times in the past.

Strong Habitat Segregation by Sex   We have found in recent years that some species have strong patterns of habitat segregation by age and/or sex. These species will be more susceptible to habitat loss than those with less rigid habitat segregation by these factors. As winter habitat becomes limiting in species where females are forced into less desirable habitats, female survival rates may go down, which will have a strong negative effect on reproductive success in subsequent summers. Although some sort of equilibrium might be reached in time, populations of species with such habitat segregation will always be lower than those with a more equitable sort of dispersion system. That a number of studies have shown skewed breeding sex ratios characterized by a lack of females is already alarming. We might want to examine sex ratios among breeding species to determine which species need to have intensive studies on winter ecology and habitat segregation in the near future. Certainly, species where habitat loss will more strongly affect females will decline more rapidly than species where this is not a problem.

Special Cases   For a few species of Neotropical migrants, some special situations may exist that could be important with regard to winter limitation. A few years ago, thousands of Swainson's Hawks were found dead in Argentina because of poisoning. A plague of grasshoppers there was ruining crops, so farmers used a pesticide made in the United States to control the grasshoppers. Unfortunately, the hawks that were eating the grasshoppers also died in vast numbers. Because these losses got much attention, the chemical industry was able to shift to a different pesticide almost immediately, such that this kind of loss was pretty much a single event. Whether the loss of so many birds had a major effect on Swainson's Hawk populations is still under debate.

The Dickcissel winters in parts of South America in immense, almost unbelievable flocks. When these flocks decide to feed on crops, they can cause massive damage. To control this damage, thousands upon thousands of Dickcissels have been killed. A solution to this problem is less obvious, but in this case we might expect to see a decline in Dickcissel numbers proportional to the number killed in winter.

Other factors could serve as special cases of winter limitation. A hurricane that struck the center of a population could be a major factor, as could a drought or other extreme climatic event. Certainly, when trying to understand an observed decline in a migrant bird population, one should check all the possible factors that could be at work.

SUMMARY

It is clear that winter limitation could affect the populations of Neotropical migrant birds; it is less clear how often this has occurred in recent years. To be ready for the future, we need better information from the field on which habitats each species requires. Combining such information with such high-tech advances as remote sensing might allow us to quantitatively understand possible winter limitation. To the extent that tropical habitats are being converted from natural systems to disturbed systems, we should expect to see shifts in the composition of winter-resident bird populations, with those that thrive in disturbed sites increasing. To the extent that tropical habitat is being turned into sites that support no birds, we might expect widespread population declines. At the current time, though, we must look closely at everything that is going on with these species before we blame tropical habitat change for migrant population declines.

10 | MIGRATION ECOLOGY
A Limiting Factor?

Bird migration is one of the marvels of nature. This mass movement between breeding and wintering grounds must involve billions of birds, although I have never seen anyone try to estimate the number of birds migrating in the Neotropics the way Moreau (1972) came up with his estimate of 5 billion birds for the Old World. The appearance of singing robins or flocks of geese is a sign of spring to everyone, not just birders. Although most Neotropical migrants are nocturnal fliers, so their migrations do not provide the spectacle that flocks of geese or blackbirds might, the first appearance of singing tanagers or Whip-poor-wills in the backyard bears witness to all the movements going on in the springtime skies. If we take into account the fact that many of these migrants move between exact locations each season, follow specific routes that may cross extreme barriers, seem to have multiple ways of navigating, and do these movements through the accumulation and burning of massive amounts of fat, we should be even more impressed with the feat we are witnessing.

However, my job here is not to describe these wonders of migration. For one thing, it has been done recently in two different books. One is edited by Kenneth Able (1999) and entitled *Gatherings of Angels: Migrating Birds and Their Ecology,* and the other, edited by Frank R. Moore (2000), is entitled *Stopover Ecology of Nearctic-Neotropical Landbird Migrants: Habitat Relations and Conservation Implications.* It would be silly for me to try to reproduce the chapters of these books that were written by the researchers who have spent their lives passionately studying the various elements of migration. I would be writing about topics that neither my students nor I have ever studied. It also could easily double the size of this book.

What I must discuss, though, is how this stage of the annual cycle might serve to limit the populations of Neotropical migrant birds. What factors of these travels might make migrants vulnerable to mortality factors that could be great enough to reduce or limit populations? Have human activities affected these possible limiting factors in any way? How would we document population declines that are caused by migration limitation, given that the migrations often cover thousands of miles?

We have already discussed how evidence that the number of migrating birds crossing the Gulf of Mexico appeared to be declining was an important element in convincing scientists that Neotropical migrant birds in general were declining. We must remember, though, that documenting declines during migration does not mean that these declines are necessarily due to limitation during migration. Rather, these counts may be just a good way to follow population trends over time. Yet, the journey from a Peruvian rain forest to a Canadian parkland for an 11 g bird must have hazards. Are such hazards enough to limit populations of these migrants?

POTENTIAL FACTORS LIMITING MIGRANTS

Migration, like most natural phenomena, is a complex process to track. A typical Neotropical migrant "decides" to leave its wintering grounds presumably based on photoperiodic cues and an internal clock, although body condition may delay this decision if food is scarce. This migrant may spend a month or more moving at night when both its body condition and the local weather conditions are favorable for flight. Sometime in the middle of the night, or at least at dawn, it drops from the sky into what is most likely a site it has never seen before. It finds a habitat that it likes or at least can cope with, then tries to find enough food to replenish fat stores so that it can do the same nighttime process again as soon as possible. Obviously, many factors could get in the way of such a complex movement over such vast areas; some of these may work together at various times, further confusing our attempts to determine what is going on.

High Energetic Demands   The fuel that drives these long-distance flights is fat. Migrant birds are able to put on fat quickly if the food supply allows it. Although such unusual long-distance fliers as the

Blackpoll Warbler are able to nearly double their normal body weight before taking off on their trans-Atlantic flights, most migrants deal with smaller hops and smaller amounts of body fat. Yet, this process may still involve an increase in body weight of 30–50% on a nearly daily basis. The next time you encounter a teeming wave of migrants that makes a spring-time woods come alive, think about the fact that every hundred or so of these migrants will try to contribute to making a collective pound of fat during the day's feeding. That's a lot of insects, and it helps explain why a woodland full of migrants is such an active place.

For most migrants in most situations, accumulating enough fat does not seem to be much of a problem. If food is sparse, the bird may have to remain in a site for an extra day; if this sparseness reflects factors such as a late spring, the local delay in migration may be adaptive, for it keeps the migrant bird from getting too far ahead of its developing food source. Lack of food may also just result in a shorter trip when the next step in migration is taken; this is only a problem when the next step involves a major barrier such as the Gulf of Mexico or Great Lakes. In addition, migrants can burn up some muscle when the fat stores are depleted, but stopping is not a good option.

Although most migrants seem able to find enough food to make the trip most of the time (at least starved migrants are rarely found during normal conditions), the possibility of food's becoming limiting to a migrant is there. Certainly, this high-energy strategy may make for a stressful existence, one that may accentuate other problems that could occur during migration. On the other hand, migrants show relatively high survival rates and have a number of adaptations that ease the migratory stresses. For example, most insectivorous migrants move northward with the advance of spring. At this time of year, deciduous trees are presenting their first leaves, leaves that are low in tannins and other protective chemicals and are feasted upon heavily by many insect larvae. Migrant birds then feed on these insect larvae. As these leaves mature and develop defenses to insect herbivory, larval numbers drop, but by then the swarms of migrants are well to the north. Fall migration for most Neotropical migrants occurs before autumnal frosts have reduced the insect supply, and many fall migrants supplement their diet with the fruits that are often abundant at this time of year. The spring migration of the Ruby-throated Hummingbird has been shown to follow the flowering of the red buckeye in much of the eastern United States, a coevolved system that results in spectacular pollen movement for the plant and easy food for the hummer (Grant and Grant 1968). Orchard Oriole migration in the fall in Mexico has been shown to follow the flowering phenology of several trees, making this trip easy for these nectar-feeding orioles. For most migrant species, their lifestyle may be hectic, but it is generally one with which they can cope unless some unusual circumstances get in the way.

Habitat Reduction and Migration Obviously, for these migrants to gather such copious amounts of food requires the proper foraging habitat. A forest bird cannot get much food from a grassland; enough of the proper types of habitat must be available throughout the migratory pathways of birds to ensure that there are not habitat bottlenecks that could lead to population limitation during migration.

Is stopover habitat limiting anywhere in the area where Neotropical migrants travel during migration? Good evidence of such limitation does not exist. In fact, if we look at the distribution of forest habitats over time, we could easily come to the conclusion that life for forest migrants is easier now than it was before settlement by Europeans. At that time there was more forest in much of the eastern United States, but once one reached the prairies, the forest became much more limiting. Today, areas like Iowa, Nebraska, and much of the rest of the Great Plains have long, skinny wooded riparian corridors and hundreds of wooded farmsteads. Western Nebraska had few trees 100 years ago; today a migrant can make easy jumps from the wooded river valleys that cross the prairies (say, from the Republican River to the Platte to the Niobrara), even if one discounts the importance of woodlots.

For forest birds moving northward in the arid zone, including the southern Rocky Mountains and the area to its immediate east (such as Arizona and New Mexico), riparian habitat is about all that is available. In some cases, there is evidence that the loss of such habitat to things such as dams or the degradation of what remains due to overgrazing or introduced plants may be causing problems for migrants attempting to move through these areas (Finch and Yong 2000). Certainly, areas with healthy riparian forests support more migrants, and these migrants seem to move through the area more rapidly than those attempting to move through areas with poorer habitats. Unfortunately, though, we cannot document whether or not the use of these poorer-quality habitats is actually limiting migrant populations or is just a nuisance in the overall scheme of things.

Although we have lamented the fragmentation of habitats with regard to supporting breeding bird populations, forest or grassland fragments may be of great value to migrant birds. The problems associated with habitat fragments have to do with nest parasitism and predation, problems that are irrelevant to migrant birds. Thus, the occurrence of at least some fragments may have great value to Neotropical migrants at this time of their annual cycle.

Natural Barriers   Many Neotropical migrants have migrational patterns that mean they have to deal with some severe natural barriers. Migrants headed to southern Mexico or Central America often fly across the Gulf of Mexico, and those wintering in the West Indies obviously require some water crossing. A few species are known to fly the trans-Atlantic route from New England to northern South America. In some cases, the Great Lakes may serve as a serious barrier.

These are major steps in the journey that require special care for migrants, but they also are jumps to which the migrants seem well adapted. Most of the time they are able to fly the Gulf or the Atlantic without major mishap, although there are recorded instances of massive losses of birds when flying conditions turn against the migrants. Although these are certainly sad occasions, they also are a part of the natural history of these species. Such massive die-offs may cause declines in populations, but these are probably short-lived and they certainly would be hard to document well.

Are changes in the environment occurring because of human activities that might make these barriers more dangerous in the future? It's a good question, but one that will be difficult to answer. I have never seen global circulation models that deal with how the winds needed for migration over the Gulf of Mexico in the spring might change over time. An increase in the number and intensity of hurricanes, many of which occur during the fall migration, could also affect migrant numbers, but it remains to be seen how serious this factor might be.

Loss of habitat at staging areas where birds put on fat before undertaking these special jumps could be a problem, and one that has been documented to some degree. On the north coast of the Gulf of Mexico in the southern United States, coastal scrub habitats are important areas for trans-Gulf migrants. In the fall they provide feeding sites so that these migrants can fatten up adequately for the jump south. In the spring they serve as emergency stopping areas for those migrants that cannot make it farther inland, which is the target for most migrants at that time. These barrier islands may save hundreds of thousands if not millions of birds on those occasions when flying conditions have resulted in trans-Gulf migrants' having just enough energy to make it to the coast. For some individuals that make the mistake of flying out to sea at the end of a night's flight, these barrier areas are a welcome refuge to which they can return when dawn allows them to see their mistake.

Many of these coastal islands have been developed with beachside resorts and summer homes. The result has been a massive loss of habitat in some locations, which means that these beach areas cannot support nearly as many migrants as they could when in a natural condition. Future population trends suggest that this problem will become greater in the near future (Simons et al. 2000). Has it cost the lives of migratory birds? Undoubtedly. Has it resulted in lower overall bird populations for some species because of these losses? That is harder to say. Certainly, such development is a problem that at some point, if it has not been reached already, could limit those migrant bird populations that fly the Gulf of Mexico or other water bodies and rely on having these coastal refuges when conditions get bad.

Unnatural Barriers Human changes in habitat distribution on the ground may have resulted in a mixed bag of effects on migrants, with some areas being easier to cross because of new habitats and some being more difficult because of the loss of habitats. For all nocturnal migrants, human activities have made the flight much more dangerous by the addition of hazards in the airspace used by these migrants. Originally, the only such hazards that resulted in sometimes massive bird kills were television and radio transmission towers. Such kills occurred when flying conditions changed in such a way that birds in the air became disoriented. At those times, the lights on these towers would attract the migrants, which would then fly around the light until they had an almost inevitable collision with one of the supporting guy wires. In recent years, the addition of microwave and other towers to fuel cellular phones and more television has added tremendously to the number of towers available to attract and kill migrant birds.

Recent evidence shows that these towers kill millions of birds each year. Short of giving up better television or phone service, we are limited to solutions involving the number of towers and their placement away from major migratory pathways. Are these hazards causing enough mortality to cause population-wide declines? Once again, this is an almost impossible thing to measure. Although it is true that massive losses occur, we also know that there are billions of migrants and that migration has always involved major losses of birds. Given that there are X billion Neotropical migrant birds with about a 50–50 chance of adult survival each year, approximately X/2 billion birds are going to die somehow each year. Do these towers add a whole new component of mortality to the equations, such that they could result in declining populations by themselves, or are the losses associated with towers the kind that result in lower losses in other factors associated with migration?

Cities with tall buildings can also attract migrants in much the same way that towers do. I have a friend who works at the Field Museum in Chicago and collects hundreds of dead birds next to the tall buildings of downtown Chicago while on his way to work. It's sad, and it would be nice if there were some easy way to reduce these losses, but it is hard to document whether such losses are a critical part of the mortality schedules of Neotropical migrant bird species.

An unusual case in which tall human structures may help migrant birds appears to be occurring in the Gulf of Mexico. It has recently been shown that oil rigs out in the Gulf can serve as refuges to thousands of migrants when they are being forced down by poor flying conditions. In most cases, it appears that these rigs provide a site for the migrant to rest and wait until conditions change and the migrant can finish the trip to land. Although this is fortunate, it is also almost impossible to discover whether the number of birds saved is meaningful in light of the whole complex of factors that affect migrant bird populations.

SUMMARY

The period of time when migrant birds are moving between breeding and wintering areas is critical to the lives of these birds. Although these migrants have adaptations to allow them to maximize their chances of survival through these arduous journeys, a major segment of the population does not make it through each migration. These losses can amount to millions or even billions of birds, even under the best of conditions. Trying to determine if the conditions under which these birds have had to migrate have changed enough in the past few decades to have caused population declines is nearly an impossible task. Yet it is clear that these limiting conditions could occur under the proper circumstances. To date, determining the various costs and benefits of all the human-induced changes in habitats and barriers on bird populations has not been accomplished. Migration ecology is certainly something that we must watch in the future; as we get a better idea of how breeding ground or wintering ground limitations work, we should then be better able to determine how the various mortality factors at work during migration help determine overall population levels. As long as migrants are so difficult to follow individually, though, we will be limited in the detail that we can measure with regard to these potentially critical factors.

11 | MIGRANT BIRDS IN THE NEW MILLENNIUM
What Do We Know?

In the previous chapters, I have tried to show you both what our thinking was in 1990 when Partners in Flight was initiated and how some of our thinking has changed since then. Our thinking has changed both because we know more now than we did and because we have had time to evaluate some of the evidence presented to support the idea that Neotropical migrant birds were declining. Here I attempt to give some general answers about the current situation with regard to migrant bird populations and their conservation, but these must be recognized as generalities. In making these sweeping statements, I am committing some of the sins that I have been critical of earlier in this book. On the other hand, I think I must provide some personal ideas about the status of knowledge about migrant bird populations and conservation as we enter the new millennium.

ARE NEOTROPICAL MIGRANT BIRDS IN GENERAL DECLINE NATIONWIDE?

Several lines of evidence suggested that Neotropical migrant birds were in general decline in the late 1980s. As was noted earlier, though, the way those data were presented had some problems. Although one could compute a national average that showed a decline, in most cases that decline was the result of smaller regional declines. In some other species, the declines of the 1980s put average population levels back to where they were in the 1960s, so that the long-term data suggested both an increase and a decline but no overall change.

Making sweeping generalizations about population trends from Breeding Bird Survey or other data in the year 2000 involves the same problems as it did in 1989, but it is my personal feeling that we no longer should be concerned with widespread declines in a large number of Neotropical migrant bird species. The supporting data just are not there; if they were, I am sure we would be seeing papers detailing these continued declines that would incorporate data from both the 1980s and 1990s. Such papers have not been published. As chair of the Mewaldt-King Award Committee for the Cooper Ornithological Society, I get to look at 40 to 50 proposals annually from graduate students doing work on bird conservation. As the years go by, I am more and more struck with the fact that proposals that use migrant bird declines as part of the justification of their work must fall back on references from 1989 to 1992 to get support from the literature to justify such declines. Here we are in the year 2000, yet we must go back a decade for good references showing that Neotropical migrant populations are declining.

ARE THERE SPECIES OR SPECIES GROUPS OF CONCERN?

If the worst-case scenario of migrant declines is not true, are there still examples of declining species or groups of species about which we should be concerned? Certainly, any long-term decline is worthy of note at any spatial level, even if the species is holding its own in a major part of its range. Such concern, though, should often be tempered with the recognition that it is a regional problem, not one of national or international concern leading to the impending doom of a species.

At the time that Partners in Flight was developed, nearly all of the concern about declines was focused on migrants that lived in forest. Since then, the most convincing data about actual widespread migrant declines has come from birds found on grasslands in North America (Vickery and Herkert 1999). As a group, these species have shown the sorts of long-term, rangewide declines that justify concern. In some regions these declines are easily explained (i.e., the loss of grasslands in the East means that you just can't have as many grassland birds, but this is a positive change for forest birds), but in parts of the Midwest and Great Plains where there still seems to be sufficient habitat, the explanations for declines require more study. The observation that there are long-term data that show the continuing declines of these species while such data have not been presented for most forest-dwelling species reinforces my feeling that the declines in the latter group are not of as much concern as they were when presented in the 1980s.

It is interesting to think about why these grassland birds did not get as much press during the early development of PIF and, some argue, still don't. Certainly, the link between habitat destruction in the Tropics and population decline was not there for this group, most of which winter either in the United States or fly all the way to the pampas (where concern for wintering habitat has been noted). A conservation group cannot talk about losing an acre of rain forest and the associated decline in meadowlarks. Perhaps because most of these grassland birds are not found in backyards, are often drab in plumage, or occur mostly in the less settled portions of the country, they are less "sexy" and receive less attention. Yet, as a group they may be the ones that most justify the PIF response.

Other species or small groups of species may be showing the sorts of declines that merit much more concern and conservation attention in the future. Further analysis of such long-term data sets as the BBS should be done to try to point out species that are showing serious, long-term, and, perhaps, nationwide declines so that these species can be the focus of detailed research and conservation. Given the complexity of the spatial pattern of declines and the possible reasons causing them (including winter versus summer limitation), we need to be eternally vigilant in looking at the monitoring data that we have so that we can note those species about which we should be seriously concerned. On the other hand, we must do this honestly, recognizing the problems associated with all of these monitoring data sets and avoiding summary compilations of Neotropical migrants as a group. Species should be the unit of concern, not proportions of species or some meaningless lumping of species by some vague migrant strategy or wintering range category.

WERE THE LATE 1980S A TOUGH TIME FOR BIRD POPULATIONS?

A variety of data sets suggest that the late 1980s really were a difficult period for bird populations, such that the declines noted by a variety of sources were real. Much of the eastern United States was suffering from a severe drought during the late 1980s, a drought severe enough to reduce

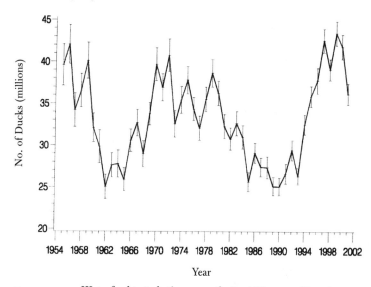

FIGURE 11.1. *Waterfowl populations over the past 50 years. Note that populations were low in the mid- to late 1980s because of drought conditions but recovered rapidly with the return of rainfall.*

nesting success (Blake et al. 1992). Given that these species have nearly 50% annual mortality, a decline in productivity can lead to a rapid decline in populations. This could easily explain some of the declines in forest birds in the East (which did not occur in the West, where the drought was not as severe) as shown both in the BBS and in wintering-ground studies. A strong correlation between stressful climatic conditions in the Midwest and the declines in grassland birds noted there has also been shown. Waterfowl populations were at their lowest at this time, as a result of continuing drought in the main part of their breeding range in the northern prairies.

As a scientist, I feel strongly that one has to believe in data that are gathered properly and analyzed appropriately. Thus, despite the concerns with BBS data, this technique showed that many species, especially Neotropical migrants, were declining in the late 1980s, during the period when intensive counts of waterfowl also showed declines. It is easy to believe that Robbins et al. (1989b) and Terborgh (1989) were correct in recognizing the data that showed widespread population declines in these migrant groups, even if they were incorrect in some of their statements about where the declines were occurring and the reasons for them.

In the case of waterfowl, the last decade has shown tremendous growth, such that duck populations are as high as they have been in the past 60 years (Fig. 11.1). We have not seen such positive changes in the other migrants, but in part this reflects the fact that ducks and warblers are different. The latter group does not show the declines as severe as those in waterfowl, which are so dependent upon breeding sites that are fairly temporary in nature, so we also do not expect warblers to increase as dramatically when drought ends.

It would be great to see if a more detailed analysis of bird monitoring data and climatic data could show more clearly if these two factors were linked in causing the declines of the 1980s. In some cases the evidence has been presented and seems clear, but further work might reveal much about how drought affects regional populations. Such knowledge would be of great importance in predicting the consequences of future droughts or, perhaps, such future phenomena as global climate change.

Is Winter Habitat Limiting to Neotropical Migrants?

Most of the early publications showing declines in Neotropical migrant populations also suggested that these declines could be explained by changing conditions on the wintering grounds (Robbins et al. 1989b; Terborgh 1989). We have already noted the difficulties involved in understanding the conditions that might lead to such population limitation during the nonbreeding season. Most important, we have shown how habitat change in the Tropics affects some species positively, such that some populations of migrants might go up while others go down, depending upon what sort of habitat changes have occurred. In addition, many recent studies have shown the variety of problems that Neotropical migrants face on the breeding grounds, providing strong data in support of breeding-season limitation.

My feeling is that there currently is little evidence of winter limitation in those North American birds that winter in the New World Tropics. Most species seem to have large wintering ranges and the ability to occur in a variety of habitat types. Even a few species that were suggested to be quite habitat-specific—e.g., Hooded Warbler and Wood Thrush (Morton 1980; Rappole et al. 1989)—have been shown to survive adequately in more disturbed sites (Conway et al. 1995).

As we gather more information about winter ranges and habitat quality for individual species, we should continue to analyze population trends and their causes. Certainly, species with limited winter ranges should be monitored closely in the future, with detailed comparisons of possible limiting factors in both breeding and wintering areas. For example, a species with declining populations that seems to show high reproduction on the breeding grounds might be examined closely for winter limitation. Species with extreme sexual segregation on the wintering grounds might also be noted and monitored closely, for they may be more susceptible to habitat limitation due to this behavioral trait. The sort of detailed examination of population trends that I suggested earlier in this chapter should include an assessment of the potential for winter limitation as a factor to explain trends. More detailed information on the winter ecology of migrants throughout their winter ranges is needed to provide a scientific basis for understanding how, why, and where winter limitation may occur.

WILL WINTER LIMITATION OCCUR EVENTUALLY?

I personally do not think that winter limitation is an important part in explaining population declines in Neotropical migratory species in the year 2000. This puts me at odds with John Terborgh, Chan Robbins, and many others, most of whom I greatly admire. I base my generalization on such factors as the severe reduction of nesting success in many sites on the breeding grounds and the fact that some species showing declines actually seem to prefer disturbed habitats in the Tropics, which suggests they should be increasing rather than declining if winter limitation is at work.

I may be wrong. If you were to compare my credentials with the two gentlemen mentioned above (Terborgh and Robbins), you should probably be on their side. On the other hand, they made their statements from the data they had at the time they published their work. I have the advantage of another decade's worth of research on both the breeding grounds and wintering grounds; I have formed my opinions from the results of that work and analyses of many other lines of evidence. I hope they are intelligent opinions; I feel strongly that they are informed ones.

If John Terborgh was wrong in his assessment that winter limitation was at work in causing the declines of the 1980s, it may be a mistake in terms of timing rather than logic. Although we can talk about how conversion of a forest into agriculture changes the composition of the winter-resident community just in the short term, the reality is that some of the habitat loss involves permanent loss of wintering habitat as the result of conversion to buildings, parking lots, or other land uses that are untenable for habitation by migrant warblers. As the population of Latin America continues to increase, it seems likely that winter habitat limitation will occur for some species sooner or later, if it has not already occurred. Once again, detailed examinations of population trends, habitat usage, and other aspects of the ecology of these migrants might allow us to predict these changes and prevent them in the future.

IS STOPOVER HABITAT CURRENTLY A PROBLEM?

As was noted earlier, gathering solid evidence showing that stopover habitat is limiting overall populations is exceedingly difficult. Although some excellent studies have been done on how migrant birds deal with large barriers such as the Gulf of Mexico (Moore 2000) or even the Great Lakes (Ewert and Hamas 1996), such situations are difficult to extrapolate to more normal conditions. In the eastern United States, where population declines seemed most pronounced in forest birds, the existence of numerous habitat fragments makes it hard to envision habitat limitation during migration. Although these forest fragments may be horrible places for trying to raise young, they most likely are excellent sites for stopping during migration. In contrast, one can see that many western regions had a bottleneck for migrants that require riparian habitats during migration, a situation that has gotten worse in recent years because of loss of riparian habitat in these regions. Although this has the potential to be limiting, these western species in general did not show long-term population declines the way that their counterparts in the East did.

Stronger cases for potential habitat limitation during migration can be made for such specialized species as Sandhill Cranes (*Grus canadensis;* Krapu 1999), White-rumped Sandpiper (*Calidris fuscicollis;* Harrington 1999), and Dunlin (*Calidris alpina;* Senner 1999). These species are distinctive because they intensively use rather small areas as staging for their migration. For example, the cranes spend several months in the spring along a few hundred miles of the Platte River in Nebraska, and the sandpipers seem to require resources from parts of the Chesapeake Bay area during their migrations. In these cases, loss of a relatively small amount of habitat could have severe consequences upon total populations.

IF THINGS ARE NOT SO BAD,
WAS PIF AN OVERREACTION?

Partners in Flight was formed to help prevent the extinction of the Neotropical migrants, which were shown to be declining. It currently calls itself the world's largest avian conservation program. If, in fact, the situation was not as severe in 1990 as we thought it was, one could ask whether the creation of PIF was an overreaction and not really necessary.

My feeling is that PIF was the proper response to the situation as it presented itself in 1990. Even if my evaluation of the situation is correct, and things are not as serious as we thought they were in 1990, the truth is that the declines shown in 1989 and 1990 were real and worthy of a serious response. Part of the PIF response involved research, and many of the pieces of evidence I have used to come to my personal conclusions about the overall situation with regard to migrant birds in the year 2000 come from research done in collaboration with PIF. Without the support and interactions that I was able to have through PIF, I would not know as much about how migrant bird populations work as I do.

Of course, I have already mentioned that I may be wrong in my final conclusions, which means that PIF is as important and urgent now as it was when it was organized 10 years ago. If this is the case, perhaps this book will serve to crystallize thought by those who can make a more convincing case for the continued widespread declines and their causes than I have seen to date.

If Neotropical migrant birds are not facing the dire circumstances suggested more than a decade ago, PIF was and still is a good idea for a variety of reasons.

PIF Got Everybody Talking Before the formation of Partners in Flight, few people cared about migrant birds at all. Even when the early studies on habitat fragmentation suggested that there might be severe local consequences to such fragmentation, few people were listening. PIF got researchers together to talk about what was going on, what it meant, and how it could be stopped. Not only did researchers from different parts of the country get together and talk, but special meetings were held so that researchers and managers could interact. With the committee structure that was developed as part of PIF, everyone was welcome to participate and there was little evidence of any pecking order among participants.

Perhaps the most important thing that PIF did was to get the various governmental agencies that had anything to do with bird conservation to work together in some fashion. Although some of this interaction occurred only after some acrimonious arguments about whose organization had legal authority to do this or that, the final result was that biologists from all the different agencies (including the Department of Defense, which controls an amazing amount of habitat) came to PIF meetings, talked to the researchers and managers who also came to these meetings, and helped in forming the conservation consensus that became characteristic of these PIF activities.

I don't think that one can overestimate how important it was to get the various biologists from these disparate agencies together, working for a common good. I say this without trying to be the least bit negative about any of the activities of these people before PIF. In dealing with government workers, I have found virtually all of them to be great people with their hearts in the right place with regard to conservation. In many situations, though, their options were limited by various directives from higher authorities or because of procedures determined by earlier goals within their agency. PIF allowed these biologists to gain the current knowledge about what was needed to protect migratory birds and then take it back to their supervisors with the leverage that these were state-of-the-art concepts that needed to be applied right away to these declining species. Some or most of these ideas would have eventually filtered through all of the agencies, but because of the way PIF worked, everything happened quickly and was easily transferred to biologists in all the governmental agencies.

PIF Was Modern and Exciting   For the two decades before 1990, there had been a gradual shift in the focus of what had originally been wildlife management. Emphasis on restoring game species was declining, in part because of the success of such restoration programs but also because fewer people were involved in consumptive uses of nature. Although the Endangered Species Act directed much effort toward listed species, the change in focus from game to nongame wildlife was occurring rather slowly, limited in part by the time it took for classically trained wildlife biologists to work their way through the retirement systems of management agencies. PIF served as a strong impetus to make rapid changes in emphasis from game to nongame among many of these agencies. That migrant birds were found nearly everywhere, that everyone cared about them, and that they were in peril could not be ignored. Representatives to PIF from these agencies were appointed, usually from among the younger employees who had a broader, often nongame-based training in wildlife biology. As these people brought the new ideas developed by PIF committees back to their agencies, they often had tremendous influence on policies. I have been continually amazed at how rapidly ideas about habitat fragmentation went from being some sort of esoteric science to a normal part of the jargon of serious conservationists. Even amateur conservationists with whom I work drop concepts of fragmentation and edge in their conversation without skipping a beat. Although the trend was already happening, PIF provided a strong, quick boost to changes in focus in many agencies.

PIF Was Proactive Rather Than Reactive   For a period of time, wildlife management seemed to have two foci, the management of harvestable species and last-ditch efforts to save endangered species. In the latter case, the situation was often desperate by the time conservation activities were initiated. The result was costly, highly manipulative, politically difficult, and often unsuccessful efforts to save wild populations of endangered species.

PIF was refreshing because, even though it was a response to serious population declines, part of its goal was "to keep common birds common." It was initiated at a time when the populations of the species of concern were still in the hundreds of thousands, if not millions. The species were still widespread, even though they were apparently declining. There was potential to preserve these species without the intensive, manipulative, and highly costly efforts required for many endangered species; rather, it appeared that populations of migrant birds were adequate, so that fairly simple habitat management would generally suffice in restoring populations locally. That activities at the level of a backyard could potentially help these species was both very real and highly attractive in selling the PIF programs to the general public.

PIF Has Been Cheap   I cannot give a lot of numbers with regard to how much money was spent on PIF activities over the past decade, but I am quite certain that PIF has operated mostly by the participation of cooperators who already were interested or active in avian conservation. Many governmental agencies at both state and federal levels have appointed PIF representatives or encouraged participation in PIF, but in most cases these positions already existed. Faculty members or graduate students who actively worked with PIF had to have "day jobs" that paid their salaries. (Actually, this was always a sore point for me when I was very active with the PIF Research Committee, because most of the governmental employees on that committee had travel funds to help them get to meetings, while I had to scrape together funds from other sources to pay my own way.)

I can think of only a few new jobs that were created as a result of PIF. Within the National Fish and Wildlife Foundation (NFWF), the agency that has coordinated most of the funded activities of PIF and helped with communication among the various PIF committees, a PIF coordinator (Dr. Peter Stangel) was named at the start of PIF. He now has a staff that helps with the administration of PIF-related grants, although they also do some non-PIF work too. PIF also has hired four regional coordinators for the development of all the conservation plans that are in the works. These are new positions that did not exist before PIF. In recent years, some of the NFWF activities have shifted to the offices of the American Bird Conservancy (ABC, formerly the International Council of Bird Preservation). Perhaps there are more staff at ABC now than before because of PIF, but if so, it is not a large number of people. ABC also accepts memberships, which help support PIF activities, but membership is totally on a voluntary basis.

As a result, what bills itself as the world's largest conservation program has been and continues to be operated primarily by people who work for different agencies in a wide variety of capacities. Support for PIF comes from the budgets that these folks have because the PIF goals are compatible with the goals of the jobs these folks hold. It is truly incredible to think that the gigantic structure that is PIF (described in Chapter 12) has been operated almost without new funding. It also is a bit scary, because it seems so easy to see something like PIF come crashing to earth if the support of all these volunteers should disappear.

IS PIF LIKE Y2K?

I began writing this chapter just a few weeks into the new millennium. Although we have quickly forgotten it, in the months before January 1, 2000, a tremendous amount of time, money, and energy was spent trying to prepare the world for the potential Y2K (year 2000) disasters that would be the result of computer shutdowns because the year 2000 on many computers would become the year 1900 (since most early computers just used the last two digits of years to save disk space). Billions of dollars were spent trying to ensure that computer systems that ran power companies, airlines, national defense, and almost everything in modern life would not shut down as the new millennium began. Despite these vast sums of money, many experts suggested that disasters were inevitable, and many people stayed home with hoarded supplies of food, gasoline, ammunition, and so forth.

Virtually nothing happened the night of January 1, 2000. The Eiffel Tower was spectacular, airlines worked, and power outages did not occur. Although some people suggested that this was because all of the money spent updating computer systems was well spent, others suggested that much of the whole Y2K disaster scenario was something concocted by groups or individuals with something to gain by these problems. Some think we may have spent billions of dollars fixing things that were already Y2K-compatible.

To me, an analogy exists between the Y2K situation and PIF. In the case of PIF, we may have had a situation with declining bird populations that required a massive, rapid response to conserve these species. Of course, I already have pointed out how this response did not cost billions of new dollars, but if the situation was not as severe in 1990 as we originally thought it was, one can question whether or not the PIF response was necessary.

I think the PIF response was totally appropriate, partly because it allowed us to gather the sort of data that have in turn allowed me to suggest that things were not as severe in 1990 as we may have thought. We did not spend a fortune, and even if we were wrong in our timing, PIF is developing state-of-the art conservation programs that will work to save migrant birds not only now but well into the future, when the many potential limiting factors we have discussed in this book will eventually be at work.

12 | PARTNERS IN FLIGHT
How It Works and How You Can Help

Part of the reason that so many people became concerned about the potential plight of Neotropical migrant bird populations is that these birds are such a dominant part of the avifauna of temperate North America. Although the first robin is a measure of spring that does not involve a Neotropical migrant, for many amateur ornithologists spring really comes with the waves of migrants and summer residents that appear in April or early May along with the greening of the environment. The thought that such an important part of the annual cycle might be disappearing was one that required a serious response, a response that resulted in the Partners in Flight program. Because these were birds of the backyard, their demise hit home much more than the problems affecting some endangered species that were confined to some limited habitat far away from home.

I have already noted some of the wonders of the PIF program with regard to its ability, in such a short period of time, to change the way that North America manages wildlife. Here I present a brief overview of how PIF is structured, how its units have operated over the last decade, and how the PIF Flight Plans have been developed as conservation plans for the new millennium. I end with some thoughts about how individuals can participate in PIF and the conservation of migrant birds.

PARTNERS IN FLIGHT: LOTS OF COMMITTEES

Attempting to develop a conservation plan for several hundred species that occur in dozens of different countries on two continents is not an easy chore. First of all, one must develop the best management plan that one can, which initially involves strong input from researchers, followed by interaction between researchers and managers. All of this must be properly communicated to interested parties in different countries, and within the larger countries it must be refined for all the different regions where Neotropical migrants may occur. Given that committees including hundreds of people from throughout the Western Hemisphere cannot generally meet cheaply and efficiently to discuss ideas, the communication process must allow feedback from those researchers or conservationists who could not be a part of the initial development of ideas to make sure the ideas are as general as possible. It is a daunting task.

Accomplishing all of these various activities requires complex partnerships among a variety of public and private entities. Obviously, for Neotropical migrants the plan must be international in scope, which means the involvement of numerous national governments. Because many conservation activities are mandated at a state or regional level, those entities must also be directly involved in the process. Nongovernmental organizations (NGOs) and corporations should be directly involved at one of these levels, depending upon whether the organization is multinational (like the Nature Conservancy) or regional in nature (like the Missouri Audubon Society). Universities have an important role in the process because they are where much of the research is done and converted into management guidelines. Finally, the public has a critical role in supporting the process through such indirect activities as political pressure for changes in funding or new laws or through direct participation in such important events as Breeding Bird Surveys.

To try to get all of the various activities accomplished with the participation of all the possible entities, Partners in Flight developed a series of working groups that were either technical or regional in nature. Four of the technical working groups focused on monitoring, research, legislation, and information/education; a fifth working group was also somewhat regional in nature, because this international working group sought to provide quick transfer of ideas and information among the other working groups and conservationists in nations where attendance by its representatives at working group meetings in the United States was often not possible.

The United States was split originally into four regional working groups, but in 1992 a boreal working group was added to cover work with migrants in boreal portions of Alaska and the Yukon. In some cases Canadian biologists participated with the regional working groups appropriate to their province, and in some cases interactions with Canada were handled through the international technical working group. These regional working groups became very important later in the life of PIF because they were the units used to hire full-time biologists for development of the Flight Plans for each of the physiographic regions within the PIF regions.

Many of the regional working groups developed their own structure, with technical working groups in research, monitoring, and information/education. In many cases, state governments became involved in these regional working groups by designating representatives to regional PIF committees and, in some cases, developing their own state responses to PIF (often with another set of committees).

One of the amazing things about PIF was that this complex hierarchy of committees actually worked very well, at least in its early years. All of the committees were run by a set of directors who were appointed by members of the committees, although being a member of any committee was pretty much determined by attendance; willingness to be active was the most important attribute to attaining a governing position. Although there were times when the turnover of participants between meetings meant that a certain amount of time was spent reinventing the wheel, all in all the committees with which I was involved were amazingly productive in their early years. Being in charge, though, meant that a lot of time was spent photocopying and mailing reports, with postage funds coming from who knows where.

Today PIF states that it has more than 200 cooperating organizations doing all of the things it does. As we go through descriptions of both the functional levels and the technical working groups, we need to keep in mind what an unusual set of circumstances it was that got so much cooperation out of such a disparate set of organizations.

Federal Agencies We have already noted the importance of PIF in getting the various agencies whose major function is managing wildlife to work together and communicate. The U.S. Fish and Wildlife Service (FWS) has legal authorization to be in charge of migratory birds through the Migratory Bird Treaty Act, but FWS historically has been accused of directing most of its efforts to waterfowl management. A look at the wildlife refuges operated by FWS supports the existence of this bias, although other activities that were part of FWS (which have been passed on to other subdivisions in recent years because of governmental reorganization) included the bird banding program, the Breeding Bird Survey, and some important nongame research done through the FWS Patuxent Refuge.

In contrast, the U.S. Forest Service (USFS) is not directly charged with preserving migrant birds, but the massive amounts of land operated by this agency support untold millions of Neotropical migrants. Because of its responsibility for developing policies that involved multiple goals for forest management, including wildlife, USFS had established quite modern management programs for its forests by 1990. It was important to get the Forest Service and the Fish and Wildlife Service to cooperate, and after some initial bickering, it seems to have happened.

Other federal agencies have become important players in PIF, several of which are a bit surprising. The Bureau of Land Management (BLM) manages 270 million acres of federally owned land; the development of management practices that included the needs of Neotropical migrants was therefore important. The National Park Service (NPS) manages nearly 80 million acres in national parks, most of which are in relatively natural conditions. The Department of Defense (DOD) may not seem like an obvious partner for PIF, but its bases include more than 25 million acres of habitat, some of it in large, relatively undisturbed parcels. The U.S. Agency for International Development (USAID) is charged with administering economic assistance in developing countries. It awarded more than $1 million to the National Fish and Wildlife Foundation for a matching grants program for projects done in Latin America with the assistance of Latin Americans. The Environmental Protection Agency (EPA) became involved because many of its regulatory powers (such as those related to the Clean Water Act and various pesticide monitoring measures) are highly beneficial to supporting the habitats that migratory birds use. The EPA also provided important information about habitat distribution through its Environmental Monitoring and Assessment Program (EMAP), a countrywide analysis of habitats using modern geographical information systems (GIS). Finally, the Cooperative Extension Service got involved in providing educational materials for teachers to use to inform their students about the problems that migratory birds face and how people can help out.

Virtually all of these federal agencies signed a memorandum of agreement in 1991 that formed the Federal Neotropical Migratory Bird Conservation Committee. This committee was the formal federal structure to ensure cooperation with the general working group structure of PIF.

State Agencies   Virtually all state conservation/natural resource agencies have gotten involved with PIF at some level. Their involvement has varied widely, in part because the nongame funding levels for the states show tremendous variation. Several states (and I refrain from naming names here to avoid leaving someone deserving out) have full-time Neotropical migratory bird coordinators, funded research projects, and extensive educational activities. States with low funding have done much less. The International Association of Fish and Wildlife Agencies, the chief umbrella group for state agencies, appointed a PIF coordinator position in 1991 to help coordinate activities and information transfer for this group.

Nongovernmental Organizations   The NGOs involved in PIF vary in size from massive international organizations such as the Nature Conservancy to small, local bird observatories. Several professional organizations (the Wildlife Society and the American Ornithologists' Union, for example) have also played important roles in PIF. The Pan American office of the International Council for Bird Preservation was very active in the early development of PIF, and with the new name of American Bird Conservancy, it serves as the current conduit for information about PIF to the public. The National Fish and Wildlife Foundation became important enough to PIF functioning that it is discussed more fully below. Although many of the NGOs were small, in numerous cases they made major contributions to PIF because of the specialized knowledge they had or the set of active conservationists who made these organizations function so well.

Corporations   Although the contributions of corporations do not match those of the various governmental agencies, several corporations have had a major impact on PIF. In most cases, the corporations became involved because of local interactions. For example, attempts to save an island sanctuary on the coast of Texas ended up involving a partnership among the Houston Audubon Society, Phillips Petroleum Company, and Amoco Production Company.

Universities   Several universities or university-related NGOs have also been instrumental in PIF. University involvement has usually been through the activity of researchers whose work has included a focus on migratory birds; many of the most active researchers can be found by checking the references in this book. Several university-related groups have also been active in PIF, including the Cornell Laboratory of Ornithology (see below) and the Organization for Tropical Studies, a consortium of more than 50 universities that operates courses and biological stations in the Tropics, especially Costa Rica.

Monitoring Working Group   The goal of the monitoring working group is to set priorities for monitoring the populations and habitats of Neotropical migrants on both the breeding and the wintering grounds. Among the group's early achievements were a monitoring needs assessment and the publication of *Handbook of Field Methods for Monitoring Landbirds,* which has become the standard reference for field methodology (Ralph et al. 1993).

Research Working Group   The research working group was exceedingly active in the early years of PIF, particularly 1991–1995. Largely through the efforts of this committee, a large symposium entitled "Status and Management of Neotropical Migratory Birds" was held at Estes Park, Colorado, in the fall of 1992. This meeting involved an impressive mix of avian researchers and avian conservationists; through presentations and committee meetings tremendous strides were made in developing management guidelines that were state-of-the-art at that time. The proceedings of this symposium appeared in two different formats. First, short versions of selected presentations appeared in a U.S. Forest Service General Technical Report (Finch and Stangel 1993); then longer versions of somewhat fewer papers were published by Oxford University Press (Martin and Finch 1995).

The research working group has not been quite as active in recent years, or perhaps because I have not been as actively involved in it, I do not know what it is doing. Several of my researcher-friends felt that researchers were not given proper attention at the PIF conference at Cape May in 1995, in part because the word was that the managers knew enough to design management plans. Given that impressive groups of researchers on migratory birds met in the fall of 1989 at Woods Hole, in the fall of 1990 for the development of PIF, and in the fall of 1992 for the Estes Park symposium, it has been a long time since a similar get-together has occurred.

On the other hand, most of the active researchers have still been doing excellent work, publishing in good journals, and making sure that the findings get incorporated into the PIF Flight Plans (see below). As long as the regional PIF personnel continue to interact with regional researchers, the Flight Plans should be state-of-the-art. Plans were recently announced for a PIF symposium in March 2002, with a focus on implementation of the bird conservation plans across the country.

Information and Education Working Group The information and education working group had as its goal the improvement of communication, education, and outreach about Neotropical migratory birds at all levels. Through a series of subcommittees, it developed slide shows for presentations on PIF, produced a packet of information entitled "Save our Songbirds" in collaboration with the National Audubon Society and the Smithsonian Institution, and edited the various newsletters that appeared early in the life of PIF. The latter duties have been taken over by the American Bird Conservancy, which publishes the journal *Bird Conservation.*

One of the products of this working group that is most visible to the general public is International Migratory Bird Day (IMBD). Usually on the second Saturday of May, this day is a chance to push the message of PIF to the public, with special emphasis on younger folks. IMBD always promotes the message of conservation throughout the New World, with emphasis on how conservation must work on breeding, wintering, and migratory sites in order to conserve migrant birds.

Legislative Working Group The legislative working group had as its goal to educate Congress and others and to attain legislatively supported funding and other resources needed for development and implementation of a coordinated and cooperative Partners in Flight program. Although this group appeared to do a great deal to educate these parties about the need for and existence of PIF in its early years, it had disappeared from the list of working groups by 1994.

International Working Group One of the major realizations from the meetings that led to PIF was that all the conservation activity possible on the breeding grounds might not be enough to save those migrant birds that were threatened by loss of adequate wintering areas. Yet, everyone was also aware that the conservation movement in Latin America was generally not as developed as that of the U.S. and that most Latin American governments did not have the resources needed to achieve adequate conservation efforts. Thus, the international working group was formed to conserve migratory birds and their associated habitats in Latin America and the Caribbean by supporting strong, capable local institutions and in-country conservation programs. Much communication was done through a regular newsletter (*La Tangara*), which announced meetings, available funding sources, and activities being done within Latin America. The international working group also was instrumental in reviewing the proposals received for funds provided by USAID for work on migrants in Latin America.

Regional Working Groups We already noted the five regional working groups for the United States. Depending on the problems faced in each region, the goals varied, but all were involved in the development of lists of priority species for their region and assessment of regional knowledge about migratory birds. In recent years, these committees have been critical in working with the regional representatives in finalizing the Flight Plans. Although some of these regional committees do not appear to meet regularly, many are still quite active. For example, the Southeast Working Group had a major symposium in Florida in January 2000.

THE NATIONAL FISH AND WILDLIFE FOUNDATION AND PIF

The National Fish and Wildlife Foundation (NFWF) was founded by Congress in 1985 to act as a catalyst for conservation by providing funds for proposals dealing with conservation of the nation's fish, wildlife, and plant resources. NFWF is independent of the government, but it is able to use federal money to fund projects that have matching funds from nonfederal sources. This match must be at least 1:1, and in many cases must exceed that ratio. For example, in 1991, NFWF committed $6.9 million in federal funds that was matched by $14.9 million in nonfederal funds.

Partners in Flight is one of four major initiatives at NFWF. Under the direction and inspiration of Amos Enos, NFWF started the Neotropical Migratory Bird Conservation Program with the meeting it sponsored in Atlanta in December 1990. Peter Stangel soon took over as PIF coordinator at NFWF, where he was instrumental in keeping the diverse set of working committees functioning while also doing his day job of funding research on Neotropical migrants. In addition to several million dollars' worth of research on migrant birds in the United States, NFWF also handled the million dollars or so of funding that was provided by USAID for projects in Latin America. In their spare time, Stangel and his coworkers also produced the PIF newsletter for at least 5 years.

It is hard to believe that PIF would have succeeded without the vision and hard work of Amos Enos and Peter Stangel and their assistants at NFWF. They provided the conceptual glue that seemed to keep the incredibly complex and potentially unworkable PIF programs going. I still disagree with some of their individual decisions (some of these disagreements have to do with their unwillingness to fund some things I thought were deserving, but others have to do with more conceptual ideas such as the need for more research), but looking back, someone or something had to serve as the catalyst that kept PIF going, and the more I think about it, it has to be the people at NFWF. Even if the need for PIF was not as desperate as we thought, we enter the new millennium with a tremendous amount of new knowledge about how to conserve these amazing birds, and we will shortly have management plans that will protect them in the future, if not today.

PIF Flight Plans

We have already mentioned the PIF Flight Plans briefly earlier, but they deserve special note. These plans are state-of the-art conservation plans being written for each of the physiographic provinces of the United States. Each plan takes into account the status of bird species in that province, with emphasis on those birds for which that physiographic province is particularly important for overall population health. The plan also provides a summary of current conditions with regard to habitats and guidelines for future management. Some of the ideas for these Flight Plans were borrowed from methods used in the North American Waterfowl Conservation Plan, but for the PIF Flight Plans a much greater variety of habitats had to be incorporated into the management schemes.

In Chapter 7 we discussed how managers recently had taken into account the need for large habitat patches to support source populations of birds. These ideas have been incorporated into Flight Plans. Although research will undoubtedly show that these guidelines are fairly primitive, the Flight Plans are currently as modern as any management plan I have ever seen. I know that for those Flight Plans being finished in the Midwest, all of the biologists and managers who know anything about the situation are being asked to read and change these plans to conform to their current ideas about what needs to be done. So often in the past, a researcher would find something out, publish it in some journal, then wait to see if the resource managers ever read the paper and adjusted their management techniques accordingly. PIF Flight Plans have the researchers involved with the managers at all levels, so that there is little time lag involved in converting a researcher's discovery into management guidelines.

IMPORTANT BIRD AREAS

Another important activity associated with PIF is the designation of Important Bird Areas (IBAs) across the country. These areas are picked because they serve a critical function in protecting Neotropical migrant birds, be it as breeding habitat, stopover habitat, or wintering grounds. The international designation of being an IBA should highlight the importance of the area to local residents, making it easier to gain local support for protection. IBAs also will probably eventually attract more tourists, which can have strong local economic effects through ecotourism. The designation of IBAs is being done internationally, with a wonderful new book covering Mexico recently released (del Coro Arizmendi and Márquez Valdelamar 2000).

PIF AND NABCI

As this book was being finished, many of the activities that were directed by PIF were being merged with the broader North American Bird Conservation Initiative (NABCI). Although this did not appear to affect most of the focal goals of PIF directly, it ideally meant that there should be less overlap or duplication of effort because different conservation efforts did not know what each organization was doing (e.g., saving grassland areas is desirable for both waterfowl and grassland birds, so now the communication between organizations can minimize effort and ensure saving areas important for both goals).

INDIVIDUAL PARTICIPATION IN PIF

If you are interested enough in migrant birds to be reading this book, you probably have already done something to benefit PIF, even if only indirectly. Nearly any bird or birding group worth its salt has signed on as a cooperator to PIF, so parts of dues you have paid to these groups may have been shunted in the PIF direction. Large national groups such as the Nature Conservancy and the National Audubon Society have also been cooperators in PIF activities, using member funds to support their activities. PIF and its cooperators can always use money, so any funds you may want to donate to help conserve migrant birds would be well put to use. The best way to find out how to do this might be to join the American Bird Conservancy, the group that has become the coordinator for most PIF activities. (The American Bird Conservancy can be reached by calling 1-888-BIRD-MAG, by email at <abc@abcbirds.org>, or on the Web at <www.abcbirds.org>. The PIF website is at <www.partnersinflight.org>.)

Serious birdwatchers with good field skills can become important active participants in PIF or contributors to migrant bird research. The Breeding Bird Survey is operated by the federal government but uses a system of state coordinators to find volunteers to run the routes. Good observers are always valuable, particularly as some states have increased the number of routes they are trying to run. For information about the BBS, check out the website at <www.mp2-pwrc.usgs.gov/bbs/>. Many states have atlasing programs that attempt to increase knowledge of the distribution and abundance of the state's birds; volunteers are valuable here too. As we have seen, participation in local Christmas Bird Counts or other censusing activities can provide important bits of information about bird populations.

The Cornell Laboratory of Ornithology offers its members a variety of opportunities to do "citizen science." One of them, Birds in Forested Landscapes, allows you to participate in a nationwide fragmentation study. Other studies focus on finding Cerulean Warblers or counting birds at feeders. In recent years, some of the results have been transferred electronically, so that you can see trends from your project on the Cornell website almost immediately. To get involved in these projects, contact the Laboratory of Ornithology at its website <http://birds.cornell.edu>.

If you want to share your knowledge and interest in birds with others, you might want to help out with local activities associated with International Migratory Bird Day in the spring. You would need to find out what your local bird group does in this regard, but volunteers are always needed for these activities. If you don't have a local group, start your own IMBD activities at your local schools. Informative packets to help with this are put out each year by the folks that sponsor IMBD. Information about IMBD can be gained at <IMBD@fws.gov> or <www.birds.fws.gov/imbd.html>.

One can help PIF at home too. Keeping track of your cat is a start. Although most residents cannot change the traits of the landscape in which they live, they can provide good nesting or stopover habitat for migrant birds in their yards. Active support of local conservation groups can result in the proper management activities on local nature reserves, making sure that management for game species is not done at the expense of migrants. If you happen to own land that supports migrant species, you might incorporate some of the ideas from this book in your management decisions.

There are lots of other things that one can do to help conserve Neotropical migrant birds and ensure that these birds remain abundant, both regionally and nationally. Although it may be true that most of these species are not declining as seriously as once thought, in many regions they face a difficult struggle to reproduce and maintain local populations. Just because things are not as serious as we thought does not mean that these birds do not need some assistance.

POSTSCRIPT

In the preceding pages, I have made the case that the situation with regard to future populations of most Neotropical migrant birds is not as severe as was suggested a decade ago. Most of these migrants are not going extinct, and many of them should continue to be plentiful as long as the world remains more or less structured the way it is. A few species of Neotropical migrants may be facing extinction if current trends continue, and in some regions, population extinction may occur if the workings of PIF are not effective. My main point, though, is that the reality of the situation, as I see it, is not one of a silent spring in the near future, but perhaps a different spring as those species that are better able to deal with human changes to their habitats on either breeding or wintering grounds do better than those that do not deal with these modifications as well.

As a scientist, I think it is important to make these points. Neotropical migrants cannot be considered a cohesive group about which generalizations can be made, particularly with regard to conservation and management. Quietly sitting back and letting the world believe that all these species face extinction, particularly if it helps me get funding for my research, might be easy and profitable, but it isn't the right thing to do. Rather, I suggest we must continue to figure out what is going on with all of the species involved so that we can figure out which ones really face long-term declines and thus are worthy of special conservation efforts.

Undoubtedly, there will be those who will take the material I have presented and use it for their own purposes. If Neotropical migrants really are not facing immediate disaster as a group, they might suggest that all is well. I have seen this happen to my friend Scott Robinson, who wrote a review in a fairly obscure journal that shared some of the ideas I have discussed here; this somehow ended up in the *New York Times* as an article called "Something to Sing About: Songbirds Aren't in Decline." He received an incredible amount of grief, not because of what he said in his review but because of how it was interpreted by the press. I predict that I will suffer some of the same consequences.

Obviously, from all the material I have shown in earlier chapters, all is not well with Neotropical migrants. On the other hand, things are not as bad as suggested by many sources. In particular, many regional populations are suffering. Yet, if I am correct in my analysis of the overall situation (and we must remember that I may be wrong in my interpretations), current conditions are not severe enough to cause the disaster that many predicted was occurring a decade ago.

Even if I am correct and Neotropical migrants are not suffering under current conditions as severely as some feared, we must remember that conditions continue to change. Continued loss and fragmentation of habitat on the breeding and wintering grounds or during migration will undoubtedly affect the total populations of some species sooner or later. We cannot continue to increase the population of the world without giving up habitat for migrant birds. As citizens of a country that consumes a disproportionate amount of the world's natural resources, we have tremendous impact upon the loss of natural resources around the world. Just because the situation with regard to Neotropical migrant bird populations may not be as drastic as once thought does not mean that it won't become drastic in the future, and perhaps the near future. My colleagues who have made the suggestions about the severity of the situation with regard to migrant populations did not use faulty logic; loss of habitat will result in declining populations. With the declines of the 1980s they suggested that we had reached some limit where habitat loss was taking effect on bird populations. Recent evidence suggests that other factors may have been more important at that time (drought, natural population cycles, etc.), but this doesn't mean that loss of habitat will not eventually be a problem.

Just because Neotropical migrants are not in general decline does not mean we lack conservation needs across the hemisphere. One of the things we have discovered in recent years is how important large areas of natural or near-natural habitat are in determining regional migrant bird populations. Such large areas are also necessary for many nonmigratory animals, including large predators, several endangered bird species, and many reptiles and amphibians. Recent ideas about how critical preservation of such large reserves has become have been presented in *Continental Conservation: Scientific Foundations of Regional Reserve Networks* edited by John Terborgh and Michael E. Soule (Soule and Terborgh 1999). These large reserves are truly critical for some of these large endangered species; for migrant birds, they may be essential sources to support regional bird populations. At the very least, they serve as insurance policies in case the situation in regions that are predominantly sink populations gets worse over time.

The situation with regard to the conservation of resident Neotropical birds in the Tropics is truly severe. Although I have suggested that Neotropical migrants as a group are not as limited by winter habitat as has been suggested by others, nonmigratory residents or those species that show short-distance, intratropical migrations suffer dramatically from habitat loss and fragmentation. With a total of several thousand species of New World tropical birds, many of them vulnerable to fragmentation and other forms of habitat loss, the extinction potential is truly frightening. Although it is true that migrants from North America seem to deal with habitat fragments rather easily during the winter, such fragmentation is locally disastrous for truly tropical species. One could envision a future where excessive fragmentation of tropical habitats created conditions that were acceptable only to Neotropical migrants from the north and weedy-second-growth tropical species. The loss of diversity of resident species would be tragic.

The world faces a crisis with regard to preserving its natural diversity. Given limited resources for conservation, perhaps it is important that we realize which species are truly in imminent danger, so that we can allocate our efforts most efficiently. My feeling is that most Neotropical migrants are not in the group that requires immediate concern; I hope I have persuaded you to agree with me.

Appendix

Lists of Migrants for Partners in Flight

The following are lists of the species that were included in Partners in Flight during its early years. The focus at that time was on land-dwelling birds that migrated to the Tropics. In recent years, the PIF umbrella has grown to include virtually all birds, and lists such as this rarely appear.

List A contains those species that breed in North America and spend their nonbreeding period primarily south of the United States. This list contains species generally recognized as "Neotropical" migrants. List B comprises those species that breed and winter extensively in North America, although some populations winter south of the United States. List C contains those species whose breeding range is primarily south of the U.S.–Mexican border and that enter the United States along the Rio Grande Valley and where the Mexican Highlands extend across the U.S. border. These populations largely vacate the United States during the winter months. List D contains those tropical species whose breeding range is restricted to the Florida Peninsula within the United States; these species withdraw from Florida during the nonbreeding season. Common and scientific names are from the seventh edition of the *Check-List of North American Birds,* published by the American Ornithologists' Union in 1998.

List "A"

Swallow-tailed Kite (*Elanoides forficatus*)
Mississippi Kite (*Ictinia mississippiensis*)
Broad-winged Hawk (*Buteo platypterus*)
Swainson's Hawk (*Buteo swainsoni*)
Merlin (*Falco columbarius*)

Peregrine Falcon (*Falco peregrinus*)
Mountain Plover (*Charadrius montanus*)
Upland Sandpiper (*Bartramia longicauda*)
Long-billed Curlew (*Numenius americanus*)
Band-tailed Pigeon (*Columba fasciata*)
Black-billed Cuckoo (*Coccyzus erythropthalmus*)
Yellow-billed Cuckoo (*Coccyzus americanus*)
Flammulated Owl (*Otus flammeolus*)
Burrowing Owl (*Athene cunicularia*)
Lesser Nighthawk (*Chordeiles acutipennis*)
Common Nighthawk (*Chordeiles minor*)
Chuck-will's-widow (*Caprimulgus carolinensis*)
Whip-poor-will (*Caprimulgus vociferus*)
Black Swift (*Cypseloides niger*)
Chimney Swift (*Chaetura pelagica*)
Vaux's Swift (*Chaetura vauxi*)
White-throated Swift (*Aeronautes saxatalis*)
Ruby-throated Hummingbird (*Archilochus colubris*)
Black-chinned Hummingbird (*Archilochus alexandri*)
Costa's Hummingbird (*Calypte costae*)
Calliope Hummingbird (*Stellula calliope*)
Broad-tailed Hummingbird (*Selasphorus platycercus*)
Rufous Hummingbird (*Selasphorus rufus*)
Allen's Hummingbird (*Selasphorus sasin*)
Olive-sided Flycatcher (*Contopus cooperi*)
Western Wood-pewee (*Contopus sordidulus*)
Eastern Wood-pewee (*Contopus virens*)
Yellow-bellied Flycatcher (*Empidonax flaviventris*)
Acadian Flycatcher (*Empidonax virescens*)
Alder Flycatcher (*Empidonax alnorum*)
Willow Flycatcher (*Empidonax traillii*)
Least Flycatcher (*Empidonax minimus*)
Hammond's Flycatcher (*Empidonax hammondii*)
Dusky Flycatcher (*Empidonax oberholseri*)
Gray Flycatcher (*Empidonax wrightii*)
Pacific-slope Flycatcher (*Empidonax difficilis*)
Cordilleran Flycatcher (*Empidonax occidentalis*)
Vermilion Flycatcher (*Pyrocephalus rubinus*)
Ash-throated Flycatcher (*Myiarchus cinerascens*)
Great Crested Flycatcher (*Myiarchus crinitus*)
Western Kingbird (*Tyrannus verticalis*)
Eastern Kingbird (*Tyrannus tyrannus*)
Cassin's Kingbird (*Tyrannus vociferans*)

Scissor-tailed Flycatcher (*Tyrannus forficatus*)
Purple Martin (*Progne subis*)
Violet-green Swallow (*Tachycineta thalassina*)
Northern Rough-winged Swallow (*Stelgidopteryx serripennis*)
Bank Swallow (*Riparia riparia*)
Cliff Swallow (*Petrochelidon pyrrhonota*)
Barn Swallow (*Hirundo rustica*)
House Wren (*Troglodytes aedon*)
Blue-gray Gnatcatcher (*Polioptila caerulea*)
Veery (*Catharus fuscescens*)
Gray-cheeked Thrush (*Catharus minimus*)
Bicknell's Thrush (*Catharus bicknelli*)
Swainson's Thrush (*Catharus ustulatus*)
Wood Thrush (*Hylocichla mustelina*)
Gray Catbird (*Dumetella carolinensis*)
Phainopepla (*Phainopepla nitens*)
White-eyed Vireo (*Vireo griseus*)
Bell's Vireo (*Vireo bellii*)
Black-capped Vireo (*Vireo atricapillus*)
Gray Vireo (*Vireo vicinior*)
Solitary Vireo (*Vireo solitarius*)
Yellow-throated Vireo (*Vireo flavifrons*)
Warbling Vireo (*Vireo gilvus*)
Philadelphia Vireo (*Vireo philadelphicus*)
Red-eyed Vireo (*Vireo olivaceus*)
Bachman's Warbler (*Vermivora bachmanii*)
Blue-winged Warbler (*Vermivora pinus*)
Golden-winged Warbler (*Vermivora chrysoptera*)
Tennessee Warbler (*Vermivora peregrina*)
Orange-crowned Warbler (*Vermivora celata*)
Nashville Warbler (*Vermivora ruficapilla*)
Virginia's Warbler (*Vermivora virginiae*)
Northern Parula (*Parula americana*)
Yellow Warbler (*Dendroica petechia)*
Chestnut-sided Warbler (*Dendroica pensylvanica*)
Magnolia Warbler (*Dendroica magnolia*)
Cape May Warbler (*Dendroica tigrina*)
Black-throated Blue Warbler (*Dendroica caerulescens*)
Black-throated Gray Warbler (*Dendroica nigrescens*)
Townsend's Warbler (*Dendroica townsendi*)
Hermit Warbler (*Dendroica occidentalis*)
Black-throated Green Warbler (*Dendroica virens*)
Golden-cheeked Warbler (*Dendroica chrysoparia*)

Blackburnian Warbler (*Dendroica fusca*)
Yellow-throated Warbler (*Dendroica dominica*)
Grace's Warbler (*Dendroica graciae*)
Kirtland's Warbler (*Dendroica kirtlandii*)
Prairie Warbler (*Dendroica discolor*)
Palm Warbler (*Dendroica palmarum*)
Bay-breasted Warbler (*Dendroica castanea*)
Blackpoll Warbler (*Dendroica striata*)
Cerulean Warbler (*Dendroica cerulea*)
Black-and-white Warbler (*Mniotilta varia*)
American Redstart (*Setophaga ruticilla*)
Prothonotary Warbler (*Protonotaria citrea*)
Worm-eating Warbler (*Helmitheros vermivorus*)
Swainson's Warbler (*Limnothlypis swainsonii*)
Ovenbird (*Seiurus aurocapillus*)
Northern Waterthrush (*Seiurus noveboracensis*)
Louisiana Waterthrush (*Seiurus motacilla*)
Kentucky Warbler (*Oporornis formosus*)
Connecticut Warbler (*Oporornis agilis*)
Mourning Warbler (*Oporornis philadelphia*)
MacGillivray's Warbler (*Oporornis tolmiei*)
Common Yellowthroat (*Geothlypis trichas*)
Hooded Warbler (*Wilsonia citrina*)
Wilson's Warbler (*Wilsonia pusilla*)
Canada Warbler (*Wilsonia canadensis*)
Yellow-breasted Chat (*Icteria virens*)
Hepatic Tanager (*Piranga flava*)
Summer Tanager (*Piranga rubra*)
Scarlet Tanager (*Piranga olivacea*)
Western Tanager (*Piranga ludoviciana*)
Rose-breasted Grosbeak (*Pheucticus ludovicianus*)
Black-headed Grosbeak (*Pheucticus melanocephalus*)
Blue Grosbeak (*Guiraca caerulea*)
Lazuli Bunting (*Passerina amoena*)
Indigo Bunting (*Passerina cyanea*)
Painted Bunting (*Passerina ciris*)
Dickcissel (*Spiza americana*)
Green-tailed Towhee (*Pipilo chlorurus*)
Chipping Sparrow (*Spizella passerina*)
Clay-colored Sparrow (*Spizella pallida*)
Brewer's Sparrow (*Spizella breweri*)
Black-chinned Sparrow (*Spizella atrogularis*)
Lark Sparrow (*Chondestes grammacus*)

Lark Bunting (*Calamospiza melanocorys*)
Baird's Sparrow (*Ammodramus bairdii*)
Grasshopper Sparrow (*Ammodramus savannarum*)
Lincoln's Sparrow (*Melospiza lincolnii*)
Bobolink (*Dolichonyx oryzivorus*)
Yellow-headed Blackbird (*Xanthocephalus xanthocephalus*)
Orchard Oriole (*Icterus spurius*)
Hooded Oriole (*Icterus cucullatus*)
Baltimore Oriole (*Icterus galbula*)
Bullock's Oriole (*Icterus bullockii*)
Scott's Oriole (*Icterus parisorum*)

LIST "B"

Osprey (*Pandion halieatus*)
Turkey Vulture (*Cathartes aura*)
Northern Harrier (*Circus cyaneus*)
Sharp-shinned Hawk (*Accipiter striatus*)
Cooper's Hawk (*Accipiter cooperii*)
Northern Goshawk (*Accipiter gentilis*)
Red-shouldered Hawk (*Buteo lineatus*)
Red-tailed Hawk (*Buteo jamaicensis*)
Ferruginous Hawk (*Buteo regalis*)
Golden Eagle (*Aquila chrysaetos*)
American Kestrel (*Falco sparverius*)
Prairie Falcon (*Falco mexicanus*)
Killdeer (*Charadrius vociferus*)
Mourning Dove (*Zenaida macroura*)
Long-eared Owl (*Asio otus*)
Short-eared Owl (*Asio flammeus*)
Common Poorwill (*Phalaenoptilus nuttallii*)
Anna's Hummingbird (*Calypte anna*)
Belted Kingfisher (*Ceryle alcyon*)
Lewis's Woodpecker (*Melanerpes lewis*)
Red-naped Sapsucker (*Sphyrapicus nuchalis*)
Yellow-bellied Sapsucker (*Sphyrapicus varius*)
Red-breasted Sapsucker (*Sphyrapicus ruber*)
Williamson's Sapsucker (*Sphyrapicus thyroideus*)
Northern Flicker (*Colaptes auratus*)
Eastern Phoebe (*Sayornis phoebe*)
Say's Phoebe (*Sayornis saya*)
Horned Lark (*Eremophila alpestris*)

Tree Swallow (*Tachycineta bicolor*)
Brown Creeper (*Certhia americana*)
Rock Wren (*Salpinctes obsoletus*)
Sedge Wren (*Cistothorus platensis*)
Marsh Wren (*Cistothorus palustris*)
Ruby-crowned Kinglet (*Regulus calendula*)
Eastern Bluebird (*Sialia sialis*)
Western Bluebird (*Sialia mexicana*)
Mountain Bluebird (*Sialia currucoides*)
Townsend's Solitaire (*Myadestes townsendi*)
Hermit Thrush (*Catharus guttatus*)
American Robin (*Turdus migratorius*)
Northern Mockingbird (*Mimus polyglottos*)
Sage Thrasher (*Oreoscoptes montanus*)
Bendire's Thrasher (*Toxostoma bendirei*)
American Pipit (*Anthus rubescens*)
Sprague's Pipit (*Anthus spragueii*)
Cedar Waxwing (*Bombycilla cedrorum*)
Loggerhead Shrike (*Lanius ludovicianus*)
Yellow-rumped Warbler (*Dendroica coronata*)
Eastern Towhee (*Pipilo erythrophthalmus*)
Cassin's Sparrow (*Aimophila cassinii*)
Vesper Sparrow (*Pooecetes gramineus*)
Black-throated Sparrow (*Amphispiza bilineata*)
Sage Sparrow (*Amphispiza belli*)
Savannah Sparrow (*Passerculus sandwichensis*)
Fox Sparrow (*Passerella iliaca*)
Song Sparrow (*Melospiza melodia*)
Swamp Sparrow (*Melospiza georgiana*)
White-throated Sparrow (*Zonotrichia albicollis*)
White-crowned Sparrow (*Zonotrichia leucophrys*)
Dark-eyed Junco (*Junco hyemalis*)
McCown's Longspur (*Calcarius mccownii*)
Chestnut-collared Longspur (*Calcarius ornatus*)
Red-winged Blackbird (*Agelaius phoeniceus*)
Eastern Meadowlark (*Sturnella magna*)
Western Meadowlark (*Sturnella neglecta*)
Brewer's Blackbird (*Euphagus cyanocephalus*)
Brown-headed Cowbird (*Molothrus ater*)
Purple Finch (*Carpodacus purpureus*)
Cassin's Finch (*Carpodacus cassinii*)
Pine Siskin (*Carduelis pinus*)
Lesser Goldfinch (*Carduelis psaltria*)

Lawrence's Goldfinch (*Carduelis lawrencei*)
American Goldfinch (*Carduelis tristis*)

LIST "C"

Common Black-Hawk (*Buteogallus anthracinus*)
Gray Hawk (*Asturina nitida*)
Zone-tailed Hawk (*Buteo albonotatus*)
White-winged Dove (*Zenaida asiatica*)
Groove-billed Ani (*Crotophaga sulcirostris*)
Elf Owl (*Micrathene whitneyi*)
Buff-collared Nightjar (*Caprimulgus ridgwayi*)
Broad-billed Hummingbird (*Cynanthus latirostris*)
Buff-bellied Hummingbird (*Amazilia yucatanensis*)
Violet-crowned Hummingbird (*Amazilia violiceps*)
Blue-throated Hummingbird (*Lampornis clemenciae*)
Magnificent Hummingbird (*Eugenes fulgens*)
Lucifer Hummingbird (*Calothorax lucifer*)
Elegant Trogon (*Trogon elegans*)
Green Kingfisher (*Chloroceryle americana*)
Northern Beardless Tyrannulet (*Camptostoma imberbe*)
Greater Pewee (*Contopus pertinax*)
Buff-breasted Flycatcher (*Empidonax fulvifrons*)
Dusky-capped Flycatcher (*Myiarchus tuberculifer*)
Brown-crested Flycatcher (*Myiarchus tyrannulus*)
Sulphur-bellied Flycatcher (*Myiodynastes luteiventris*)
Tropical Kingbird (*Tyrannus melancholicus*)
Couch's Kingbird (*Tyrannus couchii*)
Thick-billed Kingbird (*Tyrannus crassirostris*)
Rose-throated Becard (*Pachyramphus aglaiae*)
Cave Swallow (*Petrochelidon fulva*)
Colima Warbler (*Vermivora crissalis*)
Lucy's Warbler (*Vermivora luciae*)
Red-faced Warbler (*Cardellina rubrifrons*)
Painted Redstart (*Myioborus pictus*)
Olive Warbler (*Peucedramus taeniatus*)
Varied Bunting (*Passerina versicolor*)
Botteri's Sparrow (*Aimophila botterii*)
Bronzed Cowbird (*Molothrus aeneus*)

LIST "D"

White-crowned Pigeon (*Columba leucocephala*)
Mangrove Cuckoo (*Coccyzus minor*)
Antillean Nighthawk (*Chordeiles gundlachii*)
Gray Kingbird (*Tyrannus dominicensis*)
Black-whiskered Vireo (*Vireo altiloquus*)

BIBLIOGRAPHY

Able, K. P. (ed.) 1999. *Gatherings of Angels: Migrating Birds and Their Ecology.* Ithaca, N.Y.: Cornell University Press.

American Ornithologists' Union. 1998. *Check-list of North American Birds.* 7th ed. Washington, D.C.: American Ornithologists' Union.

Anders, A. D., J. Faaborg, and F. R. Thompson III. 1998. Post fledging dispersal, habitat use, and home-range size of juvenile Wood Thrushes. *Auk* 115:349–358.

Annand, E. M., and F. R. Thompson III. 1997. Forest bird response to regeneration practices in central hardwood forests. *Journal of Wildlife Management* 61:159–171.

Arcese, P., J. N. M. Smith, and M. I. Hatch. 1996. Nest predation by cowbirds and its consequences for passerine demography. *Proceedings of the National Academy of Sciences of the United States of America* 93:4608–4611.

Askins, R. A. 2000. *Restoring North America's Birds: Lesson from Landscape Ecology.* New Haven, Conn.: Yale University Press.

Askins, R. A., and M. J. Philbrick. 1987. Effects of changes in regional forest abundance on the decline and recovery of a forest bird community. *Wilson Bulletin* 99:7–21.

Baltz, M. E. 2000. Ecology winter resident warblers in southwestern Puerto Rico. Ph.D. dissertation, University of Missouri—Columbia.

Bednarz, J. C., D. Klem, Jr., L. J. Goodrich, and S. E. Senner. 1990. Migration counts of raptors at Hawk Mountain, Pennsylvania, as indicators of population trends, 1934–1986. *Auk* 107:96–109.

Blake, J. G., G. J. Niemi, and J. M. Hanowski. 1992. Drought and annual variation in bird populations. In *Ecology and Conservation of Neotropical Migrant Landbirds,* ed. J. M. Hagan III and D. W. Johnston, pp. 419–430. Washington, D.C.: Smithsonian Institution Press.

Brawn, J. D., and S. K. Robinson. 1996. Source-sink population dynamics may complicate the interpretation of long-term census data. *Ecology* 77:3–12.

Brittingham, M. C., and S. A. Temple. 1983. Have cowbirds caused forest songbirds to decline? *BioScience* 33:31–35.

Brown, J. H., and A. Kodric-Brown. 1977. Turnover rates in insular biogeography: effect of immigration on extinction. *Ecology* 58:445–449.

Burhans, D. E. 2000. Morning nest arrivals in cowbird hosts: their role in aggression, cowbird recognition, and host response to parasitism. In *Ecology and Management of Cowbirds and Their Hosts*, ed. J. N. M. Smith, T. L. Cook, S. I. Rothstein, S. K. Robinson, and S. G. Sealey, pp. 161–168. Austin: University of Texas Press.

Burke, D. M., and E. Noll. 1998. Influence of food abundance, nest site habitat, and forest fragmentation on breeding Ovenbirds. *Auk* 115:96–104.

Carson, R. 1962. *Silent Spring*. Boston: Houghton-Mifflin.

Conway, C. J., G. V. N. Powell, and J. D. Nichols. 1995. Overwinter survival of Neotropical migratory birds in early-successional and mature tropical forests. *Conservation Biology* 9:855–864.

Crick, H. Q. P., and P. J. Jones, eds. 1992. The ecology and conservation of Palaearctic-African migrants. *Ibis* 134 (Supplement 1).

Curtis, J. T., Jr. 1956. The modification of mid-latitude grasslands and forests by man. In *Man's Role in Changing the Face of the Earth*, ed. W. L. Thomas. Chicago: University of Chicago Press.

Dearborn, D. C. 1999. Brown-headed Cowbird nestling vocalizations and the risk of nest predation. *Auk* 116:448–457.

Dearborn, D. C., A. D. Anders, F. R. Thompson III, and J. Faaborg. 1998. Effects of cowbird parasitism on parental provisioning and nestling food acquisition and growth. *Condor* 100:326–334.

del Coro Arizmendi, M., and L. Márquez Valdelamar. 2000. *Áreas de importancia para la conservación de las aves en México*. Mexico City: Fondo Mexicano para la Conservación de la Naturaleza.

Diamond, J. M. 1972. Biogeographic kinetics: estimation of relaxation times for avifaunas of southwest Pacific islands. *Proceedings of the National Academy of Sciences of the United States of America* 69:3199–3203.

———. 1975. The island dilemma: lessons of modern biogeographic studies for the design of nature reserves. *Biological Conservation* 7:129–146.

Donovan, T. M., R. H. Lamberson, F. R. Thompson III, and J. Faaborg. 1995. Modeling the effects of habitat fragmentation on source and sink demography of Neotropical migrant birds. *Conservation Biology* 9:1396–1407.

Donovan, T. M., P. W. Jones, E. M. Annand, and F. R. Thompson III. 1997. Variation in local-scale edge effects: mechanisms and landscape context. *Ecology* 78:2064–2075.

Donovan, T. M., F. R. Thompson, and J. Faaborg. 2000. Cowbird distribution at different scales of fragmentation: Trade-offs between breeding and feeding opportunities. In *Ecology and Management of Cowbirds and Their Hosts,* ed. J. N. M. Smith, T. L. Cook, S. I. Rothstein, S. K. Robinson, and S. G. Sealey, pp. 255–264. Austin: University of Texas Press.

Ewert, D. N., and M. J. Hamas. 1996. Ecology of migratory landbirds during migration in the Midwest. In *Management of Midwestern Landscapes for the Conservation of Neotropical Migratory Birds,* ed. F. R. Thompson III, pp. 200–208. USDA Forest Service, General Technical Report NC-187. St. Paul: North Central Forest Experiment Station.

Faaborg, J. 1988. *Ornithology: An Ecological Approach.* Englewood, N.J.: Prentice-Hall.

Faaborg, J., and W. J. Arendt. 1989. Long-term declines in winter resident warblers in a Puerto Rican dry forest. *American Birds* 43:1226–1230.

———. 1992. Long-term declines of winter resident warblers in a Puerto Rican dry forest: which species are in trouble? *Ecology and Conservation of Neotropical Migrant Landbirds,* ed. J. M. Hagan III and D. W. Johnston, pp. 57–63. Washington, D.C.: Smithsonian Institution Press.

———. 1995. Survival rates of Puerto Rican birds: are islands really that different? *Auk* 112:503–508.

Finch, D. M., and P. W. Stangel. 1993. *Status and Management of Neotropical Migratory Birds.* USDA General Technical Report RM 229. Fort Collins, Colo.: USDA Forest Service, Rocky Mountain Forest and Range Experiment Station.

Finch, D. M., and W. Yong. 2000. Landbird migration in riparian habitats of the middle Rio Grande: a case study. In *Stopover Ecology of Nearctic-Neotropical Landbird Migrants: Habitat Relations and Conservation Implications,* ed. F. R. Moore, pp. 88–98. Studies in Avian Biology, no. 20, Cooper Ornithological Society. Lawrence, Kans.: Allen Press.

Fitzgerald, J. A., D. N. Pashley, S. J. Lewis, and B. Pardo. 1998. Partners in Flight Bird Conservation Plan for the Northern Tallgrass Prairie (Physiographic Area 40). Version 1.0. Jefferson City: Missouri Department of Conservation.

Fitzpatrick, J. W. 1980. Wintering of North American tyrant flycatchers in the Neotropics. In *Migrant Birds in the Neotropics: Ecology, Behavior, Distribution, and Conservation,* ed. A. Keast and E. S. Morton, pp. 67–78. Washington, D.C.: Smithsonian Institution Press.

Francis, C. M., and D. J. T. Hussell. 1997–1998. Changes in numbers of land birds counted in migration at Long Point Bird Observatory, 1961–1997. *Bird Populations* 4:37–66.

Francis, C. M., J. Terborgh, and J. W. Fitzpatrick. 1999. Survival rates of understorey forest birds in Peru. In *Proceedings of the 22nd Ornithological Congress,* ed. N. Adams and R. Slotow. Durban, South Africa: University of Natal.

Fretwell, S. 1972. *Populations in a Seasonal Environment.* Princeton, N. J.: Princeton University Press.

————. 1980. Evolution of migration in relation to factors regulating bird numbers. In *Migrant Birds in the Neotropics: Ecology, Behavior, Distribution, and Conservation,* ed. A. Keast and E. S. Morton, pp. 517–528. Washington, D.C.: Smithsonian Institution Press.

Friesen, L. E., M. D. Cadman, and R. J. Mackay. 1999. Nesting success of Neotropical migrant songbirds in a highly fragmented landscape. *Conservation Biology* 13:1–9.

Gauthreaux, S. A., Jr. 1992. The use of weather radar to monitor long-term patterns of trans-Gulf migration in spring. In *Ecology and Conservation of Neotropical Migrant Landbirds,* ed. J. M. Hagan III and D. W. Johnston, pp. 96–100. Washington, D. C.: Smithsonian Institution Press.

Gibbs, J. P., and J. Faaborg. 1990. Estimating the viability of Ovenbird and Kentucky Warbler populations occupying forest fragments in central Missouri, USA. *Conservation Biology* 4:193–196.

Gram, W. K. 1998. Winter participation by Neotropical migrant and resident birds in mixed-species flocks in Northeastern Mexico. *Condor* 100:44–53.

Grant, K. A., and V. Grant. 1968. *Hummingbirds and Their Flowers.* New York: Columbia University Press.

Hagan, J. M., III, T. L. Lloyd-Evans, J. L. Atwood, and D. S. Wood. 1992. Long-term changes in migratory landbirds in the north eastern United States: evidence from migration capture data. In *Ecology and Conservation of Neotropical Migrant Landbirds,* ed. J. M. Hagan III and D. W. Johnston, pp. 115–130. Washington, D.C.: Smithsonian Institution Press, Washington D.C.

Harrington, B. A. 1999. The hemispheric globetrotting of the White-rumped Sandpiper. In *Gatherings of Angels: Migrating Birds and their Ecology,* ed. K. P. Able, pp. 119–134. Ithaca, N.Y.: Cornell University Press.

Hartley, M. J., and M. L. Hunter, Jr. 1998. A meta-analysis of forest cover, edge effects, and artificial nest predation rates. *Conservation Biology* 12:465–469.

Hartshorn, G. S. 1992. Forest loss and future options in Central America. In *Ecology and Conservation of Neotropical Migrant Landbirds,* ed. J. M. Hagan III and D. W. Johnston, pp. 13–22. Washington, D.C.: Smithsonian Institution Press.

Haskell, D. G. 1995. Forest fragmentation and nest-predation: are experiments with Japanese Quail eggs misleading? *Auk* 112:767–770.

Hayden, T. J., J. R. Faaborg, and R. L. Clawson. 1985. Estimates of minimum area requirements for Missouri forest birds. *Transactions of the Missouri Academy of Science* 19:11–22.

Hayes, F. E. 1995. Definitions for migrant birds: what is a Neotropical migrant? *Auk* 112:521–523.

Hobson, K. A., and L. I. Wassenaar. 1997. Linking breeding and wintering grounds of Neotropical migrant songbirds using stable isotope analysis of feathers. *Oecologia* 109:132–141.

Hochachka, W. M., T. E. Martin, V. Artman, C. R. Smith, S. J. Heijl, D. E. Andersen, D. Curson, L. Petit, N. Mathews, T. Donovan, E. E. Klaas, P. B. Wood, J. C. Manolis, K. P. McFarland, J. V. Nichols, J. C. Bednarz, D. M. Evans, J. P. Duguay, S. Garner, J. Tewksbury, K. L. Purcell, J. Faaborg, C. B. Goguen, C. Rimmer, R. Dettmers, M. Knutson, J. A. Collazo, L. Garner, D. Whitehead, and G. Geupel. 1999. Scale dependence in the effects of forest coverage on parasitization by Brown-headed Cowbirds. *Studies in Avian Biology* 18:80–88.

Holmes, R. T., and T. W. Sherry. 1988. Assessing population trends of New Hampshire forest birds: local vs. regional patterns. *Auk* 105:756–768.

Holmes, R. T., T .W. Sherry, and L. Reitsma. 1989. Population structure, territoriality, and overwinter survival of two migrant warbler species in Jamaica. *Condor* 91:545–561.

Hoover, J. P., and M. C. Brittingham. 1993. Regional variation in cowbird parasitism of Wood Thrushes. *Wilson Bulletin* 105:228–238.

Howe, R. W., G. J. Davis, and V. Mosca. 1991. The demographic significance of "sink" populations. *Biological Conservation* 57:239–255.

Howell, C. A., S. C. Latta, T. M. Donovan, P. A. Porneluzi, G. R. Parks, and J. Faaborg. 2000. Landscape effects mediate breeding bird abundance in Midwestern forests. *Landscape Ecology* 15:547–563.

Hussell, D. J. T., M H. Mather, and P. H. Sinclair. 1992. Trends in numbers of tropical- and temperate-wintering migrant landbirds in migration at Long Point, Ontario, 1961–1988. In *Ecology and Conservation of Neotropical Migrant Landbirds,* ed. J. M. Hagan III and D. W. Johnston, pp. 101–114. Washington, D.C.: Smithsonian Institution Press.

James, F. C., C. E. McCulloch, and D. A. Wiedenfeld. 1996. New approaches to the analysis of population trends in land birds. *Ecology* 77:13–27.

Johnston, D. W., and J. M. Hagan III. 1992. An analysis of long term breeding bird censuses from eastern deciduous forests. In *Ecology and Conservation of Neotropical Migrant Landbirds,* ed. J. M. Hagan III and D. W. Johnston, pp. 75–84. Washington, D.C.: Smithsonian Institution Press.

Johnston, J. P., W. J. Peach, R. D. Gregory, and S. A. White. 1998. Survival rates of tropical and temperate passerines: a Trinidadian perspective. *American Naturalist* 150:771–789.

Karr, J. R., J. D. Nichols, M. K. Klimkiewicz, and J. D. Brawn. 1990. Survival rates of birds of tropical and temperate forests: will the dogma survive? *American Naturalist* 136:277–291.

Keast, A., and E. S. Morton, eds. 1980. *Migrant Birds in the Neotropics: Ecology, Behavior, Distribution, and Conservation.* Washington, D.C.: Smithsonian Institution Press.

Ketterson, E. D., and V. Nolan, Jr. 1983. The evolution of differential bird migration. *Current Ornithology* 3:357–402.

Krapu, G. L. 1999. Sandhill Cranes and the Platte River. In *Gatherings of Angels: Migrating Birds and Their Ecology,* ed. K. P. Able, pp. 103–117. Ithaca, N.Y.: Cornell University Press.

Latta, Steven. 2000. Ecology and population regulation of Neotropical migratory birds in the Sierra de Bahoruco, Dominican Republic. Ph.D. dissertation, University of Missouri–Columbia.

Lefebvre, G., B. Poulin, and R. McNeil. 1994. Temporal dynamics of mangrove bird communities in Venezuela with special reference to migrant warblers. *Auk* 111:405–415.

Levins, R. 1968. *Evolution in Changing Environments.* Princeton, N.J.: Princeton University Press.

MacArthur, R. H., and E. O. Wilson. 1967. *The Theory of Island Biogeography.* Princeton, N.J.: Princeton University Press.

Marra, P. P., and R. L. Holberton. 1998. Corticosterone levels as indicators of habitat quality: effects of habitat segregation in a migratory bird during the nonbreeding period. *Oecologia* 116:284–292.

Marra, P. P., K. A. Hobson, and R. T. Holmes. 1998. Linking winter and summer events in a migratory bird by using stable isotopes. *Science* 282:1884–1886.

Martin, T. E., and D. M. Finch, eds. 1995. *Ecology and Management of Neotropical Migratory Birds: A Synthesis and Review of Critical Issues.* New York: Oxford University Press.

Mayfield, H. 1975. Suggestions for calculating nest success. *Wilson Bulletin* 87:456–466.

McCoy, T. D. 2000. Effects of landscape composition and multi-scale habitat characteristics on the grassland bird community. Ph.D. dissertation, University of Missouri–Columbia.

Moore, F. R. (ed.). 2000. *Stopover Ecology of Nearctic-Neotropical Landbird Migrants: Habitat Relations and Conservation Implications.* Studies in Avian Biology, no. 20, Cooper Ornithological Society. Lawrence, Kans.: Allen Press.

Moreau, R. E. 1972. *The Palearctic-African Bird Migration Systems.* New York: Academic Press.

Morris, D., and F. R. Thompson III. 1998. Effects of habitat and invertebrate density on abundance and foraging behavior of Brown-headed Cowbirds. *Auk* 115:376–385.

Morse, D. H. 1980. Population limitations: breeding or wintering grounds? In *Migrant Birds in the Neotropics: Ecology, Behavior, Distribution, and Conservation,* ed. A. Keast and E. S. Morton, pp. 505–516. Washington, D.C.: Smithsonian Institution Press.

Morton, E. S. 1980. Adaptations to seasonal changes by migrant land birds in the Panama Canal Zone. In *Migrant Birds in the Neotropics: Ecology, Be-*

havior, Distribution, and Conservation, ed. A. Keast, and E. S. Morton, pp. 437–453. Washington, D.C.: Smithsonian Institution Press.

Munn, C. A. 1985. Permanent canopy and understory flocks in Amazonia: species composition and population density. *Ornithological Monographs* 36:683–710.

Newton, I. 1998. *Population Limitation in Birds.* London: Academic Press.

O'Conner, R. J., and J. Faaborg. 1993. The relative abundance of the Brown-headed Cowbird *Molothrus ater* in relation to exterior and interior edges in forests of Missouri. *Transactions of the Missouri Academy of Science* 26:1–9.

Orell, M., K. Lahti, and J. Matero. 1999. High survival and site fidelity in the Siberian Tit *Parus cinctus,* a focal species of the taiga. *Ibis* 141:460–468.

Paton, P. W. C. 1994. The effect of edge on avian nest success: how strong is the evidence? *Conservation Biology* 8:17–26.

Peach, W., S. Baillie, and L. Underhill. 1991. Survival of British Sedge Warblers *Acrocephalus schoenobaenus* in relation to west African rainfall. *Ibis* 133:300–305.

Peterjohn, B. G., J. R. Sauer, and C. S. Robbins. 1995. Population trends from the North American breeding bird survey. In *Ecology and Management of Neotropical Migratory Birds: A Synthesis and Review of Critical Issues,* ed. T. E. Martin and D. M. Finch, pp. 3–39. New York: Oxford University Press.

Petit, D. R., J. F. Lynch, R. L. Hutto, J. G. Blake, and R. B. Waide. 1993. Management and conservation of migratory landbirds overwintering in the Neotropics. In *Status and Management of Neotropical Migratory Birds,* ed. D. M. Finch and P. W. Stangel, pp. 70–92. USDA Forest Service General Technical Report RM-229. Ft. Collins, Colo.: USDA Forest Service Rocky Mountain Forest and Range Experiment Station.

Pollock, K. H., J. D. Nichols, C. Brownie, and J. E. Hines. 1990. Statistical inference for capture-recapture experiments. *Wildlife Monographs* 107:1–97.

Porneluzi, P. A., and J. Faaborg. 1999. Season-long fecundity, survival, and viability of Ovenbirds in fragmented and unfragmented landscapes. *Conservation Biology* 13:1151–1161.

Pulliam, H. R. 1988. Sources, sinks, and population regulation. *American Naturalist* 132:652–661.

Ralph, C. J., G. R. Geupel, P. Pyle, T. E. Martin, and D. F. DeSante. 1993. *Handbook of Field Methods for Monitoring Landbirds.* USDA Forest Service General Technical Report PSW-GTR-144. Albany, Calif.: USDA Forest Service Pacific Southwest Research Station.

Rappole, J. H., E. S. Morton, T. E. Lovejoy III, and J. L. Ruos. 1983. *Nearctic Avian Migrants in the Neotropics.* Washington, D.C.: U.S. Fish and Wildlife Service.

Rappole, J. H., M. A. Ramos, and K. Winker. 1989. Wintering Wood Thrush movements and mortality in southern Veracruz. *Auk* 106:402–410.

Remsen, J. V., Jr. 2001. The true winter range of the Veery (*Catharus fuscescens*): lessons for determining winter ranges of species that winter in the Tropics. *Auk* 118:838–848.

Robbins, C. S. 1979. Effects of forest fragmentation on bird populations. In *Management of North Central and Northeastern Forests for Nongame Birds*, ed. R. M. DeGraaf and K. E. Evans, pp. 198–212. USDA Forest Service General Technical Report NC-51. St. Paul: USDA Forest Service North Central Experiment Station.

Robbins, C. S., D. Bystrak, and P. H. Geissler. 1986. *The Breeding Bird Survey: Its First Fifteen Years, 1965–1979.* U.S. Fish and Wildlife Service Resource Publication 157. Washington, D.C.

Robbins, C. S., B. A. Dowell, D. K. Dawson, J. Colon, F. Espinoza, J. Rodrigez, R. Sutton, and T. Vargas. 1987. Comparison of Neotropical winter bird populations in isolated patches versus extensive forest. *Acta Ecologica/ Oecologia General* 8:285–292.

Robbins, C. S., D. K. Dawson, and B. A. Dowell. 1989a. Habitat area requirements of breeding forest birds of the middle Atlantic states. *Wildlife Monographs* 103:1–34.

Robbins, C. S., J. R. Sauer, R. S. Greenberg, and S. Droege. 1989b. Population declines in North American birds that migrate to the Neotropics. *Proceedings of the National Academy of Sciences of the United States of America* 86:7658–7662.

Robbins, C. S., B. A. Dowell, D. K. Dawson, J. A. Colon, R. Estrada, A. Sutton, R. Sutton, and D. Weyer. 1992a. Comparison of Neotropical migrant landbird populations wintering in tropical forest, isolated fragments, and agricultural habitats. In *Ecology and Conservation of Neotropical Migrant Landbirds*, ed. J. M. Hagan III and D. W. Johnston, pp. 207–210. Washington, D.C.: Smithsonian Institution Press.

Robbins, C. S., J. W. Fitzpatrick, and P. B. Hamel. 1992b. A warbler in trouble: *Dendroica cerulea.* In *Ecology and Conservation of Neotropical Migrant Landbirds*, ed. J. M. Hagan III and D. W. Johnston, pp. 549–562. Washington, D.C.: Smithsonian Institution Press.

Robinson, S. K. 1992. Population dynamics of breeding Neotropical migrants in a fragmented Illinois landscape. In *Ecology and Conservation of Neotropical Migrant Landbirds*, ed. J. M. Hagan III and D. W. Johnston, pp. 408–418. Washington, D.C.: Smithsonian Institution Press.

Robinson, S. K., F. R. Thompson III, T. M. Donovan, D. R. Whitehead, and J. Faaborg. 1995. Regional forest fragmentation and the nesting success of migratory birds. *Science* 267:1987–1990.

Sauer, J. R., and S. Droege. 1992. Geographical patterns in population trends of Neotropical migrants in North America. In *Ecology and Conservation of Neotropical Migrant Landbirds*, ed. J. M. Hagan III and D. W. Johnston, pp. 26–42. Washington, D.C.: Smithsonian Institution Press.

Sauer, J. R., B. G. Peterjohn, and W. A. Link. 1994. Observer differences in the North American breeding bird survey. *Auk* 111:50–62.

Schneider, D. 1997. Requiem for the songbird: Perilous decline puzzles scientists. *Christian Science Monitor*, June 10.

Senner, S. E. 1999. Converging North: Dunlins and Western Sandpipers on the Copper River Delta. In *Gatherings of Angels: Migrating Birds and Their Ecology*, ed. K. P. Able, pp. 135–148. Ithaca, N.Y.: Cornell University Press.

Sherry, T. W., and R. T. Holmes. 1995. Summer versus winter limitation of populations: what are the issues and what is the evidence? In *Ecology and Management of Neotropical Migratory Birds: A Synthesis and Review of Critical Issues*, ed. T. E. Martin and D. M. Finch, pp. 85–120. New York: Oxford University Press.

Simons, T. R., S. M. Pearson, and F. R. Moore. 2000. Application of spatial models to the stopover ecology of trans-Gulf migrants. In *Stopover Ecology of Nearctic-Neotropical Landbird Migrants: Habitat Relations and Conservation Implications*, ed. F. R. Moore, pp. 4–14. Studies in Avian Biology, no. 20, Cooper Ornithological Society. Lawrence, Kans.: Allen Press.

Soule, M. E., and J. Terborgh. 1999. *Continental Conservation: Scientific Foundations of Regional Reserve Networks.* Washington, D.C.: Island Press.

Staicer, C. A. 1992. Social behavior of the Northern Parula, Cape May Warbler, and Prairie Warbler wintering in second-growth forest in southwestern Puerto Rico. In *Ecology and Conservation of Neotropical Migrant Landbirds*, ed. J. M. Hagan III and D. W. Johnston, pp. 308–320. Washington, D.C.: Smithsonian Institution Press.

Stevens, W. K. 1997. Something to sing about: songbirds aren't in decline. *New York Times*, June 11.

Temple, S. A., and J. R. Cary. 1988. Modeling dynamics of habitat interior bird populations in fragmented landscapes. *Conservation Biology* 2:340–347.

Terborgh, J. 1974. Preservation of natural diversity: the problem of extinction prone species. *BioScience* 24:715–722.

Terborgh, J. W. 1980. The conservation status of Neotropical migrants: present and future. In *Migrant Birds in the Neotropics: Ecology, Behavior, Distribution, and Conservation*, ed. A. Keast and E. S. Morton, pp. 21–30. Washington, D.C.: Smithsonian Institution Press.

———. 1989. *Where Have All the Birds Gone?* Princeton, N.J.: Princeton University Press.

Tewksbury, J. J., S. J. Hejl, and T. E. Martin. 1998. Breeding productivity does not decline with increasing fragmentation in a western landscape. *Ecology* 79:2890–2903.

Thomas, L. 1996. Monitoring long-term population change: why are there so many analysis methods? *Ecology* 77:49–58.

Thompson, F. R., III. 1994. Temporal and spatial patterns of breeding Brown-headed Cowbirds in the Midwestern United States. *Auk* 111:979–990.

Thompson, F. R., III, and W. D. Dijak. 2000. Differences in movements, home range, and habitat preferences of female Brown-headed Cowbirds in three Midwestern landscapes. In *Ecology and Management of Cowbirds and Their Hosts,* ed. J. N. M. Smith, T. L. Cook, S. I. Rothstein, S. K. Robinson, and S. G. Sealy, pp. 100–109. Austin: University of Texas Press.

Thompson, F. R., III, W. Dijak, and D. E. Burhans. 1999. Video identification of predators at songbird nests in old fields. *Auk* 116:259–264.

Thompson, F. R., III, S. K. Robinson, T. M. Donovan, J. Faaborg, and D. R. Whitehead. 2000. Biogeographic, landscape, and local factors affecting cowbird abundance and host parasitism levels. In *Ecology and Management of Cowbirds and Their Hosts,* ed. J. N. M. Smith, T. L. Cook, S. I. Rothstein, S. K. Robinson, and S. G. Sealy, pp. 271–279. Austin: University of Texas Press.

Van Horn, M. A., R. M. Gentry, and J. Faaborg. 1995. Patterns of pairing success of the Ovenbird (*Seiurus aurocapillus*) within Missouri forest fragments. *Auk* 112:98–106.

Vega Rivera, J. H., J. H. Rappole, W. J. McShea, and C. A. Haas. 1998. Wood Thrush postfledging movements and habitat use in northern Virginia. *Condor* 100:69–78.

Vickery, P. D., and J. R. Herkert. 1999. *Ecology and Conservation of Grassland Birds of the Western Hemisphere.* Studies in Avian Biology, no. 19, Cooper Ornithological Society. Lawrence, Kans.: Allen Press.

Villard, M.-A. 1998. On forest-interior species, edge avoidance, area sensitivity, and dogmas in avian conservation. *Auk* 115:801–805.

Walkinshaw, L. H. 1983. *Kirtland's Warbler.* Bloomfield Hills, Mich.: Cranbrook Institute of Science.

Whitcomb, R. F., J. F. Lynch, P. A. Opler, and C. S. Robbins. 1976. Island biogeography and conservation: strategy and limitations. *Science* 193:1030–1032.

Whitcomb, R. F., C. S. Robbins, J. F. Lynch, B. L. Whitcomb, M. K. Klimkiewicz, and D. Bystrak. 1981. Effects of forest fragmentation on avifauna of the eastern deciduous forest. In *Forest Island Dynamics in Man-Dominated Landscapes,* ed. R. L. Burgess and D. M. Sharpe, pp. 125–205. New York: Springer-Verlag.

Wilcove, D. S. 1985. Nest predation in forest tracts and the decline of migratory songbirds. *Ecology* 66:1211–1214.

———. 1988. Changes in the avifauna of the Great Smoky Mountains, 1947–1983. *Wilson Bulletin* 100:256–271.

Wilcove, D. S., and S. K. Robinson. 1990. The impact of forest fragmentation on bird communities in eastern North America. In *Biogeography and Ecology of Forest Bird Communities,* ed. A. Keast, pp. 319–331. The Hague, Netherlands: Academic Publishing.

Winter, M. 1998. Effect of habitat fragmentation on grassland nesting birds in southwestern Missouri prairie fragments. Ph.D. dissertation, University of Missouri—Columbia.

Woodworth, B. L. 1999. Modeling the population dynamics of a songbird exposed to parasitism and predation and evaluating management options. *Conservation Biology* 13:67–76.

Wunderle, J. M. 1992. Sexual habitat segregation in wintering Black-throated Blue Warblers in Puerto Rico. In *Ecology and Conservation of Neotropical Migrant Landbirds,* ed. J. M. Hagan III and D. W. Johnston, pp. 299–307. Washington, D.C.: Smithsonian Institution Press.

Zimmerman, J. L. 1988. Breeding season habitat selection by the Henslow's Sparrow (*Ammodramus henslowii*) in Kansas. *Wilson Bulletin* 100:17–24.

Author Index

Subject Index

American Bird Conservancy, 193
applied biogeography, 37–40, fig. 4.2, fig. 4.3
archipelago studies, 41, fig. 4.4
area-sensitive species: defined, 43; generalized about, 43–45; minimum areas, 49
Association of Field Ornithologists, 24
austral migrant, 3

banding stations, 27, 28; population trends, 28
BBIRD: defined, 82; parasitism study, 82–83
Bird Conservation Area (BCA): described, 111, fig. 7.4; tested, 112
Blackbird
—Red-winged: on fragments, 42
—Yellow-shouldered: parasitism, 62
Blue Jay, 26, 42: as predator, 68, 70, 71; in Smokies, 48
Bobolink: population declines, fig. 1.1
Bobwhite, Northern, 64
body condition: and blood hormone levels, 147–148; described, 145–148, fig. 9.3; fat scores, 146–147
Breeding Bird Census (BBC): defined, 25; population trends, 25
Breeding Bird Survey (BBS): analytical problems, 21–22; cowbird distributions, 60, fig. 5.1; data-gathering problems, 15–17; early results, 5; evidence for declines, xiii, 4–10; general value, 22–23; importance, 12; methodology, 5, 13–15; physiographic provinces, 14, fig. 2.1, 18; route locations, 14, fig. 2.1; spatial variation, 17–19, fig 2.2; temporal variation, 19–21, fig. 2.2, fig. 2.3
Bunting
—Indigo, 55: late fledging, 89; parasitism, 58; populations in MOFEP, 105; predation, 69; winter habitat, 131
—Painted: population declines, fig. 1.1
Bureau of Land Management, 186

Cardinal, Northern: in clear-cuts, 107
Chat, Yellow-breasted: populations in MOFEP, 105
Christmas Bird Count: and cowbirds, 58; described, 25, 26; population trends, 26
clear-cut: caveats about using, 107; effects on populations, 104–107, fig. 7.3; as even-aged management, 103; value, 102–103